A Mountain of Difference

Cornell University

Oona Paredes

A Mountain of Difference

The Lumad in
Early Colonial Mindanao

SOUTHEAST ASIA PROGRAM PUBLICATIONS
Southeast Asia Program
Cornell University
Ithaca, New York
2013

Cornell Southeast Asia Program Publications
640 Stewart Avenue, Ithaca, NY 14850-3857

Studies on Southeast Asia No. 61

Printed in the United States of America

ISBN: hc 978-0-87727-791-0
ISBN: pb 978-0-87727-761-3

Cover: designed by Kat Dalton

To

my sister Kagay
and other friends amongst the Higaunon
whose unique spirits have illuminated
my research and my life
in the most unexpected ways

and

the late Father Peter Schreurs MSC,
who helped me begin my own
conversation with the past

TABLE OF CONTENTS

MAP OF MINDANAO

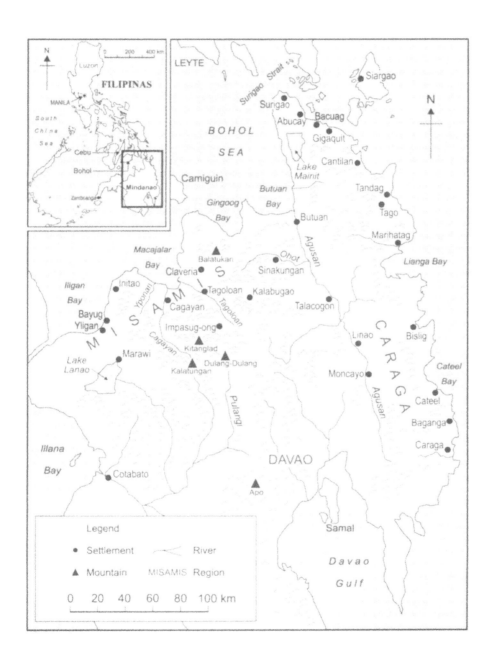

MAP OF SOUTHEAST ASIA
IN THE 1800S

ACKNOWLEDGMENTS

This book is dedicated to my sister Kagay, to Tahak and *datu* Budluwa, and other friends among the Higaunon who have illuminated my research and my life in the most unexpected ways, and to the late Father Peter Schreurs MSC, who helped me begin my conversation with the past.

The archival research for this book was undertaken for my doctoral program, and made possible by the Wenner-Gren Foundation for Anthropological Research in the form of a generous dissertation research grant, and by residential fellowships from the Newberry Library of Chicago, the Vatican Film Library at St. Louis University in Missouri, and the Escuela de Estudios Hispanoamericanos in Sevilla, Spain. An extended period of writing and revision was sponsored by the American Association of University Women, through its 2009–2010 American Fellowships program. A Faculty of Arts and Social Sciences Book Grant from the National University of Singapore provided additional support in the final stages. Earlier field research that ultimately led to this archival study was supported by the US National Science Foundation's Graduate Research Fellowship Program, and by Arizona State University through the Graduate College, the former Program for Southeast Asian Studies, and the Sociocultural Anthropology Program of what is now the School of Human Evolution and Social Change.

The reader will no doubt find various defects and inadequacies in my work, and for such things I am solely to blame and beg forgiveness. That said, whatever merits my work may possess, I freely attribute to the fact that, as I muddled through the past few years, I encountered rather serendipitously many others—academics and civilians alike—who forced me to think much more profoundly than I otherwise would have, had I been left entirely to my own devices. It was indeed my blind fortune to meet so many people who gave so freely of their time, and I hope that they can appreciate how much they were a part of the particular intellectual and cultural journey that this work involved.

First and foremost, the present work is inconceivable without the pioneering work of Mindanao's often iconoclastic "local" scholars. I would like to recognize their significant influence on how I think about the Lumad world today—especially Augusto Gatmaytan, Rudy Buhay Rodil, Mardonio Lao, Elena Maquiso, Victorino Saway, Bebito Aniscal, Edvilla Talaroc, Dionisio Yumo, Domingo Non, Bro. Karl Gaspar CSsR, Heidi Gloria, Linda Montilla-Burton, Macario Tiu, and Fr. Albert Alejo SJ. I also thank the dedicated personnel of NGOs like Anthrowatch and Balay Mindanaw for affirmation and synergy in the *bukid*.

To the Orden de los Augustinos Recoletos, Provincia de San Nicolás de Tolentino, I owe a particularly profound *utang kabubut-on* for generously granting me access to their private archive in Marcilla, and allowing me to work in their *convento* through Holy Week in 2005. I especially thank Hmno. Alfonso, P. Fr. Santiago Marcilla, and P. Fr. Miguel Flores, and the archivist P. Fr. José Manuel Bengoa, for patience, good humor, and avuncular kindness. To be sure, none of this would have gone so well without the late Father Peter Schreurs's reportedly epic letter of introduction, which I was told would have secured me an audience with the Pope.

I must also thank, from my time in Spain: Loli Alamo Martell, Alfonso Alvarado Bravo, Sra. Teresa Carra Lorente, Magdalena Diéz and family, Rita and Conchi Goñi, Hector Huerto, George Lovell, Isabel Marín, Caroline Mènard, Geno Mendola, Rocío Minguet Medina, Enrique Orce, Esther Palacios, Guillermo Pastor Nuñez, Louise Iseult Paradis, Aurora Pérez Vázquez, Tristan Platt, Florentino Rodao, Alison Stuart, Paul Sweeney, and Francisco Taborda Ocampo. In Chicago and St. Louis: Bro. Bill Biernatzki SJ, Bruce Calder, Susan L'Engle, Mark and Cole Lycett, Stepanka Magstadtova, Hannah Rosen, Richard Turits, and Elizabeth Wright. In the ensuing storm and its aftermath: Jojo Abinales, Donna Amoroso, Barbara Watson Andaya, Jiemin Bao, Thomas Borchert, Mona Misa Cladis, Signe and Dan Cohen, Patricia Durante, Jane Ferguson, Suzanne Flanegin, Louanna Furbee, Mel and Margaret Gopen, Michael Grinfeld, Frances Hayashida, Larry Hollingworth, Sherry Hubbard, Tracy Pilar Johnson, Christy and Mario Jugador, Annabelle Fortich Jugador and family, Manolita Jugador, Rissa Katigbak, Michael and Judy Laffan, Vina Lanzona, Lee and Barbara Lyman, Tiki and Doug Magee, Chito and Pet Misa, Francis and Lai Misa, Kathleen Morrison, Lance and Laura Ostman, Craig and Fran Palmer, Cheree Quizon, Paul Rodell, Lisa Sattenspiel, Mark Schulze, Julaine Stiers, Heidi Swank, Eric Tagliacozzo, Steve Tanner, Bill Thomas, Grace and Abel Vega, Shawna Victor, and Stephnie Wriedt.

Over the years, some key conversations helped me bring the book to life; special thanks to Joel David, Melanie Tan Uy, Felix Vergara, Ayi Hernandez, Jojo Abinales, Michael Laffan, Itty Abraham, and Vince Rafael. My doctoral supervisory committee —Jim Eder, John Chance, and John Martin—somehow managed the delicate balance of giving me the freedom to make my own mistakes whilst making sure I didn't get away with too many of them.

The final revisions were completed during my first year with the National University of Singapore, where I have received such wonderful support for writing and research. I thank especially Phil Daquila, Goh Beng Lan, Chie Ikeya, Irving Chan Johnson, Douglas Kammen, Pattana Kitiarsa, John Miksic, Tim Barnard, Michael Feener, Mika Toyota, Patrick Daly, Tukta Kitiarsa, Millie Rivera, Brenda Yeoh, Khairudin Aljunied, and a colorful array of campus interlopers including Barbara and Leonard Andaya, Shane Barter, Anne Blackburn, Arunima Datta, Foo Shu Tieng, Janet Hoskins, Lin Idrus, Steve McKay, Merle Ricklefs, Teren Sevea, Xiang Biao, and Yeoh Seng Guan. I also thank Mdm. Moli Peariasamy, Mdm. Rohani bte Sungib, and Ms. Sharifah Alawiyah Alhadad, who still help me get my act together daily.

I am indebted to Cornell SEAP Publications for transforming the manuscript into a book, especially to Deborah Homsher for her faith in the project, and for painstakingly editing the text, with Fred Conner, over several rounds. Two anonymous reviewers provided extensive comments and critical suggestions that allowed me to develop the text into something better. Sarah Demb and John Chance read through the first complete draft and helped me reorganize the text; Grace Vega reviewed my Spanish translations over one very long Missouri winter; and Mdm. Lee Li Kheng, created the original maps that appear in this book.

Last but never least, Lucas and Jess always kept a straight face whenever I claimed to be working. This book bears witness to their fearless, infinite love, and irrepressible sense of humor.

Iyan dà.

THE PROBLEM OF HISTORY

> I, too, face the problem of history: what to retain, what to dump, how to hold onto what memory insists on relinquishing, how to deal with change.
> –Salman Rushdie, *Shame*[1]

> But first they had to reclaim themselves from the anonymous stew into which history had flung them.
> –Luis H. Francia, *Eye of the Fish*[2]

Despite all appearances to the contrary, this ethnohistory of north Mindanao's indigenous upland peoples—the Lumad—is rooted firmly in the present, not in the past. So this is where I should begin: with a reflection of how our experience of the present colors this reading of the past. In fact, let us begin with one particular Lumad's perception of the colonial past. In 1995, I interviewed the Higaunon *datu*[3] Mansumayan in the uplands of Naawan in western Misamis. He was the least conspicuous of all the *datus* I met, dressed as poorly and unassumingly as he was, going without the elaborate beading and red accoutrements favored by most *datus*. Clearly, he was respected, but his status as a *datu* could not be attributed to any obvious markers of power, such as charisma, wealth, or aggressiveness. Instead, he had a quiet, self-effacing air, secure in the knowledge that he was the wisest of the lot. Sitting contentedly in his little house, exceedingly amused that I had walked for almost two hours just to listen to him talk, Mansumayan outlined for me the major conflicts that had happened there over the decades, from the American occupation through Martial Law to the time of Mabalao.[4] But when I asked about an earlier time, the colonial period, when the *Kachila*, or Spaniards, were converting people to

---

[1] Salman Rushdie, *Shame* (New York, NY: Vintage International, 1981), p. 92.

[2] Luis H. Francia, *Eye of the Fish: A Personal Archipelago* (New York, NY: Kaya Press, 2001), p. 58.

[3] A *datu* is an indigenous male authority figure among the Higaunon, whose equivalent is found in all Lumad groups. As I explain in Chaper Five, *datu* is regularly glossed by lowlanders as "chieftain," but there are fundamental questions as to the precise nature of datuship among the Lumad.

[4] *Datu* Mabalao was Ricardo de la Camara, who in the late 1970s was claimed by some to be the "supreme *datu* of the Higaunons." A minor but nonetheless problematic local figure, in 1977 he was kidnapped from his home in Agusan del Sur by the New People's Army and was never seen again. This took place in the time when Higaunons first joined the armed communist insurgency for political and other purposes. See Oona T. Paredes, "Higaunon Resistance and Ethnic Politics in Northern Mindanao," *The Australian Journal of Anthropology* 8,1 (April 1997): 270–90.

Christianity, he told me the following in no uncertain terms: "Dear girl, we were never colonized, because the *Kachila* were never here."

Some weeks later and further to the east, I remarked on this in the presence of the *datu* Mandilguwan, who, sitting on the front porch of the missionary's house in the uplands of Gingoog, was growing increasingly irritated by the mere fact that I was there, talking to him. Indeed, I had established myself as a *bona fide* annoying person the week before, arriving as I did with a contingent of city folk who countered the "unnatural" peace and quiet of the mountains by playing a transistor radio at full volume through the night. Addressing me curtly in Binisayá,[5] the settlers' language, the *datu* dismissed my question by saying that, well, obviously, those *Kachila* didn't get to them, either.

At that point in time, everyone I had talked to—from the Lumads to the NGO workers who purported to help them, to the scholars of local history and anthropology—was so sure of the *Kachila*'s irrelevance to their history that I felt silly for bringing up the question. In fact, the defining features of the Lumad colonial experience had already been established by Mindanao historian Rudy Rodil in his article so aptly titled "The Resistance and Struggle of the Lumad in Mindanao."[6] The truism was that Lumads were not like "normal" lowland Filipinos because they successfully resisted any and all Spanish influence, fought violently against missionaries, colonizers, and settlers alike, and therefore preserved their traditional culture, which we now treasure as part of the Philippines' pre-Hispanic heritage.

However, I already knew from standard colonial accounts[7] that northern Mindanao was one of the earliest places where Spaniards, beginning with Magellan in 1521, made first contact, and that missionaries had officially been there since 1596. I also knew that the incarnation of the Recoletos (discalced Augustinians)[8] as an

---

[5] Technically, a northern Mindanao variant of Cebuano Visayan.

[6] B. R. Rodil, "Pagtututol at Pakikibaka ng mga Lumad sa Mindanaw, 1903–1935," *Mindanao Focus Journal* 29 (1990): 10–32.

[7] See Peter Schreurs, *Caraga Antigua 1521–1910: The Hispanization and Christianization of Agusan, Surigao, and East Davao* (Cebu: University of San Carlos Publications, 1989), for a missionary-centered account of this aspect of Mindanao history that is completely absent from what is probably the most often cited historical summary of the Christianization of the Philippines, that by Phelan. See John Leddy Phelan, *The Hispanization of the Philippines: Spanish Aims and Filipino Responses, 1565–1700* (Madison, WI: University of Wisconsin Press, 1959).

[8] The Recoletos are Religious (as opposed to Secular) clergy—either priests (*padre*) or brothers (*hermano*)—who are members of the Order of Augustinian Recollects (Orden de los Agustinos Recoletos). Religious clergy take a vow of obedience and belong to a religious order; Secular clergy are under the authority of a local bishop and do not belong to a religious order, nor do they follow rules of cloister or take vows of obedience. The Recoletos are one of the Catholic mendicant orders, which strive towards a more ascetic existence than do regular Religious orders, and utilize the prefix *fray* (nom. *fraile*), from the Latin *Frater*, meaning "brother." Hence, they use the titles *Padre Fray* (abbreviated as P Fr) and *Hermano Fray* (H Fr). Historically, the mendicant orders did not own property either individually or collectively, and were dependent entirely on alms for subsistence; thus, they were classed as "begging friars." The Recoletos, in particular, are often referred to in texts as the *Agustinos descalzos*, literally "shoeless" Augustinians, to differentiate them from the regular Augustinian clergy. In this study, I use the term *Recoleto* instead of the English "Recollect" because it is the more familiar term to Filipino audiences, and also to keep the Iberian cultural context of the study period more consciously in mind. The common suffix for members of this order is *OAR*, but I have seen a few instances of *ORSA*, for Orden de los Recoletos de San Agustín. They originated as a mendicant movement within the older Order of Saint Augustine (Orden de San Agustín, OSA), but became an entirely separate Religious order in the late sixteenth century.

order came principally through their Mindanao missions, and that their mission at Linao, deep in the interior of what is now Agusan del Sur, was established in 1614. This was centuries before any government resettlement policies were implemented, before the trickle of lowlanders from the north would become the deluge that permanently altered the political and cultural landscape of Mindanao. So it is certainly a mystery how centuries of mission work by the Recoletos has been forgotten by all but a determined few.[9]

Moreover, why should we assume, just because the indigenous people of Mindanao did not dress, talk, or behave exactly as the lowlanders to their north, that they could not have experienced significant and meaningful colonial contact? In the early colonial period, the people on the coast were as indigenous or *lumad* to Mindanao as those we find in the interior today, as the categories of lowland vs. upland, or coastal vs. interior, were not mutually exclusive as they have now become. The bottom line is that, even if the *datu*s no longer remembered it, the *Kachila* had, in fact, been in the uplands of northern Mindanao and had, indeed, lived among their ancestors. And clearly a large number of those ancestors became and remained converts, such that the Recoleto missions in Mindanao were sustained well into the nineteenth century, the period when many of these missions were turned over under protest to the reconstituted Jesuit order.[10] So why should we assume there is only one possible or conceivable path of cultural evolution, i.e., that of the explicitly Hispanized and Christianized lowland Filipino, that can result from such contact?

We do know, based on the historical records analyzed by William Henry Scott and Felix Keesing, that significant and sustained contact with Spanish, and later American, colonial officials in northern Luzon island manifested itself in the evolution of "Igorot" as a distinct category of ethnicity.[11] Given that the Igorot and the Lumad are equally distinct from the lowland Filipino, can we not, by simple logical inference, entertain the notion of a similar process having taken place among the Lumad, even in the absence of conclusive historical research?

The Recoletos remain active all over the world, including the Philippines, although these days they are a well-financed missionary operation and regularly utilize footwear.

[9] Schreurs, and, of course, the Recoletos themselves, pointed the finger at the Jesuits as the ultimate source of this blatant omission. The inter-Religious conflicts between Jesuits and the other Religious orders are beyond the scope of this study, but are well-documented. The Recoleto archive in Marcilla (Navarra), Spain, contains press clippings, testimonials, and briefs relating to this deep-rooted territorial conflict as it played out in the Philippines.

[10] After decades of political intrigue due to clashes with other Religious orders, the Jesuits were formally suppressed and disbanded by Pope Clement XIV in 1773, after which they were ejected from all their mission fields except Russia. See Giulio Cordara, *De Suppressione Societatis Iesu Commentarii*, ed. John Murphy SJ (Chicago, IL: Jesuit Way, 1999); and Jonathan Wright, *God's Soldiers: Adventure, Politics, Intrigue, and Power: A History of the Jesuits* (New York, NY: Doubleday, 2004). In the Philippines, the suppression was pre-dated by a *real cedula*, or royal decree, dated December 10, 1757 (Archivo General de Indias [hereafter AGI], Filipinas, 335, leg 17, f13v-15v), and Jesuits were officially removed from the Philippine islands by 1768, returning only after Pope Pius VII officially restored their order in 1814.

[11] Felix Keesing, *The Ethnohistory of Northern Luzon* (Stanford, CA: Stanford University Press, 1962); William Henry Scott, *The Discovery of the Igorots: Spanish Contacts with the Pagans of Northern Luzon* (Quezon City: New Day, 1974). See also Gerard Finin, *The Making of the Igorot: Contours of Cordillera Consciousness* (Quezon City: Ateneo de Manila University Press, 2005).

This leads to even broader questions about both the Lumad and the Philippine colonial experience. First, given the complexity and heterogeneity of colonialism, especially within the Philippine experience, was not the totality of this experience equally complex and heterogeneous? Second, given that the Philippine state and the Filipino as citizen are by and large postcolonial phenomena, why not approach Lumad peoples as Southeast Asians in their own right, rather than as subcategories of the Filipino? In other words, can we not build a Lumad ethnohistory within the context of the larger region, rather than as an inconsequential footnote of Philippine colonial history? The result is therefore something of a thought experiment, one that would historicize the Lumad through not only a determined peek through the parchment curtain but also a candid reinterpretation of the random vignettes of Lumad life that we do glimpse.

REPOSITIONING THE MISSIONARY

The victimology of Western colonial expansion is well-established: the colonizers' technological and strategic advantages over non-Europeans resulted in the "corruption" of indigenous culture by foreign influences, aggravated by the oppressiveness of state-sponsored Christian missionization, the unfairness of forced labor and taxation, the enrichment of Europeans and European entities at the expense of native peoples, the suppression of any and all indigenous autonomy through physical violence and other forms of abuse, and the evolution of a native intelligentsia with occidental frustrations. But human experiences and endeavors, especially cross-cultural ones, form a much more complex, intricate tapestry than this single thread would allow us to weave. For starters, in most cases colonial powers could not have dominated their subjects so thoroughly without the active participation of natives.

I do not mean to say that we should ignore the hegemonizing qualities of Christian missionary work, or stop questioning the missionaries' individual compulsions and motives. While I would argue that the friar abuses shown in José Rizal's novels, *Noli Me Tangere* and *El Filibusterismo,* are not representative of the totality of Christian missionary work in this period, this "image problem" was not spun from pure fiction.[12] There is always tremendous potential for abuse in the inherently unequal relationship between Western missionary and non-Western native, an imbalance stemming from gross inequality in wealth, education, access to information, and access to and familiarity with advanced technology. And, ultimately, the missionary presence in the colonial Philippines was backed by a military presence that was the source of many actual abuses. There can therefore be no pretensions of naïveté claimed for missionaries who, as *de facto* agents of Spanish colonialism, coveted and coaxed power from their target communities.

That said, we cannot simply dismiss the work of these missionaries as mere "hegemony" or presume that any native would—and should—have rejected or resisted any foreign influence out of hand. Whether particular cases of conversion were the result of free choice or spiritual seduction, the converted would have had their own complex motives for acting. By stepping outside of an inflexible "resistance" frame that, by definition, requires designating natives as victims and

---

[12] José P. Rizal, *Noli Me Tangere* (Manila: National Historical Institute, 1995 [1887]), and *El Filibusterismo* (Manila: National Historical Institute, 1996 [1891]).

demonizing missionaries (basically, Christian evangelical propaganda in reverse), we at least allow ourselves to acknowledge the on-the-ground complexity of the relationship between indigenous Filipinos and Roman Catholicism.

I draw from my own experience under Martial Law in the Philippines (1972–81) to say that the Roman Catholic Church is multifaceted, sometimes downright paradoxical. Many Filipinos saw the Church hierarchy turning a blind eye to, even publicly blessing, the Marcos dictatorship despite the openness of its violence and abuse of basic human rights. Ironically, in many instances this violence was knowingly directed against religious workers: priests and nuns—both local and foreign—risked their lives "on the ground" to aid and protect the most powerless communities, especially the ethnic minorities and the urban poor, and for these acts of defiance against the state, many were branded as insurgents, some even targeted for murder. In effect, the Church in the Philippines at that time was both a collaborator and also the only real refuge from the dictatorship. In a similar way, the Church in colonial times incorporated in its single body both the administrative structure that, in certain areas, abused the *indios* and engaged in the theft of native property and resources, while elsewhere, that same structure supported the missionaries on the ground who did what they strongly believed was necessary to improve the lives (spiritual or otherwise) of native peoples and protect the rights and welfare of the faithful under their responsibility. In the first mission period, committed missionaries sought to protect their charges even at the risk of being singled out by Muslim raiders for abduction, torture, and murder.

Even bearing in mind the missionary enterprise's "imperialism of good intentions"[13] in the specific case of the early Spanish colonial period, there remained the quantifiable interpersonal relationships that developed between Catholic missionaries from Europe and the indigenous peoples of Mindanao. Unlike modern evangelical Protestant missionaries I have observed, who, by and large, regularly deflect away attention from themselves in order to focus on the transmission of religious doctrine, it has always been common for Catholic priests methodically to endear themselves to communities at the parish level. Their goal is to achieve a position of complete paternal trust within their target communities in a way that befits their job title of "Father." The communication of doctrine, in turn, is a lifelong process that unfolds as part of this socially intense relationship. In a manner of speaking, the missionary priest is himself the medium and the message of the Catholic mission, for to be a priest is literally to embody the Catholic faith.

The late Mindanao historian and Dutch missionary priest, Peter Schreurs, believed that Filipinos are special for what he saw as their total embodiment of the Catholic faith, arguing that this trait may well be the Filipinos' primary contribution to humanity.[14] I cannot bring myself to reduce Philippine culture to such a gross oversimplification, but all the same, I recognize that it is a great disservice to Philippine scholarship to pretend that we can somehow still isolate a discrete "authentic," purely indigenous culture or identity free of all Spanish or Catholic contamination. Unlike the limited cultural infusion vis-à-vis the United States, limited despite a century of gross globalization, the extended cultural intercourse between the Philippines and Spain is impossible to parse out today, and who can say

---

[13] See Hans Joas, *War and Modernity: Studies in the History of Violence in the Twentieth Century* (Cambridge: Polity Press, 2002), p. 40.

[14] Personal communication, Tilburg, Netherlands, April 1, 2000.

with authority that it would have been possible to do so even within the first century of colonial rule? Every contact has its consequences, every action a reaction, no matter how small. As we will see in the chapters that follow, even those who managed to emerge from the historical stew of the colonial period as "non-Christian" were affected significantly by the presence of Christian missionaries in their territories.

This fact underlines the significance of the missionary presence *per se*, which will be discussed in greater detail in Chapter Two. For this preface, perhaps it is enough simply to remind everyone that the long-term presence of Recoleto missionaries in the population centers of both the coast and riverine interiors of northeast Mindanao—centuries before these regions were overrun by Visayan and Tagalog settlers, until the end of the colonial period—is an incontrovertible fact of history. As we attempt to reconceptualize the ethnohistory of Lumad peoples, the Recoletos lurk ever in the background, like Chekhov's gun that we know has to be fired at some point in their story. It is simply inconceivable that, over three centuries of residence, the Recoletos would not have had a tangible cultural impact on indigenous peoples. It is time to recognize them as a meaningful element of the Lumad past.

The current model of Lumad ethnogenesis remains fundamentally flawed for precisely this reason. It is based almost entirely on the upstreaming of "salvage" ethnographies produced at the turn of the nineteenth century, during the demographically tumultuous, and therefore socially tumultuous, transition period between Spanish and American colonial administrations. It is an "ethnographic present" of questionable value, premised on highly unlikely conditions of cultural isolation and stasis that ignore key historical developments.[15] This model also defines the Lumad not in terms of who they are or what they have endured, but largely as the undeveloped negative of lowland, mainstream Filipinos, i.e., they are what the Filipino would still be if not for the forced baptism in colonial waters. The renowned Southeast Asianist Leonard Andaya rightly cautions us, "Too often the story of Southeast Asia has been structured according to ethnic struggles, a presentist approach that obscures the flexibility of ethnic identities in the past."[16]

A meaningful Lumad ethnography and history must therefore reveal something more interesting, more human, and more substantial than the popular, romanticized image of an emphatically un-Hispanized peoples who somehow escaped all colonial influence and oppression and, whenever possible, violently resisted it. The

---

[15] Henry Dobyns and Robert Euler, addressing the same deficiency in Native American ethnography, use one individual's life history to illustrate just "how utterly unrealistic the concept of the 'ethnographic present' was and is … Ethnohistorical studies of cultural change during four decades have demonstrated that no 'traditional ethnographic present' ever existed. Yet studies continue to be published presenting data in an 'ethnographic present' that ignores preceding key events that shaped the defectively depicted situation." See Henry F. Dobyns and Robert C. Euler, "The Nine Lives of Cherum, The Pai Tokumhet," *American Indian Quarterly* 22,3 (1998): 363. Quoting Eminie Wheeler-Voegelin, they also point to the problem of a research artifact that similarly plagues Philippine ethnography: "The majority of ethnological reports on North American Indian cultures that were written by American-trained ethnologists during the period 1910–40 were couched in the 'ethnographic present' and purported to describe the 'aboriginal' cultures of various Indian groups." See Erminie Wheeler-Voegelin, "The Northern Paiute of Central Oregon: A Chapter in Treaty-Making," *Ethnohistory* 3,1 (1956): 1.

[16] Leonard Andaya, *Leaves of the Same Tree: Trade and Ethnicity in the Straits of Melaka* (Singapore: NUS Press, 2010), p. 5.

combination of historical evidence and modern-day observation shows us that the truth lies somewhere in the reconciliation of both scenarios. Despite the undeniable colonial contact and conversion that took place over many centuries, Lumad peoples managed to maintain a level of cultural distinctiveness in the course of the many transformations wrought by colonization and conversion, a distinctiveness that misleads most observers to conclude by deductive reasoning that such processes, and therefore such contact, could not have taken place.

Alas, it is surprisingly easy to look at such politically disadvantaged minorities as the Lumad and imagine them having mounted a romantic, but futile, resistance to change, modernity, and inevitable detribalization. In the Philippines, a patriotic sense of outrage at one's historical powerlessness and colonial victimization finds its purest expression in this sort of romanticism. As such, nostalgia is quite insidious and may be even a more serious problem than sourcing in terms of its effects on local history or anthropology. As culturally specific as it is universally human, nostalgia is

> ... a mourning for the impossibility of a mythical return, for the loss of an enchanted world with clear borders and values ... a secular expression of a spiritual longing for an absolute, a home that is both physical and spiritual, the edenic unity of time and space before entry into history. The nostalgic is looking for ... memorable signs, desperately misreading them.[17]

From this perspective, people like the Lumad are mourned in the very act of celebrating them, and the "victims of progress" model remains popular for framing the plight of indigenous/tribal minorities, despite arguments against this limited view.[18] Although Lumad peoples have, at times, attempted to turn this stereotype to their own advantage, they only cage themselves further through self-fetishization.

It is certainly not difficult to appreciate the weighty national stakes involved in perpetuating a timeless image of the Lumad and other tribal peoples as true representatives of a native Filipino essence, especially in the absence of any grand political, literary, or monumental inheritance from the pre-Hispanic past.[19] But weightier existential matters are at stake for Lumad peoples, because they are not benefited by a paternalistic approach that forces them into socially and politically essentialized foreign categories and compels them to play exoticized "Ethnic" in order to receive legal or other recognition.[20] Instead, they are plagued by the same dilemma of conformity as tribal peoples in the Americas and elsewhere, who, when they do break out of these ethnic straitjackets, risk castigation by outsiders as "politically incorrect Indians."[21]

---

[17] Svetlana Boym, *The Future of Nostalgia* (New York, NY: Basic Books, 2001), p. 8.

[18] For example, as outlined in John Bodley, *Victims of Progress* (Palo Alto, CA: Mayfield Publishing Company, 1982). See also James F. Eder, *On the Road to Tribal Extinction: Depopulation, Deculturation, and Adaptive Well-Being among the Batak of the Philippines* (Berkeley, CA: University of California Press, 1987).

[19] See Benedict Anderson, "The Rooster's Egg: Pioneering World Folklore in the Philippines," *New Left Review* (March–April 2000): 47–62.

[20] See Oona T. Paredes, "Discriminating Native Traditions among the Mindanao Lumad," *Old Ties and New Solidarities: Studies on Philippine Communities*, ed. C. Macdonald and G. Pesigan (Quezon City: Ateneo de Manila University Press, 2000), pp. 74–90.

[21] This phrase was first used against Amazonian Indians in Brazil who were condemned for legally selling off their own mineral and timber resources in order to pay for modern

The "wave migration" theory of Philippine ethnic differentiation, popularized in the previous century by the American ethnologist H. Otley Beyer, goes even further by asserting that people like the Lumad were culturally different because they were descended from a less evolved race of humans, biologically separate from mainstream lowland Filipinos.[22] While this alleged genetic imperviousness to culture change has been explicitly discredited in academic circles, its vestiges remain deeply embedded in popular thinking. Wave migration still surfaces in elementary school textbooks in which present-day Lumad cultural forms, including modern ethnic subdivisions, are represented as examples of precolonial Philippine culture.[23] It also remains implicit in current academic research. For example, in an archaeological study of feasting practices in precolonial central Philippines, the archaeologist Laura Junker relies heavily on Fay-Cooper Cole's description of early-twentieth-century Lumads in Bukidnon province in north Mindanao to describe and analyze chiefdoms that existed in the Visayas roughly five centuries *prior* to Spanish contact. Junker thereby unintentionally affirms Beyer's assertions.[24] If the problem lies in the

---

conveniences. See Jack Epstein, "Brazil Indians Defend Sale of Gold, Trees," *Dallas Morning News*, November 6, 1993, p. 20A.

[22] See H. Otley Beyer, *Philippine and East Asian Archaeology and its Relation to the Origin of the Pacific Islands Population* (National Research Council of the Philippines, Bulletin 29, 1948). Beyer's wave migration theory was basically a scientistic reflection of colonially informed racial categorization that projected twentieth-century socio-economic conditions into prehistoric times, and in many ways justified the superior position of groups in power—including that of Euro-American colonizers. In fact, it had absolutely no basis in archaeological, linguistic, genetic, or other scientific or ethnographic evidence. See William Henry Scott, *Cracks in the Parchment Curtain and Other Essays in Philippine History* (Quezon City: New Day Publishers, 1982), pp. 8–12, 29. But for decades, Beyer's wave migration theory was treated with very little skepticism and underwent refinement by respected Philippine anthropologists, and was a common feature of anthropological monographs of the American colonial period. As utilized, for example, in Fay-Cooper Cole, *The Bukidnons of Mindanao*, Chicago Natural History Museum Fieldiana 46 (Chicago, IL: Chicago Natural History Museum, 1956); and John M. Garvan, *The Manóbos of Mindanáo* (Washington, DC: United States Government Printing Office [USGPO], 1941), pp. 10–13. Wave migration theory also appears in the introduction to Madigan's article mentioned in Chapter Three. See Francis Madigan SJ, "The Early History of Cagayan de Oro," *Philippine Studies* 11,1 (1963): 76–130. See Filomeno V. Aguilar, "Tracing Origins: Ilustrado Nationalism and the Racial Science of Migration Waves," *Journal of Asian Studies* 64,3 (2005): 605–38, for the most informed discussion of this theory and its impact on Philippine national identity.

[23] See, for example, Estella Capina, ed., *Isang Bansa, Isang Lahi* (Metro Manila: Vibal Publishing House, 1994), pp. 68–71. This practice of "upstreaming" is a common tool in ethnohistory, but its uncritical application, as practiced by Beyer and others, has a parallel in the upstreaming and essentializing of Hutu and Tutsi ethnicities in colonial and postcolonial Rwanda. While this essentializing of Lumad differentiation is regarded by most Filipinos and Philippinists as quite harmless, it is, in fact, a negative experience for Lumad peoples. The later Rwandan genocide may be an extreme consequence of such essentialism, but deadly conflict is not an unusual outcome in terms of general human behavior. Hence the gravity I give to this issue. See Jan Vansina, *Le Rwanda Ancien: Le Royaume Nyiginya* (Paris: Karthala, 2001), and "History Facing the Present: An Interview with Jan Vansina," *H-Africa*, 2001, www.h-net.org/~africa/africaforum/vansina interview.htm, accessed November 30, 2007. See also John K. Chance, "Mesoamerica's Ethnographic Past," *Ethnohistory* 43,3 (1996): 380.

[24] See Cole, *The Bukidnons of Mindanao*. See also Laura L. Junker, *Raiding, Trading, and Feasting: The Political Economy of Philippine Chiefdoms* (Honolulu, HI: University of Hawaii Press, 1999). While the latter study is important in so many ways, Junker's direct use of postcolonial datuship from an egalitarian minority group in the highland interior of a large island like Mindanao to describe pre-contact chiefdoms among stratified lowland majority groups in a

sparseness of the conventional historical record, then the antidote to this destructive nostalgia is a reexamination of our sources for this period of Philippine—and Lumad—history.

I pursued archival research in the hope of uncovering something previously missed, either in the form of unidentified or underutilized documents, or records that may have been misinterpreted or mistranslated, or perhaps whole categories of information that may have been dismissed as insignificant because, in pertaining to such a peripheral area as northeast Mindanao, such materials could contribute nothing to the grander perspective of Philippine national history and consciousness. In order to carry out archival research on the Lumad, therefore, it was necessary for me to go to Spain, where I would face a reckoning in terms of my own ethnic identity.

REPOSITIONING HERITAGE

I come from a family that is proud to be brown, but I know that quite a few *Kachila* ancestors married into the indigenous gene pool, part of the same process of miscue and *mestizaje* that took place throughout Southeast Asia and the Americas, with every encounter of Western expansion, and with every meeting or clash of peoples since time immemorial.[25] Some sort of Iberian ancestry comprises a good quarter of my blood quantum, and on some level it always made me uneasy that this ancestry is traceable, despite the fact that I could never be mistaken for a European. I would console myself that, unlike some families of mestizo descent, at least we knew whose side we were on. At the very least, we had no pretensions of being better than anyone, nor of being anything other than Filipino. I was proud of the fact that—to use the Manila colloquialism that mocks the more loathsome of the bourgeoisie—at least we were not like those awful *"konyo* kids."[26]

I had immersed myself in African studies as an undergraduate, therefore, my reference for this experience—my visit to Spain—was not from Filipino or Latino literature, but from the African-American writer Eddy Harris, who wrote poignantly of his pilgrimage to Africa, during which he hoped to rediscover his roots, only to find that he was entirely of the West—that he was not, and never would be, African. I had prepared myself for a similar "disappointment." Indeed, that was how I felt *before* I began my research. If anything, I felt a great sense of trepidation about having to defend myself culturally or intellectually against my people's former

---

small Visayan island is problematic. There are also some rather serious issues with regard to the representativeness of Cole's description of the Bukidnon; see Oona T. Paredes, "Describing Higaûnon Culture," *Kinaadman* 20 (1998): 53–74.

[25] See Richard Rodriguez, *Brown: The Last Discovery of America* (New York, NY: Penguin, 2002); and James A. Clifton, ed., *Being and Becoming Indian: Biographical Studies of North American Frontiers* (Chicago, IL: Dorsey Press, 1989). "*Mestizaje*" originally referred to cultural and sexual interaction between Europeans and non-Europeans in the Americas, and the highly racialized hierarchies and complex power inequalities that evolved in those settings. I invoke it here in a broader sense to refer to the similar exchanges, tensions, and ambiguities of contact situations elsewhere.

[26] This term is based on a common Spanish-derived expletive, which is also a vulgar term for female genitalia. It has been used to mock upper-class Filipinos who aspire to "whiteness" in part by being either unwilling or unable to communicate in an indigenous Philippine language.

colonial masters. My interest in Spain was then purely academic: I would not have gone there if not to gain access to the archives.

Nothing therefore can adequately describe the irony of being a Filipina in Spain, of walking into the core of this foreign Hispanic world and feeling instantly and eerily at home. I found that living spaces were arranged "correctly," and the sounds of the city familiar. I realized that, despite the language barrier, I saw a familiar order in the superficial chaos of the crowded bars, markets, and streets. I was neither surprised nor rattled by the cozy inertia of local people, nor by a public infrastructure that, like everything in my Third World childhood, seemed to run on serendipity rather than efficiency. I also found that the peculiar attitudes and idiosyncrasies that often bothered me about my homeland—things that grated on the Western end of my spectrum of sensibilities—were the very same ones that rankled me about Spaniards and Spain. It came to the point where I began to hear what I thought were Tagalog words sprinkled into everyday speech.[27]

It truly shocked me that my initial experience of Spain—in particular, the city of Sevilla—was of an impossible *déjà vu*. Filipinos are notorious for being so heavily "Americanized," yet even the United States felt properly foreign the first time I set foot in it as a young immigrant. In contrast, I felt a resonance with Spain that, to this day, remains impossible to describe, except to say that when I got there I felt that I had not traveled at all. And it was there, in the land of the *colonialista*, that I finally began to accept that Filipinos are part of this blended Spanish cultural family after all, for better or for worse.

This aspect of my research experience is relevant beyond standard anthropological positioning because it became an integral part of my whole process of data collection. As a registered scholar, legitimated by an official letter from my home university, I was given daily access to data sources that are, for the most part, neglected by other scholars who do not have either the financial and institutional support, or the linguistic skills, to take advantage of these sources.[28] This type of archival research can be particularly intimidating for Filipino scholars in other ways, and almost seems more trouble than it is worth when English translations of important Spanish originals are widely available in both print and digital formats.[29] However, working from previously translated sources has many inherent problems, the most fundamental of which would be the potential for mistranslation and decontextualization. As shown in alarming detail by Spanish historian Gloria Cano, it is intellectually perilous to use translations uncritically and take them at face value, even—or perhaps especially—when dealing with widely accepted publications.[30]

---

[27] For example, *coger* (to take) in subjunctive present, second person formal, is *coja*, which is pronounced and used just like the verb *kuha*, in both Cebuano and Tagalog.

[28] For more on my experience of conducting archival research in original Spanish-language sources, see Oona T. Paredes, "Working with Spanish Colonial Records and Archives: Reflections and Practicalities," *Kyoto Review of Southeast Asia*, 2006, http://kyotoreview sea.org/Paredes_final.htm, accessed May 24, 2012.

[29] For example, the fifty-five-volume "Blair and Robertson" compendium of translated published and unpublished Spanish documents is now widely accessible in both print and digital format. The Bank of the Philippine Islands released the complete series on CD-Rom in 2005, and about half of the volumes are also available online via the Gutenberg Project, at www.gutenberg.ph/, accessed May 24, 2012. See Emma H. Blair and James A. Robertson, *The Philippine Islands, 1493–1898* (Cleveland, OH: Arthur H. Clark Company, 1903–1909).

[30] Gloria Cano, "Evidence for the Deliberate Distortion of the Spanish Philippine Colonial Historical Record in *The Philippine Islands, 1493–1898*," *Journal of Southeast Asian Studies* 39

The value of returning to primary sources is not simply in the act of reading them in the original archaic Castillian. Methodologically, in fact, I found it extremely valuable to struggle through the original scripts themselves and handle the centuries-old paper and vellum on which they were written, because the exercise helped me return these texts to their appropriate "untranslated" foreignness. Though it took significantly more time, this process contributed greatly to my own ability to detach the texts from their extant and prior ideological usage vis-à-vis Philippine nationalist history. The tactility of this process removes any presumptions of narrative familiarity that we might have with the texts: it shocks us intellectually into reading them anew. Though in the end I could not rely solely on primary sources for this book, I made use of them whenever the opportunity arose, and the experience has undoubtedly changed not only the way I will read all source materials but also the way I see the "pastness" of the Philippines, and the way I reflect on its history and its historicity.

Likewise, I learned much from the novel viewpoints of the countless researchers and archivists I encountered in and out of the archives, and beyond the reach of Philippine political and cultural concerns. I was therefore compelled to broaden my perspective to accommodate these unfamiliar realities, all of which contributed something unique to my understanding of what constitutes colonialism and the many permutations of what we often generically refer to as "the" colonial experience, as if it were a single story simply being retold.

The fact that I was Filipina in Spain also added another, equally interesting layer that made me take a second look at the relationship of the colonial experience to the formation of modern Filipino identities. While in Spain, I was an object of curiosity to others, like a distant cousin who had grown up elsewhere and was visiting for the first time. This state of simultaneous familiarity and foreignness gave me the opportunity to see not only how Spaniards and Americanos responded to me,[31] but also how these two groups responded to each other. I found their mutual animosity—a love–hate relationship that existed despite, or perhaps because of, their greater cultural proximity and more intertwined histories—perplexing, to say the least. Not a few of the Americanos I met, all fellow PhD students, went so far as to express a shocking derision of Spain and Spaniards on a daily basis, even in public. Ironically, I was also cornered several times by Spaniards who wanted to know whether Filipinos also hated them like the Americanos did—and if not, then why not?

One Spanish *profesora* complained of having to endure Mexicans of European descent condemning all Spaniards as colonialists and racists, and to her face, no less. In her view, it was the height of hypocrisy to blame people like her for colonial injustices because it was, after all, the Spanish ancestors of those same Mexicans who left Spain and did the colonizing, while *her* ancestors stayed behind and had nothing to do with oppressing any Americanos. She was clearly incensed by this ugly association with colonialism, but I could only shrug agreeably as she looked to me for some kind of atonement, as if it were in my power to exonerate a select few on

(2008): 1–30. See also G. Cano, "Blair and Robertson's *The Philippine Islands, 1493–1898:* Scholarship or Imperialist Propaganda?," *Philippine Studies* 56,1 (2008): 3-46.

[31] I use the term *Americano* here as Spanish speakers do, in reference to the peoples of Mexico, Central America, South America, and the Caribbean. *Hispanoamericano*, in common academic use in Spain, is apparently offensive to (at least some) Americanos. This is true of the Anglicized term "Hispanic" as well.

behalf of all *indios* past and present. I was therefore impressed by the Spaniards' puzzlement and regret that Filipinos, being somewhat more agreeable on the surface than those angry Americanos, were not better integrated into the Spanish-speaking world. I began to feel astonished that, despite the anger, hatred, and violence of the Philippine Revolution—during which my great-grandmother Esperanza Tronqued reportedly broke her own prominent nose so she would not be killed for resembling her Spanish father—Filipinos just don't seem to have those kinds of issues.

That said, I personally found it rather difficult to veer away from the selective nationalist history I learned in school. It bordered on an existential crisis to admit that the primary sources reflected such a remarkably different picture from the national memory. But my research in Spain, coupled with daily encounters with the Americanos, highlighted two basic facts that ultimately forced me to reconfigure my understanding of the overall Philippine colonial experience under Spain. The first is that, even at the apex of the colonial period, physical and psychological violence against Philippine natives was never comparable to the Spanish occupation of the Americas.[32] To assert that anything close to this was a quotidian fact of Philippine life under Spanish rule belittles the well-documented genocide and further persecution of Amerindians.[33]

The second is that, in the battle for cultural hegemony between colonizer and colonized, it was clearly the indigenous Filipino who prevailed. This is most apparent when we consider the vitality of indigenous languages then as well as now. Spaniards find it incomprehensible that, after over three hundred years in the islands, *Castellano* never managed to secure an enduring foothold. With the negligible exception of two Spanish creole languages of limited circulation, native Philippine languages remain alive and well. And in those that are inflected by a significant number of Spanish loan words, all vestiges of Iberian speech are conjugated mercilessly into indigenous linguistic molds.

If these two fundamental realities do not seem like much, let us make an intimate, experiential contrast with the Americano perspective, which is neatly summarized in the words of a Colombian acquaintance who once scolded me that Filipinos were lucky, for we never experienced the demographic extremes of extermination and replacement. "I hate Spain and all the Spaniards!" he loudly proclaimed one day at a grocery store (to my great discomfort). "They killed almost

---

[32] See Thomas R. Berger, *A Long and Terrible Shadow: White Values, Native Rights in the Americas, 1492–1992* (Seattle, WA: University of Washington Press, 1991); Bartolomé de las Casas, *Bartolomé de Las Casas: A Selection of His Writings*, trans. George Sanderlin (New York, NY: Knopf, 1971); Kenneth Kipple and Stephen Beck, eds., *Biological Consequences of European Expansion, 1450–1800* (Aldershot: Ashgate Press, 1997); and David Stannard, *American Holocaust: Columbus and the Conquest of the New World* (New York, NY: Oxford University Press, 1992). However, see also Matthew Restall, *Seven Myths of the Spanish Conquest* (Oxford: Oxford University Press, 2004).

[33] Nor should we forget the absolute animal brutality of other forms of colonization. The Spanish scholar Ana Crespo Solana, of the Instituto de Historia in Madrid, attributed Dutch cruelty in Surinam to an intolerant Calvinist doctrine that did not allow for the idea that non-whites had souls, and to the notable absence of religious conversion as a Dutch colonial objective. Whereas Spanish Catholicism and related colonial policies had innumerable faults, at least it was explicit about the underlying humanity of colonial subjects; uncivilized and heathen though they were, they were acknowledged as possessing souls in need of saving. Presentation by Ana Crespo Solana, Mesas Redondas lecture series, Escuela de Estudios Hispanoamericanos, Sevilla, Spain, March 15, 2005.

everyone, they took my land, they took my culture, they took my language! We have nothing left of our own!" His Andean features were of little consolation, he explained: "All I have left is my Atahualpa[34] face!"

Given this perspective, it would be disingenuous for Filipinos or Philippinists to reify their own victimization when studying the Spanish colonial period, because once the Americano experience is allowed to resonate against our own, it does so loudly, even deafeningly, and only then can we comprehend what it truly means to be defeated, colonized, and reduced as a people. The more I learned through my research and through my colonial "step-siblings"—Colombians, Peruvians, Mexicans, and other Americanos—the more I recognized that a more insidious type of "colonial mentality" keeps us handcuffed to someone else's history. Maybe it's time to conduct a proper autopsy of the past four-odd centuries and, in the process, finally resolve our selves in the postmortem of our colonial experience. Perhaps asking different questions of the colonial past will enable us to understand why the Philippines seems to be frozen in a difficult and seemingly endless postcolonial moment, trapped in what the poet Luis Francia calls "the straitjacket of … defeat and colonialism."[35]

There is, indeed, a profound internal conflict over modern Filipinos' Spanish heritage, thanks to our intimate emotional and intellectual relationship with the Catholic Church. That Catholicism is embedded in the very DNA of Philippine nationhood is glaringly obvious to its non-Catholic citizens, who are forced to accommodate it at every turn, even when dealing with a purportedly secular government. I embody that conflict as well, and now come full circle to confess that, as someone from north Mindanao who was raised and educated squarely within the Hispanized Philippine Catholic tradition, I cannot claim a true separation from my own subject. While neither the European missionaries nor the Lumad are "my people" in the strict ethnological, political, cultural, social, or even biological sense, I also cannot assert a purist's objectivity on the basis of "otherness," whether mine or theirs. This has been a surprisingly personal journey, in which I have had to resolve many contradictions that complicate my own identity, family history, beliefs, sense of nationalism, and understanding of my place on this planet, which, from a grand historical perspective, has always been very, very small. "There is," as the American essayist Richard Rodriguez laments, "such a betrayal in writing about one's family."[36]

Any introspective Filipino scholar must realize that confronting and critiquing either the colonial period or the issue of religious conversion involves critiquing something that is woven into our very conception of self. This confrontation is particularly acute for those generations weaned on Teodoro Agoncillo and Renato Constantino.[37] Reynaldo Ileto, the historian, captures this predicament nicely in his foreword to the aptly titled volume *More Hispanic Than We Admit*:

---

[34] Atahualpa was the sixteenth-century Inca ruler who encountered Francisco Pizarro and his men in 1532. Pizarro later captured and executed Atahualpa, beginning the Spanish conquest of the Inca Empire.

[35] Francia, *Eye of the Fish*, p. 34.

[36] Richard Rodriguez, public lecture at the University of Missouri–Columbia, sponsored by the Center for the Literary Arts, November 13, 2008.

[37] See Teodoro Agoncillo, *History of the Filipino People* (Quezon City: Malaya Books, 1967); Renato Constantino, *The Philippines, vol. 1: A Past Revisited (Pre-Spanish to 1941)* (Quezon City:

> To publicly admit of the Hispanic in us has been a vexing issue ... Admission would seem to be reverting to an earlier view that relegated Philippine history to chapters of the history of Imperial Spain. Admission would seem to downplay the possibility of recovering a pre-Hispanic culture that Spanish conquest and conversion had destroyed. Admission would seem to challenge the narrative of resistance to colonial rule, from scattered revolts to the revolution against Spain, that serves as the backbone of textbook histories.[38]

Thus is nostalgia a cage for all Filipinos, not just ethnic minorities like the Lumad. I have no doubt that this will remain the smelly *carabao* in the room for a few more intellectual generations to come.[39] Once we do manage to take the fuller historical and cultural context of the Philippines into account, I hope it becomes easier to see that we have all shared, contributed to, and own the same messy and emotionally charged history. From where I stand, it is not a history of defeat, but one of heady survival and triumph, setting us apart within the world of former Spanish colonies. It is a history that defines *all* Filipinos.

Yet as I argue for the recognition of an equally significant colonial experience among the Lumad, I would also argue for decoupling this experience from the dominant narrative of Philippine nationhood, if only to underline the fact that this book is about events that took place before any notions of nationhood, much less its expression or its inevitability, had materialized. To be sure, history, even something as clearly delineated as Philippine history, is never just a single, unified storyline. This work is presented not as an alternative story, but as an additional, complementary one that allows us to appreciate the surprising degree of cultural and political liminality that was possible within the colonial context.

The chapters that follow present historical vignettes of the Lumad colonial experience from the beginnings of Spanish contact in the late sixteenth century to the early Carlist Wars of the nineteenth century, the period immediately preceding the drastic political transformations in Spain that resulted in a burst of institutional intensification that became the now-familiar form of colonial governance and experience in the Philippines. I intentionally dwell on the long centuries before the beginnings of what became the *Katipunan*, well before José Rizal and his now iconic indictment of colonial and clerical abuse, and the revolution on the northern island of Luzon,[40] because the story of the Lumad simply cannot be presented, much less analyzed, through the conventional framework of Philippine colonial history. That history dwells on the Hispanization and oppression of lowland cultural groups—particularly Tagalog and Visayan *indios* who had more regular and intensive contact with Spaniards and Spanish administration—and maps out the process of

---

Tala Publishing Services, 1975). But see also Glenn May, *A Past Recovered* (Quezon City: New Day, 1987), and Nick Joaquin, *A Question of Heroes* (Pasig City: Anvil, 2005).

[38] Reynaldo C. Ileto, Foreword, *More Hispanic Than We Admit: Insights into Philippine Cultural History*, ed. Isaac Donoso (Metro Manila: Vibal Publishing, 2008), p. v.

[39] *Carabao* is the Philippine word for water buffalo.

[40] The *Katipunan*, formed in 1892, was the most viable revolutionary organization formed by native Filipinos in their struggle against colonial rule. José Rizal's novels were widely considered revolutionary for their gratuitous depiction of corruption and abuse by Spanish friars.

Hispanization in a way that makes it difficult to go beyond that single story of how Filipinos became and remain a people. In contrast, from the Lumad perspective, the nation itself was but a belated subplot of their own story; and from that perspective, there was certainly nothing inevitable about how anything would turn out.

CHAPTER OUTLINE

This is not an attempt to establish the definitive (ethno)history of Lumad peoples in Mindanao. That project cannot be accomplished until more scholars of Mindanao are called to study the phenomenon of the Lumad, and the colonial history of Mindanao, at a more significant level than has been undertaken to date. With this book, I focus instead on several touchstones that, taken together, begin to show us the contours of a Lumad ethnohistory. This approach gives us an episodic rather than a continuous history, a limitation that reflects the fragmentary nature of the documentary coverage of this area. However, the robustness of each episode allows us to begin moving away from conjectural history, and towards a more substantial one.

"Las Dychas Yslas" situates Mindanao in the early colonial period, when the archipelago itself was still a poorly defined entity, loosely referred to in Spanish correspondence as "those islands."[41] Here we encounter the Lumad and try to parse out who they were during this period in history, at the very beginning of the colonial encounter, in contrast to how we routinely define them today.

"Blessed are the Peacemakers" introduces an important set of actors in the Lumad story: the Order of Augustinian Recollects, or Recoletos. As a fledgling Spanish order at the time, they chose to make northeast Mindanao a major area of focus, sending some of their very first missionaries there at the beginning of the seventeenth century. This means the history of the Recoleto order and that of the Lumads were both unfolding at the same time, across the same landscape. I would argue that in order to understand the Lumad at that particular moment in time, we also need to understand who the Recoletos were and the mission they were attempting to carry out, in order to contextualize properly the archival record they left behind.

"Blood Brothers and the Enemies of God" tells the story of how the Kagayanon Lumad people, led by the *datu* Salangsang, converted to Christianity after the arrival of two Recoletos in 1622. It describes the dangerous conditions under which this encounter took place, and how that danger contributed to both the bonds that developed between missionaries and Lumads, and the battlefield conversions that followed. This turn of events made possible a major reorganization of Lumad life, including the relocation of their settlement farther downriver, in what eventually grew into the present-day city of Cagayan de Oro.

"Treachery Most Foul" is about a little-known bloody uprising led by erstwhile Karaga Lumad converts around the small Spanish garrison of Tandag, in the province of Caraga in 1631. The revolt was a deep betrayal for the Recoletos, who had regarded many of the rebels—local elites who had forged close working relationships with the local Spanish regiment—as friends and protectors. It likewise

---

[41] The recurring phrase was "*las dychas yslas*," which is literally "the said (or aforementioned) islands," but for the context in which it was used, the English prose equivalent would be "those islands."

reverberated among the Karaga themselves, a majority of whom actively turned against kinfolk in protecting Recoleto lives, suppressing the revolt, and luring escaped rebels out of hiding afterwards. I draw from eyewitness accounts and inquest testimony to outline the sequence of events in Caraga and frame them within the social world of the Tandag mission.

In this chapter, I point to the dual nature of conversion, arguing that, just as a strong Christian identity had developed among Karaga converts in a very short time, the Recoletos were likewise "converted" to the Lumad world, such that they began to imagine them within the context of shared Christian values and "brotherhood," particularly in contrast to the Karaga's former allies, the Magindanaw "Moros." I also make special note of the peculiar case of María Campan, a female convert who was singled out for condemnation in the inquest despite the fact that she was not accused of conspiracy or murder in the revolt. Campan's case reveals the dissonance between Lumad and Spaniard worldviews relative to gender, and how they erupted in this particular instance.

"Your Slaves Who Shall Serve You" presents three letters containing official requests for Spanish patronage by three different Lumad communities in the early eighteenth and nineteenth centuries. These letters provide a rare glimpse of Lumad political life in the early colonial period and show very clearly the limitations of Spanish colonial power vis-à-vis Mindanao during these periods. Contradictions within the texts suggest that the Lumad were well aware of this reality, and show their willingness to exploit this political gap for their own gain. One letter, transcribed in an archaic Visayan dialect from 1722, also provides a possible linkage with oral historical traditions from northern Mindanao that point to a rupture within one Lumad community. This rupture appears to have culminated in the rejection of mission life by at least one kin group, and was signaled by their migration into the mountainous interior, where they could stay true to their ancestral spiritual laws.

The final chapter, "The Golden Cane," explores the surprising Spanish colonial origins of several oral traditions and shared symbols of indigenous political authority and law that remain culturally significant among many modern-day Lumad groups. These symbols, which are widely believed to be precolonial in origin, prove essential to understanding how profoundly embedded the colonial experience is in Lumad cultures. The possible role of Spanish colonial administration in the development of modern indigenous leadership is also highlighted.

As an afterword, "Respecting Place" closes the book by returning to the issue of situating Lumads within, rather than without, the Philippine colonial experience. The theme of "place" echoes the locative task of situating the Lumad historically and geographically, as well as exploring how centuries of contact with missionaries and other Spanish agents marked the lives of colonial-era Lumadnon in northeast Mindanao.

CHAPTER 1

LAS DYCHAS YSLAS:
THE AFOREMENTIONED ISLANDS

The early Spanish colonial period opens at a time when the island of Mindanao and its people—indeed all of what is now the Philippine archipelago—were still in the process of becoming historic, a time when, in retrospect, the colonial project was still unsettled and subject to reexamination. While the spiritual conquest of the Americas had been well underway for many decades, the Philippine archipelago was politically inchoate, and, as a political or even cultural unit, it was both meaningless and inconsequential. The indigenous peoples of Mindanao, ancestors of today's Lumadnon, were just beginning their encounter with Iberian missionaries and the radically different world from which they came.

Most early records I came across in the archives spoke rather generically of *las dychas yslas*, those "aforementioned islands," or, when they wanted to be more specific, *las yslas del poniente*, the islands of the West. Only much, much later was this entire oceanic assemblage named after King Philip II of Spain to become *Filipinas*, the Philippines.[1] Even then, it was always bundled administratively—and archivally— with the Marianas,[2] until the end of the Spanish colonial era. As a nascent mission field, moreover, it was still being conceptualized and spiritually mapped during this era. As such, what we now regard as the centers and the peripheries of the indigenous colonial experience were yet to be determined. At the point where this study begins, there is nothing specifically peripheral about northeast Mindanao, the Lumad peoples, or the Recoleto missions that were about to be established there ... except in the sense that Southeast Asia itself was peripheral, being that it was not Europe. Soon thereafter, however, the presence of Muslim peoples in their new colony, too soon after the Reconquista, definitely colored how Spaniards thought of Mindanao. So it was that colonial accounts, when they did bother to mention Mindanao, focused primarily on the "problem" of its indigenous Muslims, whom they branded as "Moros," after their Moorish nemeses in the recently concluded Spanish Reconquista.

Those accounts that deal with the rest of the island usually state that the first Catholic mission in Mindanao was established by Jesuits in Butuan in 1596, and

---

[1] The name was coined by Ruy Lopez de Villalobos during his disastrous 1543 expedition and initially referred only to the Visayan islands of Samar and Leyte.

[2] The Mariana Islands were formerly known as *Las Islas de los Ladrones*, or "islands of thieves," because the early Spanish explorers had some very unpleasant experiences there, in sharp contrast to their much more congenial reception in the Philippine archipelago. See Laurence Bergreen, *Over the Edge of the World: Magellan's Terrifying Circumnavigation of the Globe* (New York, NY: HarperCollins, 2003). This contrast was a recurring theme in some of the early reports, or *relaciones*, about the Philippine archipelago.

leave it at that.[3] However, as with history's persistent questions regarding Magellan's expedition in 1521, the complicating facts of what came before and after that 1596 Jesuit mission are equally, if not more, important.[4] Only when we are mindful of this wider context can we come to a wider understanding of the day-to-day realities of mission life—for both the missionaries and the missionized—in what, at the time, was a wild and unpredictable land by Western standards. Some argue that it remains so today, that Mindanao and its denizens retain much of their danger-tinged colonial mystique.[5]

The most basic thing we should know about the contact history of Mindanao is that there was considerable Spanish and Portuguese contact prior to 1596. The Magellan expedition, in fact, came ashore and interacted with several settlements on the northern coast of Mindanao in 1521 before moving on to the Visayas region, where the explorers would take part in the iconic events that marked the beginning of the Spanish colonial era: the First Mass at Limasawa, the bequest of the Santo Niño Christ-child figure to the people of Cebu, and the Battle of Mactán in which the *datu* Lapu-Lapu killed Magellan. After that rather inauspicious beginning, other Iberian expeditions—both Spanish and Portuguese—made contact, traded with, and sometimes hurriedly baptized the natives. All these contacts involved the marking of territory in a long-running boundary dispute between Spain and Portugal.[6]

---

[3] Francisco I. Alcina SJ, *Historia de las Islas e Indios de Bisayas* (1668), transcription by Victor Baltazar (Philippine Studies Program Archives, Regenstein Library Special Collections, University of Chicago, Chicago, IL, 1962); Francisco Colín SJ, *Labor Evangélica, Ministerios Apostólicos de Obreros de la Compañía de Jesús, Fundación, y Progresos de su Provincia en las Islas Filipinas* (Madrid: Joseph Fernandez Buendia, 1663); Francisco Combés SJ, *Historia de las Islas de Mindandao, Iolo, y sus Adyacentes*, vols. 1–8 (Madrid: W. E. Retana, 1897 [1667]); Horacio de la Costa SJ, *Selected Studies in Philippine Colonial History*, ed. R. Paterno (Metro Manila: Philippine Province of the Society of Jesus / Ateneo de Manila University Press, 2002).

[4] See Peter Schreurs MSC, "The Search for Pigafetta's 'Mazaua,'" *Kinaadman* 18,1 (1996). I refer those curious about mission history *per se* to Schreurs's missionary-focused, but nonetheless seminal, *Caraga Antigua 1521–1910: The Hispanization and Christianization of Agusan, Surigao, and East Davao* (Cebu: University of San Carlos Publications, 1989). This book provides an excellent foundation regarding the nature and reach of the early Spanish missions there, not to mention the considerable presence of another religious order, the Recoletos, in this area between 1596 and the 1870s. The Jesuit missions from the latter half of the nineteenth century on are more than adequately covered in Schreurs's three-volume annotated translation of Pablo Pastells's *Misión de la Compañía de Jesús de Filipinas en el siglo XIX* (Barcelona: Tip. y Lib. Editorial Barcelonesa S. A., 1916). See Peter Schreurs MSC, *Mission to Mindanao 1859–1900, from the Spanish of Pablo Pastells SJ*, vol. 1 (Cebu: University of San Carlos Publications, 1994). Both volumes II and III were published by Claretian Publications (Quezon City, 1998).

[5] See Mark Turner et al., eds., *Mindanao: Land of Unfulfilled Promise* (Quezon City: New Day Publishers, 1992). See also Marites Vitug and Glenda Gloria, *Under the Crescent Moon: Rebellion in Mindanao* (Quezon City: Ateneo Center for Social Policy and Public Affairs / Institute for Popular Democracy, 2000), and Marites Vitug and Criselda Yabes, *Jalan-Jalan: A Journey Through EAGA* (Pasig City: Anvil Publishing, 1998).

[6] The territorial dispute in the colonial theater between Spain and Portugal was generated by the provisions of the Treaty of Tordesillas in 1494. The Treaty of Zaragoza was signed in 1529, purportedly to resolve this dispute in the "division" of Asia-Pacific territories, but it only fueled further competition in the Philippine archipelago. While Spain relinquished the rest of Southeast Asia to Portugal, the Crown claimed a prerogative to conquer the Philippine islands, which were referred to in diplomatic correspondence at the time as *las yslas del poniente,* or the westerly islands. In retrospect, we can clearly see that the repeat expeditions to Mindanao were attempts by both Spain and Portugal to create what, in modern political parlance, is called "facts on the ground."

As previously noted, for the first century of contact, the archipelago remained an undefined geographical entity whose southern boundary was still under debate.[7] Prior to the formal colonization of what would become *Filipinas*, the coastal populations of north and east Mindanao encountered four more expeditions sent from Spain via the Americas: those of Loaisa in 1526, Saavedra in 1528, Villalobos in 1543, and Legazpi and Arellano in 1565; and two Portuguese expeditions sent from nearby Maluku: those of Pinto in 1534–35 and de Castro in 1538. While there exists no extended monograph describing these encounters—at least, nothing equivalent to that of Alvar Nuñez Cabeza de Vaca, the sixteenth-century Spaniard who was stranded "alone" among Amerindians for eight long years in what is now the Gulf Coast and Southwestern United States[8]—it is worth noting that some of these expeditions, all of which passed through Mindanao waters, were also tasked to rescue members of previous expeditions who had been either taken hostage or enslaved by natives, or were otherwise stranded on the island. Fleeting though they were, these encounters produced written reports that provided clues to precolonial lifeways in the region.[9]

The early Spanish explorations culminated in the conquest mission of 1565, when Miguel Lopez de Legazpi officially claimed the Philippine archipelago for the king of Spain. Initially basing himself in Cebu,[10] Legazpi became the first governor of "Filipinas," and the lands in northeast Mindanao were among the very first to be distributed as *encomiendas* (government-regulated trusts) to members of Legazpi's expedition.[11] The bureaucratic history of Mindanao's *encomiendas* is a fascinating topic in itself, but for the purposes of this study it is sufficient to say that the *encomenderos* (trustees) had limited success in administering their new trusts in Mindanao, in part because of their isolation.[12] Apart from introducing the paper

---

[7] At one point, a few parts of the eastern Indonesian archipelago were included in this new Spanish claim, over the objections of Portugal, even after the Treaty of Zaragoza was signed in 1529. For this treaty, see the Archivo General de Indias (hereafter AGI) in Sevilla, Spain: (AGI, Patronato, 49, R.9/17-4-1529).

[8] Alvar Nuñez Cabeza de Vaca, *Naufragios y Comentarios* (Barcelona: Espasa-Calpe, 1999 [1542]).

[9] Schreurs, *Caraga Antigua*, pp. 48–50. See also William Henry Scott, *Barangay: Sixteenth-Century Philippine Culture and Society* (Quezon City: Ateneo de Manila University Press, 1994).

[10] Spanish Manila was established much later, in the 1570s, in the vicinity of an indigenous Muslim-controlled settlement called Maynilad on the northern island of Luzon. According to Quirino, "Not until about 1590, long after the founding of the City of Manila by Miguel Lopez de Legazpi, did Luzon appear in … European maps." Carlos Quirino, *Philippine Cartography, 1320–1899* (Manila: Carmelo and Bauermann, 1959), p. 21.

[11] Originally from the Basque province of Gipuzkoa in northern Spain, Legazpi was accompanied on this expedition by other Basques, including his nephew Juan de Salcedo, and fellow Gipuzkoan Fr. Andrés de Urdaneta, who, prior to his ordination as an Augustinian, had been soldier and sea captain and, in both those capacities, had also traveled decades earlier to island Southeast Asia, specifically Mindanao, as part of García Jofre de Loaisa's expedition in 1525. All three were based in Mexico at the time the Legazpi conquest expedition was planned and authorized.

[12] Chapter Five refers to some issues related to *encomienda* taxation in the Lumad areas. Legally speaking, an *encomienda* was a trust over people, as opposed to land, under which the trustee, or *encomendero*, had the responsibility to collect taxes and tribute on behalf of the Spanish Crown, to provide for religious instruction, and to protect and maintain the well-being and good health of the lands and people under the *encomienda*. The trusteeship also involved the allotment of indigenous labor for public works projects. I am indebted to the Meso-

bureaucracy of the *encomienda* and the machinations of the mission enterprise, Spain more or less neglected the northeastern regions of Mindanao militarily until the late eighteenth century due to more pressing concerns elsewhere, including but not limited to suppressing the Moros, fighting off a hostile takeover attempt by the Dutch in 1647,[13] attacks on Manila by the Chinese,[14] and the English occupation of Luzon in 1762.[15]

Therefore, it was really not a major contact event when, in 1596, two unarmed Jesuits from Spain arrived in the international trading port of Butuan, on the northeastern coast of Mindanao island, to establish missions among the ancestors of those we now refer to as the Lumad. According to Jesuit narratives, they were welcomed like royalty, and the baptism of willing natives achieved with seemingly little or no effort.[16] This was, of course, not the first time Iberians had set foot on Mindanao's shores and, to the locals, the missionaries would have seemed like just the latest in a long line of foreign transients to these parts, including traders and the odd mutineer or captured slave left behind by previous European expeditions.[17] In this context, the receptiveness of the locals is not all that surprising, whether due to some innate Southeast Asian fascination with novelty or simply the fact that, historically, no white visitor had ever stayed for very long. In keeping with this trend, the pioneer Jesuit mission, and the mark they left in terms of conversions, was likewise short-lived, and the mission eventually abandoned due to lack of personnel.[18]

This changed a decade later with the arrival of a handful of *frailes* (friars) of the newly created mendicant Orden de los Agustinos Recoletos, an order constituted in

---

Americanist John Chance for this important clarification. In the Philippines, an *encomienda* was inheritable within one family for a limited number of generations (not in perpetuity), and only if notarized documentation was provided, with supporting testimony from local officials, to prove that the trust was managed up to the Crown's benevolent standards (on paper, at least). Writs of *encomienda* for northeast Mindanao, archived at the Archivo General de Indias, indicate that this standard was rather difficult to achieve in the Lumad areas, and *encomiendas* in that region were more often than not summarily vacated due to non-fulfillment of contractual obligations vis-à-vis the Spanish Crown, and passed on to another, more promising *encomendero*.

[13] This particular event was a late extension of the Eighty Years' War between Spain and the Netherlands into the larger colonial theater, a conflict that had major implications for the future decline of Spain as a naval and colonial power. The many *"robos y ataques de holandeses"* are mentioned in numerous official documents, including (AGI, Filipinas, 30, N.7/02-08-1625) and (AGI, Filipinas, 9, R.2, N.34/1661), and further hostilities over a century later in (AGI, Estado, 45, N.5/29-12-1778).

[14] For example, the Chinese pirate known as Limahong attacked in 1574, and in 1662, the military leader Koxinga, or Zheng Chenggong, attacked the islands as he demanded tribute from Spain. He appears in Spanish records as a "pirate" named "Cogsenia," as mentioned in (AGI, Filipinas, 9, R.2, N.34/1661).

[15] This took place under the watch of Simon de Anda y Salazar. See Antonio Molina, *Historia de Filipinas* (Madrid: Ediciones Cultura Hispanica del Instituto de Cooperacion Iberoamericana, 1984), Tomo I, Cap. 6. Incidentally, the rise of Philippine national hero Diego Silang, who fought against Spain, came about in the midst of the political instability that ensued from the English invasion.

[16] De la Costa, *Selected Studies*. See also H. de la Costa SJ, *The Jesuits in the Philippines, 1581–1768* (Cambridge, MA: Harvard University Press, 1961).

[17] Schreurs, *Caraga Antigua*, pp. 48–50.

[18] De la Costa, *The Jesuits in the Philippines*, pp. 154, 165–66, 171, 319.

northern Spain for the very purpose of planting Catholic missions in its newest colony. The Recoletos were distinguished from the main Augustinian Order as the *Agustinos descalzos*, literally "shoe-less Augustinians," a reference to their vow of poverty. Their fate in Mindanao would be one of frustration, discomfort, and suffering, punctuated by the occasional violent death. But they also achieved surprising success in Christianizing the area, particularly with warrior-chieftains whose often dramatic public conversions incited their own followers to convert. Granted, doctrinal adherence under these conditions may have been unlikely, but the conversions were nonetheless heartfelt enough that there are documented cases of Lumad warriors loyally defending the lives of missionaries and fighting alongside Spanish troops against their Muslim neighbors, with whom they were historically allied, and once even against their own brethren. It is this curious relationship, in part, that forms the unifying thread of not only this book but also the colonial experience of all Lumad groups.

Spain officially claimed possession of what is now the Philippine archipelago in 1565, along with a host of other Pacific territories. Nonetheless, on the island of Mindanao, colonial agents remained vastly outnumbered and outgunned by "ferocious" natives well into the nineteenth century. Even towards the end of the colonial period, officials complained that Spain possessed only a sliver of coastline. Lumad treaties with the colonial state were few and far between, and were therefore always celebrated despite being economically negligible and politically conditional.

Regardless of Spain's pretense that it maintained control over Mindanao, it was not logistically possible for these foreigners to compel any Lumad community to accept their presence, much less their religious or social authority. In this context, the idea that prominent Lumad leaders willingly and publicly accepted the supernatural authority of powerless strangers and adopted a foreign religion seems absurd in the face of the anti-imperialist and subaltern approaches that now teach us to anticipate indigenous resistance to religious conversion and colonial authority, particularly if a military imbalance favors the indigenous side of the equation. A ready acceptance of the missionaries by Lumad leaders is particularly striking because baptism into Christianity required major behavioral changes that would have been onerous for men of high status, including: keeping only one wife, and, consequently, returning bride payments received from the families of other wives;[19] freeing all slaves; ceasing all raiding, revenge-killing, and other aggressive behavior that was once considered critical to male status enhancement; and accepting the authority of strange men with no inherent status, with whom they shared no kin ties.

We know from comparing the early conquest history of the Spanish Americas to the Iberian colonization of the Philippines that there are no real similarities, except perhaps that a similar cast of characters, albeit of a later generation, was involved in the latter. But the passage of time made quite a difference, because by the time the expedition of the Basque captain Miguel Lopez de Legazpi arrived in the archipelago to undertake, in an official capacity, the colonization of the Yslas del Poniente, some of the most egregious errors of conquest had already been made, and the *conquista* (military conquest) as official policy was on the road to abolition, officially replaced

---

[19] For example, the Butuanon *datu* Silongan, who was converted by the Jesuits at the end of the sixteenth century, was reportedly "bound by the chains of his six wives, and the huge dowries he had given for them." Eventually he kept his "legitimate" wife, whose name was María Payo, and their son was sent to be schooled by Jesuits in Cebu, together with other Butuanon boys. See Schreurs, *Caraga Antigua*, pp. 108 and 115, respectively.

as modus operandi by its milder-mannered cousin *pacificación* (pacification) in 1573.[20] Likewise, the missionaries who accompanied Legazpi and those who were to follow were already operating in a different paradigm, one informed by the legacy of Bartolome de las Casas, a former *encomendero* who turned to the priesthood after witnessing Spanish atrocities in the Americas.[21]

This change in approach involved a paradigm shift that was subtle, and yet which profoundly changed the way the later contact experiences unfolded. In writing about the aggressive and religiously violent conquest of the Americas in the sixteenth century, Nicholas Cushner explains how those encounters officially began with the *Requerimiento*, a legal document that was read aloud by conquistadors, through which unwitting natives were informed that they were required to submit to the "legitimate" authority of the Spanish Crown and were subject to religious proselytization. It also spelled out the dire consequences of resisting conquest and colonization.

> A half-century before [c. 1510], the reading of the unintelligible document was invariably followed by the roar of cannon and the screams of Spanish soldiers. But times had changed, somewhat. The intervening years witnessed bitter debates in Spain over the legitimacy of the conquest, the way it was carried out, and the obligations to the Indians. By 1565, Spaniards were not so sure of the righteousness of their cause.[22]

In other words, had Magellan survived the Battle of Mactan and proceeded to claim the islands for Spain, he would have done so through the *Requerimiento*. But by 1565, when Legazpi made the journey for the purpose of colonizing the islands for Spain, the *Requerimiento* had already been abolished, thanks in part to public condemnation by de las Casas. And in theory at least, if the natives refused to cooperate, there was nothing a Spanish conquistador could legally do. This is not to say that these new guidelines were strictly or consistently followed, or that no illegal actions were creatively rationalized on paper, or that the drive for glory and personal enrichment that characterized the conquest of the Americas had been completely erased. After all, the military culture that was nurtured in Spain over the long centuries of the violent Reconquista, which ended only in 1492, was still dominant.[23] It was, in fact,

---

[20] The original documentation of Legazpi's colonization of the Yslas del Poniente is found in the Archivo General de Indias, Spain, including the original orders for *conquista y contratación* (AGI, Patronato, 23, R.6 and R.8), for *pacificación* (AGI, Patronato, 23,R.21), and detailed reports of the explorers' observations and fascinating cultural impressions (AGI, Patronato, 23, R.9 to R.10, and R. 17).

[21] Bartolomé de las Casas, *Bartolomé de las Casas: A Selection of His Writings*, trans. George Sanderlin (New York, NY: Knopf, 1971); cf. Hugh Thomas, *Rivers of Gold: The Rise of the Spanish Empire, from Columbus to Magellan* (New York, NY: Random House, 2003).

[22] Nicholas Cushner, *Why Have You Come Here? The Jesuits and the First Evangelization of Native America* (New York, NY: Oxford University Press, 2006), p. 35.

[23] "The process of the Reconquest as a whole is of conceptual significance. It defined the character of the Middle Ages in Spain, which differed from that prevailing elsewhere in Western Europe. Forced to give precedence to war rather than letters for the better part of a millennium, the Spaniards were the military champions of the Christian faith. Spain became a society organized for war, with a greater percentage of its population positioned as nobles, knights, and warriors, as well as its own crusading ideals and military orders." Angus MacKay, "Reconquest of Spain," in *The Reader's Companion to Military History*, eds. Robert

the Reconquista that gestated this "peculiar blend of church and state unity," in which "evangelization was considered a joint effort that obligated civil as well as religious authority," that characterized Spanish colonialism around the world, including the Philippines.[24] Nevertheless, this new official thinking meant a world of difference in that colonization and missionizing were now to be undertaken within the parameters of an operational paradigm in which the objects of conquest were granted specific rights, as opposed to one in which they were not.

While conversion by physical force or other direct forms of compulsion may have been initially possible in the Americas,[25] it was neither desirable nor possible in the Philippines, not under this post-de las Casas paradigm. Nor would it have been a successful strategy in the face of the logistical and cultural challenges specific to the Philippines at the time of contact. These included: the considerably fewer Spaniards on the ground, due to the challenges of traveling from Spain or even Mexico; better indigenous resistance to European diseases than in the Americas, coupled with European vulnerability to diseases endemic to Southeast Asia;[26] the existing sophistication and knowledge of the natives regarding the capabilities and motives of the Europeans, based in part on the prior occupation of nearby Malacca by the Portuguese in 1511; the lack of a major centralized, hierarchical political power, such as a kingdom, that could be conquered by capturing its head; the fact that iron-based weaponry, including heavy swords and cannons of indigenous design, were already being produced locally by specialist guilds of *panday*, or craftsmen; and, finally, the eager acceptance of foreigners and foreign cultural trends that characterized early modern Southeast Asia.[27]

With *pacificación*, however, Catholic missionaries became the *de facto* face of colonial power in Filipinas to most *indios*. The role of missionaries as interlocutors between Lumad and Spanish worlds in the pericolonial context of Mindanao in the first mission period did not happen by accident. It was part and parcel of a legal arrangement between the Catholic Church and the Spanish Crown called the *Patronato Real*, under which missionaries "played a key role in the Spanish plan of conquest and colonization."[28] The missionaries' role is also documented in the

---

Cowley and Geoffrey Parker (Boston, MA: Houghton Mifflin, 1996), p. 381.

[24] Cushner, *Why Have You Come Here?*, pp. 28–29.

[25] Even then, the Spaniards did not conquer the Americas solely by brute force. They apparently still had to engage in persuasion to secure local cooperation, for example, by providing material incentives "to encourage the hesitant and entice the indifferent." Cushner, *Why Have You Come Here?*, pp. 71–75.

[26] Ken de Bevoise, *Agents of Apocalypse: Epidemic Disease in the Colonial Philippines* (Princeton, NJ: Princeton University Press, 1995).

[27] See Barbara Watson Andaya, "Historicizing 'Modernity' in Southeast Asia," *Journal of the Economic and Social History of the Orient* 40,4 (1997). This regional attraction and openness to "the foreign" included patterns of aligning politically with foreigners, and calling on them as neutral parties to resolve disputes. See David Henley, *Jealousy and Justice: The Indigenous Roots of Colonial Rule in Northern Sulawesi*, Comparative Asian Studies Series 22 (Amsterdam: VU Uitgeverij, 2002). This attraction and openness to "the foreign" is also found throughout the wider Austronesian world. See John Barker, ed., *Christianity in Oceania: Ethnographic Perspectives*, ASAO Monograph 12 (Lanham, MD: University Press of America, 1990).

[28] Cushner, *Why Have You Come Here?*, pp. 28–29. The *Patronato Real*, or royal patronage, was put into place after the Reconquista to bring the various religious orders under the political control of the Crown in exchange for funding and other crucial support that enabled the clergy to undertake expansion into the New World and other colonial territories.

archival record of the first mission period, during which colonial-era missionaries seem to have regarded themselves as mediators not only between the Lumad and the spiritual world of Christianity, but also between the Lumad and the general European milieu characterized by both mission-planting and colonialism, which together introduced European styles of warfare, settlement, government, adjudication, taxation, dress, transportation, and modes of religious practice. The missionaries, in fact, seem to have considered themselves quite distinct from other Europeans in the colonial matrix: morally superior, politically more astute, and more sensitive culturally, not least because of their level of interaction with the Lumad— much like anthropologists, in other words, except clothed in cassocks and Scripture. Moreover, in order to convert the Lumad, missionaries would have had to live with them day by day, learn their languages, and know them as individuals, in the course of conveying Catholic doctrine and preaching their Gospel. They would have had to immerse themselves in the Lumad world in order to bring it in line with the world of Christianity. So what was this world like?

AN *INDIO* BY ANY OTHER NAME?

As we place the Lumad within a regional understanding of Southeast Asia in the early colonial period, it is important to clarify who exactly the Lumad are. The term "Lumad" is a modern political term that refers to the indigenous peoples of Mindanao who did not convert to Islam prior to, during, or after the Spanish colonial period. It is a Cebuano Visayan word that literally means "born from the earth," and despite its etymology, it is used widely today for collective self-reference across eighteen culturally related, but nonetheless distinct, ethnolinguistic groups. In other words, it identifies not one ethnic group but an ethnic category, which Leonard Andaya defines in his history of Malayu ethnicity as

> a loose and generalized collectivity to which groups attach themselves or are assigned by outsiders because of certain shared characteristics. While the members of an ethnic category acknowledge some common cultural relationship, their interpersonal and intergroup relationships are limited.[29]

In reference to island Southeast Asia, Andaya further notes the characteristic fluidity of ethnicity in this extremely diverse part of the world, observing that supposed ethnic "groups" like the Orang Asli, Orang Laut, Penan, Kayan, Kelabit, and Kenyah are actually ethnic categories that "do not form social units or a distinct social system and may not even share the same language and culture."[30] With regard to the Philippines, one can compare my use of "Lumad" with the widely accepted ethnic category names of "Igorot," which is used in reference to uplanders in the mountainous interior of northern Luzon, and "Moro," which refers to the indigenous Muslims of the Philippines, as noted above. Both Igorot and Moro categories are made up of groups that have much less in common with each other than do the groups that constitute the Lumad. However, the terms "Igorot" and "Moro" remain

---

[29] Leonard Andaya, *Leaves of the Same Tree: Trade and Ethnicity in the Straits of Melaka* (Singapore: NUS Press, 2010), pp. 6–7.

[30] Ibid. For the Borneo categories, Andaya cites Jerôme Rousseau, *Central Borneo: Ethnic Identity and Social Life in a Stratified Society* (Oxford: Clarendon Press, 1990).

commonly used blanket terms despite their external derivation and historical origins, and the even greater linguistic and cultural diversity of the various ethnic groups that fall within these categories. In contrast, a majority of the Lumad do have shared ancestors, origin myths, and common linguistic origins. In Mindanao, "Lumad" has been embraced by the younger post-Martial Law set as a shorthand way of distinguishing the island's indigenous uplanders from the equally indigenous Muslim groups, who have co-opted the formerly derogatory Spanish term *Moro*, and from the various Filipino settler groups that have taken over Mindanao.[31]

Using the term "Lumad" in reference to the colonial area is definitely anachronistic, but it is useful for several reasons, not least of which is the lack of an already established term for this category of people during earlier periods. In lieu of contriving yet another name, I argue that it is appropriate to apply this modern label to an earlier time period for several reasons. The first is that, ironically, despite the term's wholly modern provenance, using the generic "Lumad" in reference to the colonial era helps us avoid "upstreaming" errors inherent in the application of internal twentieth-century ethnolinguistic distinctions to prior centuries. The various native terms used in historical accounts indeed resemble some of the Lumad group names today, like *manobo, subano, mandaya, bukidnon*. But they cannot be directly associated with present-day tribal names because, until the late nineteenth century, these terms were actually used in the same generic way as the Spanish word *montés*—as a broad reference to local people living away from population centers or other loci of political power.[32] When later colonial-era observers wished to be more precise, which was not often, a more specific locative label was used, based on the name of the closest identifiable—that is, named and mapped—settlement or river tributary. For example, the Lumad living closest to the Cagayán river were called the Kagayanon, and so with the Agusanon, Pulangion, Tagoloanon, Adgawanon, Butuanon, and so on.[33] While the older riparian nomenclature is still used for reference within some groups, other "official" group names—derived in part from published ethnographic descriptions—are becoming the standard for self-reference, as various Lumad communities become more involved with government, NGOs, and other outside entities. For example, the peoples of the Cagayán and Tagoloán rivers we encounter in chapters three and five, respectively, would be Higaunons today. Finding the boundaries between these modern names—e.g., Higaunon, Bukidnon, Manguangan, Banuwaon, Talaandig, Tagakaolo, Kalagan, Mandaya, Manobo—is also difficult, as these groupings are not entirely discrete, relying for the most part on self-identification, which often depends on who is asking or being asked, and which may vary from community to community.[34]

Conversely, as mentioned above, the earlier colonial descriptions of Mindanao indicate that the ancestors of today's Lumad may have had much more in common with each other than their descendants do with each other. We know first of all that

---

[31] The Visayan plural form of Lumad is *Lumadnon*.

[32] Oona T. Paredes, "People of the Hinterlands: Higaûnon Life in Northern Mindanao, Philippines" (MA Thesis, Arizona State University, 1997), pp. 27–34.

[33] John M. Garvan, *The Manóbos of Mindanáo* (Washington, DC: US Government Printing Office, 1941), pp. 1 *passim*. See also Carmen Ching Unabia, "Gugud: A Bukidnon Oral Tradition," *Asian Folklore Studies* 44 (1985): 206.

[34] On the difficulty of keeping track of fluid social identity in Southeast Asia, see also Peter V. Lape, "A Highway and a Crossroads: Island Southeast Asia and Culture Contact Archaeology," *Archaeology in Oceania* 38,2 (2003): 106.

the various Lumad groups had mutually intelligible languages, and a missionary could preach from the east coast all the way through to the deep interior and come out the north coast without learning a new language. Francis Madigan notes that a missionary arriving in Butuan on the north coast, from the Caraga area on the east coast, "found he was able to preach to them immediately in their local dialect since this was very similar to that of Caraga whose rudiments he had mastered in Gigaquit."[35] This is no longer the case with Lumad language variation today. Though today all but one of the Lumad groups in northeast Mindanao speak a language belonging to the Manobo sub-family, people who self-identify as members of the same group may, in fact, speak very distinct dialects.[36] Among the Higaunon, for example, the verbal and written language in Bukidnon province is different enough from the dialects of eastern Misamis Oriental that they sound "odd" to each other, and are frequently regarded as different languages by outsiders.[37]

We also know that the Lumad were tied to each other through kinship, with extensive consanguineal and affinal relationships among political elites throughout northeast Mindanao, ties that they sometimes also shared with Visayan elites. No studies have been conducted to determine the genealogical relationship of today's Lumads to today's Visayans, but we do know that, in the sixteenth century, at least, some members of elite Lumad families, or *principales*, in Cagayán and Butuan were related affinally—that is, by marriage—to other elites living on the islands of Cebu, Bohol, and Leyte.[38] This means the Lumads in Mindanao had regular dealings with peoples in the Visayas, enough to use the language and to intermarry. According to William Henry Scott, in fact, the northern and eastern regions of Mindanao—in both the coast and the interior—were part of the Visayan culture area, which is true.[39] However, it does not mean the people living in these areas were Visayans themselves. In fact, these regions were just as much a part, if not even more so, of the political and cultural realm of Moro polities like the Magindanaw sultanate, to which they paid tribute and rendered service as allies in raids on the Visayas. Lumadnon also had equally regular dealings and some degree of intermarriage with Moro groups. For example, the direct linguistic, genetic, and historical connection between Butuanons and Tausug is widely acknowledged.[40] And the oral traditions of Lumad and Moro groups preserve the memory of a shared past that has long been

---

[35] Francis Madigan SJ, "The Early History of Cagayan De Oro," *Philippine Studies* 11,1 (1963): 84–85.

[36] The exception being the Mamanwa, a Negrito group in Surigao.

[37] The dialect of the Higaunon language spoken in Bukidnon is commonly referred to by the Visayan term Binukid (literally, "mountain speech"). One linguist estimates only an 81 percent similarity between the two dialects. See Scott Munger, "An Analysis of the Semantic Structure of a Higaonon (Philippines) Text" (Masters Thesis, University of Texas at Arlington, 1988), p. 14. However, my understanding is that the degree to which Manobo languages are mutually intelligible (or not) is similar to the limited mutual intelligibility of Norwegian, Danish, and Swedish.

[38] Schreurs, *Caraga Antigua*, p. 113. See also Rolando O. Borrinaga, "Lapu Lapu in Biliran? A Tentative Hypothesis," *Kinaadman* 17 (1995): 207–14.

[39] Scott, *Barangay*, p. 161.

[40] Ibid., p. 164.

intertwined.[41] Yet no one would argue that the Lumad should be categorized as Moros.

The term "Visayan" itself refers to a large and quite diverse linguistic family whose roots lie in the scattered islands of the central Philippine archipelago, including Cebu, Bohol, Panay, Negros, Leyte, and Samar. The Lumadnon link to the Visayas in terms of language was probably quite strong in the pre-colonial period, which is not surprising, considering it was the main trade language for the central and southern Philippine archipelago. We know that the indigenous populations of Mindanao could communicate with outsiders in a "Visayan" language, and that Recoleto missionaries were able to move between mission assignments around the Visayas and Mindanao without having to learn a new language. The Recoletos wrote of having to learn "Bisaya" in both Cagayán and Butuan. Furthermore, the Recoleto P. Fr. Tomás de San Jerónimo wrote a *Vocabulario de la lengua cebuana y peculiar de Cagayán y Tagoloán* in which he identifies the language spoken in northern Mindanao as being a unique variant of Visayan, just as Cebuano was a distinct variant of Visayan spoken on the capital island of Cebu.[42] But this does not mean that Mindanao was already overrun by settlers from Cebu and Bohol in the sixteenth century, as it is today. The Spaniards, in fact, differentiated the *Bisaya* themselves—who were also known as *pintados*, the painted ones, and were distinguished for being tattooed from head to toe—from the *naturales*, or natives, whom they encountered repeatedly on Mindanao.

Last but not least, we know from archaeology that, despite these long-standing ties with the Visayas and elsewhere, there have been people and polities in northeast Mindanao since the ninth century, and perhaps even since "time immemorial." The Agusan region of Mindanao, particularly Butuan, was clearly involved in the region's international maritime trade, and even hosted the occasional trading party from China. The residents produced styles of gold jewelry, accessories, and other wares, some with religious significance, that evoked Indic references—a clear sign that even in a "backwater" like Mindanao, local people were aware of regional and international trends. However, regional experts like John Miksic note that the Agusan gold was not only locally manufactured, it was locally designed as well, with remarkable art motifs and production values that were distinct not only from those produced in the Visayas, but also distinct from gold objects created elsewhere in Southeast Asia and India.[43] While we know little else about the cultures that crafted the artifacts that are now exhibited as national treasures at the Ayala Museum in Metro Manila, we can say with confidence that they were indeed "local"

---

[41] In this book there are numerous references to the intimate political connections that bound the Lumads and Moros, who were historically their allies, in the early colonial period. See also Herminia Meñez Coben, *Verbal Arts in Philippine Indigenous Communities: Poetics, Society, and History* (Quezon City: Ateneo de Manila University Press, 2009), p. 242. Coben cites Carmen Ching Unabia's "Bukidnon Flood Myth," in *Philippine Folk Literature: The Myths*, ed. Damiana Eugenio (Quezon City: University of the Philippines Press, 1993), pp. 241–42; and Carmen Ching Unabia, *Tula at Kuwento ng Katutubong Bukidnon* (Quezon City: Ateneo de Manila University Press, 1996), pp. 275–78. See also Unabia, "Gugud."

[42] Francisco Sábada del Carmen OAR, *Catálogo de los Religiosos Agustinos Recoletos de San Nicolás de Tolentino desde el Año 1606 en que Llegó la Primera Misión á Manila, hasta Nuestros Días* (Madrid: Imprenta del Asilo de Huérfanos del Sagrado Corazón de Jesús, 1906), pp. 102–4, 148, 151.

[43] See Florina H. Capistrano-Baker, John Guy, and John Miksic, eds., *Philippine Ancestral Gold* (Singapore: NUS Press, 2012), especially pp. 138–61, 193–257.

to Mindanao. In other words, even if these populations might have originated from the Visayas region or maybe even farther afield in prehistoric times, by the time the Spaniards arrived in the sixteenth century, they would have been rightly considered indigenous, or *lumad* to Mindanao. And it is from these Lumad that the various modern-day tribes of Lumadnon are descended in the genetic sense.

While Lumad groups today have highly comparable settlement patterns, systems of political leadership, legal systems, and religious practices, they appear to have had even greater commonalities in previous centuries. The Recoletos, for example, "found that the natives of Agusan had the same customs and religious practices as the Caragans of the east coast; only their social behavior was a little less wild."[44] Similarly, "the Kagayanos differed little from [people in] Butuan and Caraga" except in terms of relative "civility" or receptivity towards the Spaniards.[45] In terms of political organization, Lumad communities seem to have been, on the whole, also similar in that they were all acephalous and, in the eyes of Iberian missionaries, tending towards anarchy. Political organization revolved around a *datu*, a semi-hereditary male authority figure who, in classical anthropological typology, would fall somewhere between a "big-man" and "chief."[46] Whether he was more like one than the other would have depended entirely upon the level of stratification and the prominence of particular descent groups in a given community. Other studies deal more directly with this issue,[47] though only Schlegel's study of Tiruray adjudication provides a definitive description of this wide-ranging indigenous political and legal role.[48] Nonetheless, all of them point to the *datu* as embodying the "man of prowess" concept that still informs political organization in Southeast Asia.[49]

Datu is more an achieved political status than an office. The role not only requires that a candidate demonstrate a certain amount of "prowess" or natural political ability to arbitrate local community conflicts and achieve consensus, it also requires years of education, the appropriate rites of passage, as well the approval

---

[44] Schreurs, *Caraga Antigua*, p. 137.

[45] Madigan, "The Early History of Cagayan De Oro," pp. 90–91.

[46] Marshall Sahlins, "Poor Man, Rich Man, Big-man, Chief: Political Types in Melanesia and Polynesia," *Comparative Studies in Society and History* 5,3 (1963): 285–303.

[47] Garvan, *The Manóbos of Mindanao*. See also William Biernatzki SJ, "Bukidnon Datuship in the Upper Pulangi River Valley," *Bukidnon Politics and Religion*, ed. A. de Guzman and E. Pacheco (Quezon City: Ateneo de Manila University Press IPC Papers 11, 1973), pp. 15–50; Fay-Cooper Cole, *The Bukidnon of Mindanao*, Chicago Natural History Museum Fieldiana 46 (Chicago, IL:, Chicago Natural History Museum, 1956); Dionisio L. Yumo, "Power Politics of the Southern Agusan Manobo," *Mindanao Journal* 15 (1988): 3–47.

[48] Stuart A. Schlegel, *Tiruray Justice: Traditional Tiruray Law and Morality* (Berkeley, CA: University of California Press, 1970). Among the Tiruray, the figure equivalent to a *datu* is the *kefeduwan*. He is called *timuay* among the Subanen.

[49] "Prowess" in Southeast Asia is a form of personal potency that remains a critical aspect of political success, even in the present day. It can be lost and enhanced through everyday activities and ritual acts; it is demonstrable in a variety of ways, including but not limited to: success in warfare, the acquisition of a large personal following, and eloquence in public debate. See Schlegel, *Tiruray Justice*, on how a Lumad leader's prowess is considered equally critical to the peaceful adjudication of conflict as to revenge-raiding. See also O. W. Wolters, *History, Culture, and Region in Southeast Asian Perspectives* (Ithaca, NY: Cornell Southeast Asia Program Publications, 1999); and John Walker, *Power and Prowess: The Origins of Brooke Kingship in Sarawak* (Honolulu, HI: University of Hawaii Press, 2002).

and recognition of other established *datu*s before one can "make" *datu* and properly carry the title. The general consensus among modern-day Lumadnon seems to be that, while datuship tends to run in families, such that the son of a *datu* is normally expected to become a *datu* himself, a good *datu* is born and not made. In other words, recognition of the *datu*s' authority is not contingent upon their membership in any particular descent group; instead, it is a man's innate abilities that recommend him to this special status. In many communities, therefore, an able man who has no remembered "noble" ancestry can still gain recognition as a *datu*, perhaps because the quality of his ancestry is implied by his personal prowess. However, the duties and community responsibilities that come with this status are onerous enough— requiring *datu*s to spend much of their time away from their families and their farming in order to adjudicate, attend meetings with other *datu*s, deal with state officials, and fulfill other obligations—that even men who otherwise seem well-suited to be *datu*s may choose not to "make" *datu*.[50]

While today a Lumad man can enhance his status in the community by displaying his prowess in adjudication and peacemaking, this path to traditional leadership once coexisted very intimately with the *bagani,* or warrior, complex, in which men achieved higher status in proportion to the prowess they demonstrated through success in warfare. In fact, even today, a propensity for violence remains widely regarded as a mark of raw masculinity throughout the archipelago, in both the lowlands and the uplands. At one time, therefore, the most common avenue for demonstrating leadership qualities—common even up to the early twentieth century—was through participation in collective violence, most often in the form of raids against other Lumad settlements. Raymond Kelly explains that the prevalence of collective violence in a society depends on the presence of certain cultural factors that structure warfare as a culturally meaningful social act, such as the linking of prowess and status to violence. In the case of "warlike" societies, in which warfare appears endemic, such ideas survive in various ways, and can be deeply entrenched and sustained over generations on a semi-religious or mythic level.[51] Until very recently in Lumad societies, raiding and other aggressive behavior remained an important avenue for displaying physical and spiritual prowess and enhancing male social status, for establishing leadership and accumulating political capital, for building and reinforcing alliances with neighbors, and for acquiring trade goods.[52]

---

[50] One Higaunon man I know very well, the cousin and close confidante of a popular *datu* in Misamis Oriental province, is one such example. He is in his early fifties, and has long been regarded by others, including his cousin, as intelligent, honest, fair-minded, objective, collegial, and eloquent enough to make a very good *datu*, such that his opinion is often sought (rather than simply allowed, as is everyone else's) in community meetings. He also comes from a respected descent group with solid land rights in his area. However, knowing the amount of time and energy his *datu* cousin is required to commit to his responsibilities, and seeing how it interferes with farming and family obligations, such that his cousin's wife and children are often left "alone" to fend for themselves, he flatly refuses to undergo formally the process of "making" *datu*.

[51] Raymond Kelly, *Warless Societies and the Origin of War* (Ann Arbor, MI: University of Michigan Press, 2000). See also Kenneth George, *Showing Signs of Violence: The Cultural Politics of a Twentieth-Century Headhunting Ritual* (Berkeley, CA: University of California Press, 1996); and Janet Hoskins, "The Headhunter as Hero: Local Traditions and Their Reinterpretations in National History," *American Ethnologist* 14,4 (1987): 605–22.

[52] Laura L. Junker, *Raiding, Trading, and Feasting: The Political Economy of Philippine Chiefdoms* (Honolulu, HI: University of Hawaii Press, 1999). See Reynaldo Ileto, *Magindanao 1860–1888:*

Among the Lumad, the relationship of warfare to political prowess is ethnologically apparent from the documented existence of warrior complexes, in which males achieved greater social and political status as warriors—*bagani* or *magani*—according to the number of enemies they killed on raids.[53] We know that they were often distinguished by special clothing and accessories with "varying shades of red, the intensity of which indicated the number of enemies killed," including a black color produced by the "saturat[ion of] ... the darkest red dyes."[54] The *bagani* also obtained access to a special war deity common within a widespread Lumad religious practice known as *busaw*, *tagbusaw*, or *talabusaw*, and they often assumed the highest leadership roles, including that of *datu*. The explicit link to the *busaw* spirit means that the *bagani* and others who engage in violence are regarded as being under the direct influence of—and, in some cases, possessed by—a supernatural being that embodies humanity's aggressive impulses. The *busaw* is "fed" by blood and alcohol, and its potency is claimed to be so great that, when inebriated, it blinds its subjects with the urge to destroy everything in their paths.[55] Among Lumads in the present day, the *bagani* remains an important cultural figure. With the post-colonial decline of revenge-raiding, baganiship is almost never fully actuated as a political role, but the qualities of aggressiveness and potential for violence in men still command respect in themselves, reflecting the persistence of the *bagani* as idealized male hero.[56]

Not surprisingly, another thing colonial-era Lumadnon shared was the experience of raiding, or *pangayaw*. A review of ethnographic and historical accounts shows that raiding, for revenge and for slaves, was once a recurring fact of Lumad life. Lumad groups raided each other, and they were raided in turn by more organized Islamicized "Moro" groups to their west. Raiding was, in fact, a vital economic activity throughout the central Philippines and elsewhere in island Southeast Asia during this period.[57] *Pangayaw*, in turn, was an important engine for

---

The Career of Datu Uto of Buayan (Ithaca, NY: Cornell Southeast Asia Program Publications, 1971) for a biographical study of one particular "man of prowess" from the Magindanaw area.

[53] Garvan, *The Manóbos of Mindanao*, p. 141; Junker, *Raiding*, pp. 336–69; and Cole, *The Bukidnon of Mindanao*. See Leslie E. Bauzon, "The Bagani as Folk Hero among the Lumads of Northeastern Mindanao," *Diliman Review* 45, 2–3 (1997): 50–58. See also Fay-Cooper Cole, *The Bagobos of Davao Gulf* (Manila: Bureau of Printing, 1911); and Fay-Cooper Cole, *The Wild Tribes of Davao District, Mindanao*, Publication 170 (Chicago, IL: Field Museum of Natural History, 1913).

[54] Coben, *Verbal Arts*, pp. 252–53. See also Joy Dadole, "The Talagbusao Phenomenon of the Bukidnon People," *Kinaadman* 11: 43–53, and Cole, *The Bukidnon of Mindanao*, p. 96.

[55] Garvan, *The Manóbos of Mindanao*, pp. 214–15. See also Dadole, "The Talagbusao Phenomenon ... ," pp. 46 passim; and Coben, *Verbal Arts in Philippine Indigenous Communities*, pp. 252–53.

[56] This phenomenon is now beginning to be studied under the rubric of *rido*, a term used primarily among the Moro groups of western Mindanao. However, its cultural aspects in relation to the supernatural world or constructions of masculinity remain underexplored. See Wilfredo M. Torres III, *Rido: Clan Feuding and Conflict Management in Mindanao* (Makati: Asia Foundation/USAID, 2007). *Pangayaw* still takes place in Lumad areas to this day. At press time, there has been an unresolved series of killings in the provinces of Misamis Oriental and Agusan del Sur, all involving *datu*s.

[57] See F. A. A. Gregorij, "Aantekeeningen en Beschouwingen Betrekkelijk de Zeerovers en Hunne Rooverijen in den Indischen Archipel, Alsmede Aangaande Magindanao en ee Soolo-archipel," *Tijdschrift voor Neêrlandsch-Indië* 7,2 (1845): 300–37; Thomas Kiefer, *The Tausug: Violence and Law in a Philippine Moslem Society* (Prospect Heights, IL: Waveland Press, 1986);

political organization and an avenue for the development of leadership potential among Lumad males.

Acknowledging the significance of collective violence is therefore one possible key to interpreting evidence of the bonds that formed between Lumads and Recoleto missionaries. Although such acts of collective violence are obvious examples of male bravado, bolstered by conditions of a seemingly "warlike" society, there is more to *pangayaw* than mere aggression. It is notable, for example, that the willingness of Lumad men to fight both *with* and *on behalf of* individual missionaries, discussed in chapters that follow, required going directly against both their powerful neighbors and erstwhile allies, the Magindanaw Moros, and sometimes their own kin. Taking on such profound risks to their political system, security, and moral obligations demonstrates the creation of social bonds strong enough to override all these concerns. And this is an important point to remember as we reconsider the missionary question. But before we can begin do so, we must first put the Lumad in their proper place, both literally and figuratively.

A MOUNTAIN OF DIFFERENCE

Ask anyone in Mindanao today where to find the Lumad, and they would invariably answer that Lumadnon are mountain people who, naturally, live in the *bukid*, or mountains. They are often referred to as *taga-bukid*, a local Visayan term that in most contexts is loaded with simpleminded, nature-loving, primitive tribal connotations and directly contrasted to the "normal" people who live in the coastal, lowland towns. Mountains are where such wild and unpredictable creatures as spirits, armed rebels, and inscrutable tribal people dwell. In other words, they are as far as you can get from civilization. Locating "mountain people" in the mountains would be unproblematic but for the fact that Lumad oral traditions point very clearly and unambiguously to their coastal origins, as discussed further in Chapter Six. For example, prose *gugud* narratives from central Mindanao, as well as storylines from the widely shared *Ulagíng* sung epic, revolve around the displacement of Lumads from lowland communities, often triggered by such problems as environmental disasters, harassment from settlers, or colonial interference.[58] How, then, should we read this disparity? And where should we properly locate the Lumad in terms of Mindanao's history? Perhaps the disparity is simply a matter of translation.

In Chapter Five, I review a set of documents relating to the founding of the mission of Tagoloán in the colonial province of Misamis in northern Mindanao. The documents, dated 1722, refer to correspondence regarding *los prinzipales Infieles de los Montes y Riveras … de Tagoloán*,[59] which most people would translate literally as "the

---

James Warren, *The Sulu Zone 1768–1898: The Dynamics of External Trade, Slavery, and Ethnicity in the Transformation of a Southeast Asian Maritime State* (Quezon City: New Day, 1985).

[58] Unabia, "Gugud," pp. 206, 207, 222–24. See also the equally detailed work of Elena Maquiso, *Ulahingan, An Epic of the Southern Philippines*, Ulahingan Series 1 (Dumaguete: Silliman University Press, 1977); and Elena Maquiso, *Ulahingan, An Epic of the Southern Philippines: The Adventures of Impehimbang and Nebeyew; Begyasan's Visit to Insibey*, Ulahingan Series 2 (Dumaguete: Silliman University Press, 1990); Ludivina Opeña, "Olaging: The Battle of Nalandangan," *Kinaadman* 1,1 (1979): 151–227; Francisco Col-om Polenda, "Ulegingen: A Prose Retelling of a Mindanao Epic," trans. Richard Elkins, *Kinaadman* 16,2 (1994): 101–225; and Tranquilino Sitoy, "The Bukidnon Ascencion to Heaven," *Philippine Magazine* 34,354 (1937): 445–66.

[59] Document from the private archive of the Recoletos in Marcilla, Spain (Archivo Provincial

heathen chieftains of the mountains and rivers of Tagoloán."[60] Today, in the same general area, the lowland city of Tagoloán in present-day Misamis Oriental province includes both coastal and inland areas. From the correspondence, it is clear that the Tagoloán of 1722 did not correspond exactly to today's lowland city: the earlier town was a group of settlements located away from the coast, built around a small lake. Given such factors as recurring typhoons and raids, not to mention the lack of arable land, very few settlements on Mindanao would have been established on exposed beachfront property the way they are today. This was not peculiar to minor settlements like Tagoloán: to reach even the major "coastal" trading town of Butuan required navigating a few kilometers up a tributary river in those days.[61]

The words *el monte* and *montés,* adjectives that mark things as being from the hinterland, were regularly applied throughout the Spanish colonial period to refer to the indigenous peoples of Mindanao—i.e., the ancestors of those to whom we have referred since the late twentieth century as the Lumad. Today, the word *montés* is translated consistently into English as "mountain people," and, in historical reports of Mindanao that mention its indigenous peoples, *montés* is routinely substituted with the corresponding Visayan term *taga-bukid,* which also explicitly refers to mountains. Another similar term, "upland," is a universal term of reference for ethnic minorities in Southeast Asia, and it likewise conjures images of things "montane," or, in some manner elevated, or, at the very least, sloped or hilly. It is a relatively accurate reflection of present-day *realpolitik* in the Philippines and most of Southeast Asia, where the line between ethnic minorities and the most dominant national groups is most accurately discussed within the framework of a literal upland–lowland divide.[62] It is also true that, by the final decades of Spanish rule, towards the end of the nineteenth century, the term *montés* came to be associated principally with Lumads who by then were located deep in the mountainous interior of Mindanao, especially in what is now the very aptly named Bukidnon province, from the Visayan root word *bukid,* or mountain. As the twentieth century drew closer, terms of reference for Lumads and other ethnic minorities became increasingly specific in terms of elevation. Given this loaded etymology, and the fact that Mindanao does have true mountains of considerable elevation, visible even from coastal areas, it would be difficult today for someone familiar with the topography and geography of Mindanao to believe that the lowland Tagoloán region of either the past or the present—even in its most elevated interior reaches, and even in relation to the coast—could ever be regarded as a "montane" or authentically "upland" sort of place.

---

de los Agustinos Recoletos, Marcilla, Spain, hereafter ARM), leg 61, num 3, doc HN25, f5r.

[60] *Principales,* in a wider sense, pertains not only to the chieftains themselves but to others (men, women, children) belonging to a wider group ascribed with special authority or status, i.e., local "nobility" or "chiefly" families. A broader interpretation of the term *infiel* is discussed later in this volume with reference to conceptions of political allegiance and religious conversion.

[61] Schreurs, *Caraga Antigua,* p. 137.

[62] That said, the divide remains a political rather than literal one. The Muslim minority groups of the Philippines—most of whose members either reside in lowland areas (including neighborhoods in Metro Manila), occupy whole islands, or, in the case of some groups, are primarily seafaring and sea-dwelling—have also been referred to as "uplanders." See, for example, Renato Rosaldo, ed., *Cultural Citizenship in Island Southeast Asia: Nation and Belonging in the Hinterlands* (Los Angeles, CA: University of California Press, 2003).

But the Spaniards were not necessarily making mountains out of coastlines in this case, because in Spanish, *el monte* can, in fact, refer to land that is forested or otherwise covered with vegetation because it is *inculto,* or uncultivated. *Montés* therefore encompasses things that are also "uncultivated" in the broader sense of being unrefined, uncouth, uncivilized, rustic, or even simply "wild" in English, drawing on the same notions from which the word "pagan" originally evolved.[63] Classifying upriver Tagoloán as *el monte,* and its people as *montés,* makes more sense within the context of this term's broader definitions. Moreover, despite the implication of "wildness" and other negative, animalistic connotations that the word conjures in English, it is obvious that the Spaniards thought the Lumad to be rational human beings with whom they could negotiate, and who could certainly comprehend catechism. For this reason, I opt for the less offensive—yet still geographically informative—adjective "hinterland" when translating *montés* with reference to the Lumad.

With this clarification, we can begin to understand that when Spanish documents refer to *las tribus monteses de Misamis,* they do not mean "the mountain tribes" or even the "wild tribes" of Misamis, but those who have not yet cottoned on to, much less adopted, Western notions of "civilization." As we will see, this is no simple matter of semantics because both the Spanish and English terms amount to statements regarding the place of the Lumad in Mindanao's cultural and political geography, as well as its physical geography. To assume that the *monteses* referred to in historical texts are only those who actually lived in the mountains, deep in the interior of Mindanao, is to erase a large part of Lumad history and heritage on the basis of an oversimplified translation.

Finally, let us consider the political ramifications of the seemingly innocuous designation of eighteenth-century Tagoloán as part of *el monte* over one hundred years after missions were first planted in the region. It tells us in fairly straightforward terms that the Spanish conception of the dividing line between the coast and interior—or better yet, the conceptual line between the "backwoods" and what passed for civilization—was defined by a thin sliver of northern and eastern Mindanao's oceanfront over which colonial agents could assert their presence and negotiate their agenda. I can think of no better way to place Spanish colonial authority in Mindanao in a broader political context than by quoting directly from Spanish authorities in the early nineteenth century. More than a century after the aforementioned Tagoloán correspondence, and two centuries after missionization began in earnest, with thousands of local conversions already confirmed, Spanish colonial officials are forced to admit in a letter to their king that, with regard to Mindanao,

> the Spanish nation possesses only a very small coastal section in its two provinces of Caraga and Misamis, and the fort of Zamboanga [on the far western end of the island] with its territory. All the rest is populated by savage Tribes without any culture or civilization; or by barbarian Mohammedans, and pirates who are subjects of the King of Mindanao [Sultan of Magindanaw] who, despite the treaties and the state of peace that

---

[63] The Latin etymology of "pagan" is *paganus*—someone who, during the Roman Republic, lived a rustic, independent life in the countryside, as opposed to in the city-states, where "citizens" lived together in "settled" and "civil" communities.

the government has tried to maintain, keep conducting raids on defenseless towns and engaging in hostilities, bringing a thousand evils upon the subjects of Spain with seeming impunity because the small boats with which they conduct their pirating are so fast that they cannot be caught by ours.[64]

In other words, Spain's political reach in terms of Lumad Mindanao never paralleled the considerable social and cultural impact of its missionaries.

Direct and indirect references to conversion in northeast Mindanao describe significant missionary contact in Lumad areas, intensive contact that would have had a cultural impact. Missionary contact often led to the nominal incorporation of native settlements into the colonial administrative framework, primarily through the Catholic missions and related "services," through a haphazardly sponsored settlement program, known as *reducción*,[65] and through the equally haphazard, but relatively continuous, maintenance of these areas as *encomiendas*. Female converts are noted and celebrated in missionary accounts for their critical role in initiating and maintaining cooperative relationships between Lumads and missionaries. The active peacemaking role played by foreign missionaries was said to have contributed to the cessation of warfare by indigenous leaders whose political capital was previously cultivated through a warrior complex that encouraged revenge-raiding. Strong ties with individual missionaries even led native warriors to fight under the banner of Spain against former allies, and sometimes to fight against their own close kin in indigenous revolts. These interactions enabled the development of Christian identification among the Lumad, such that several communities actively sought not only religious conversion but also the patronage of Spanish colonial officials.

Yet centuries later, Lumad peoples were counted among what American colonial officials called the "non-Christian tribes" of the Philippines, and they have long been objectified and appropriated for nationalist and academic ends.[66] In the twentieth century, American and Filipino ethnographers even pointed to them as representatives of precolonial cultural traditions.[67] In other words, they are defined

---

[64] Archivo Histórico Nacional, Madrid, Spain (hereafter AHN), Ultramar,5155,Exp13,n6,f1r-1v. The original text is: "… en que la Nacion Española apenas posee una muy pequeña parte litoral en sus dos provincias de Caraga y Misamis, y el presidio de Zamboanga con su territorio. Todo lo demás se halla ocupado por Tribus salvajes sin cultura sin civilizacion alguna; o por Mahometanos bárbaros, y piratas sujetos al Rey de Mindanao, quienes a pesar de los tratados, y del estado de paz que se procura guardar de parte del Gobierno siempre hacen incursiones en los pueblos indefensos y practican hostilidades causando mil males a los subditos de España casi impunemente por que las pequeñas embarcaciones con que andan en su piraterías son tan veloces que no pueden ser alcansadas por las nuestras … "

[65] Despite the connotations of forced resettlement associated with this term in the Philippines—echoes of "hamletting" in the American colonial and Martial Law periods—a *reducción* is defined by the online edition of the *Diccionario de la Real Academia Española* (DRAE; http://www.rae.es) simply as a settlement of already-Christianized indians.

[66] Cf. Ian McNiven and Lynette Russell, *Appropriated Pasts: Indigenous Peoples and the Colonial Culture of Archaeology* (Lanham, MD: Alta Mira Press, 2005), on the global phenomenon of exploiting indigenous peoples for political ends.

[67] This characterization of indigenous minorities as precolonial "relics" has what I consider to be serious ramifications in the present day. Besides the social prejudice and discrimination faced by such minorities as a direct result of this stereotype, one can also find scholars applying rather uncritically the available descriptions of early twentieth-century Lumad peoples to studies concerning precolonial Philippine culture in general *as if* they were interchangeable. See, for example, the use of descriptions of twentieth-century Bukidnon and

almost entirely on "conjectural history," which even a functionalist like A. R. Radcliffe Brown would have explicitly distinguished from "authentic history."[68] Not surprisingly, the long-term significance of the early missionary encounters on Lumad culture and political organization today remains largely ignored, even by Mindanao specialists.

Producing a viable ethnohistory of the Lumad in colonial Mindanao therefore requires something more than the readily available, previously translated bits of random archival data about Lumad Mindanao distilled from the historical canon of the Philippines. Translation itself is both a linguistic and cultural act of redefinition, for our earlier sense of the Lumad had already been channeled and constricted to produce a coherent national vision. The problem is that, while this vision may accurately reflect the situation in Luzon in the final decades of the nineteenth century, it does not illuminate the frontier world of Mindanao in the sixteenth to eighteenth centuries.

As one might expect, sources for Mindanao from the early colonial period are rather sparse relative to data available for other areas of the Philippines or Southeast Asia, and more starkly so when compared to the primary sources available for other Spanish colonies. This sparseness *per se* is a very real problem, given that the data are too easily lost in the echo chamber of our received wisdom about the Spanish colonial period, creating a nonsensical, vacuous image of the Lumadnon when examined devoid of context. I certainly do not seek to neutralize any of the brutal, oppressive, or exploitative aspects of Spanish colonialism. There is nothing that justifies colonial occupation, in any form. However, when we focus too intently on its hegemonic power, and its political and economic agenda, we overlook what William Henry Scott called "the cracks in the parchment curtain" that can still tell us so much about local intentions, aspirations, and actions. Therefore, to resonate more fully with the truth of the Lumad experience, of their becoming and remaining a people within the context of the colonial experience, we must intentionally ground ourselves not only in the history told through Spanish colonial records—the only

---

Manobo culture in Junker's study of precolonial Philippine chiefdoms in the Visayas region. See Oona Paredes, "Discriminating Native Traditions among the Mindanao Lumad," in *Old Ties and New Solidarities: Studies on Philippine Communities*, ed. C. Macdonald and G. Pesigan (Quezon City: Ateneo de Manila University Press, 2000), pp. 74–90. See also Junker, *Raiding*. These particular Lumad groups are, in fact, part of an entirely different linguistic and cultural family than Visayans and, even if only for demographic and geographical reasons, were and still are markedly less hierarchical in political organization. See Richard Elkins, "A Proto-Manobo Word List," *Oceanic Linguistics* 13 (1974): 601–41; and Teodoro Llamzon, *Handbook of Philippine Language Groups* (Quezon City: Ateneo de Manila University Press, 1978). Moreover, I consider Cole's work *The Bukidnon of Mindanao* highly problematic in that, according to the Coles' own accounts (see also Mabel Cook Cole, *Savage Gentlemen* [New York, NY: D. Van Norstrand Company, 1929]), they conducted their research through interpreters from Luzon who did not speak the languages of Mindanao. At times, Fay-Cooper Cole's descriptions diverge widely from those of other researchers working in the same area. For example, a fellow researcher and contemporary of the Coles, Frank Lynch, also questioned the representativeness of Cole's monograph. See Frank Lynch, "The Bukidnon of North-Central Mindanao in 1889," *Philippine Studies* 15,3 (1967): 464–82. See also Oona Paredes, "Describing Higaunon Culture," *Kinaadman* 20 (1998): 59–60.

[68] Ioan Lewis, *Arguments with Ethnography: Comparative Approaches to History, Politics, and Religion* (Oxford: Berg, 2004), p. 12.

primary sources available[69]—but also in our broader ethnographic knowledge of Lumad peoples, including their oral traditions.[70]

A new look at the historical record of northeast Mindanao tells us this much very clearly: that many ancestors of today's Lumad peoples did convert, and that Catholic missions and missionaries played a significant role in making the Lumad who they are today. Even with our limited data, it is apparent that the Lumad peoples of northeast Mindanao were exposed to and significantly influenced by religious missionization in the early Spanish colonial period, which brought about significant transformations in their social organization, especially with regard to religious practice, warfare, and identity, as will be shown in the chapters that follow. With this study I therefore hope to complicate, out of necessity, not only the claims of a Manila-centered view of Philippine anthropology and history in general, but also a Muslim-centered view of Mindanao, in order to productively destabilize our perceptions of the early Spanish colonial period, and begin the process of marking the place of Lumad peoples within these larger histories.

---

[69] Following Vansina, we can say that colonial documents are "stable and permanent, not fluid or evanescent as oral messages are," whereas oral traditions "consist of information existing in memory," which "itself is only distinguished from other information by the conviction that the item is remembered, not dreamt or fantasized." Unfortunately, colonial documents are also the only possible contemporary sources available for this particular case, in the sense that they were created in their present form at the time the relevant events actually took place. Oral traditions, like genealogies, epics, and other unwritten traditions, in contrast, are passed along from generation to generation through individual memories, and therefore recontextualized (or actively "re-created" according to Vansina) with each remembering and retelling. Although oral traditions can be considered primary sources in a larger ethnographic sense, there is no way we can regard them as contemporary to the sixteenth century, since they have "passed from mouth to mouth, for a period beyond the lifetime of the informants." See Jan Vansina, *Oral Tradition: A Study in Historical Methodology*, trans. H. M. Wright (Chicago, IL: Aldine, 1985), pp. 12–13, 147.

[70] Data presented without reference to either published work or publicly available documents are synthesized from my own ethnographic knowledge gained from observations, notes, correspondence, and interviews with an assortment of Lumad people from earlier field visits in 1994 and 1995, and from personal correspondence with select field informants that extends to the present day.

CHAPTER 2

BLESSED ARE THE PEACEMAKERS: RECOLETOS AND THE OTHER MISSION TO MINDANAO

If the colonial experience transformed the Lumad world into what it is today, at the heart of this experience was the foundation of early Christian missions among the Lumad in northeast Mindanao. This chapter outlines the area's mission history, presenting a distilled contact scenario that came to typify interactions between pioneering European mission planters and autonomous Lumad communities, and contextualizing the complex social and political relationships that developed between Iberian missionaries and the Lumadnon in this pericolonial area.

Much of what I discuss in this chapter comes from the internal literature of the Orden de los Agustinos Recoletos, including the *Catálogo de los Religiosos* and a special issue of the Recoletos' *Boletín de la Provincia de San Nicolás de Tolentino.*[1] Both the *Catálogo* and the *Boletín* directly and extensively reference the Recoleto archives and official chronicle, referred to as the *Crónicas,* and they do so faithfully, with little embellishment save for a predictable pro-Recoleto spin. This "spin," though primarily stylistic in nature, nonetheless has some significance in terms of historical interpretation in that the Recoleto narratives tend to dwell on the extreme difficulties and humiliations experienced by their missionaries as they struggled to convert the *naturales.* As such, these reports consistently convey the smallness of their victories, betraying no sense of satisfaction or accomplishment, because there remained so

---

[1] Francisco Sábada del Carmen OAR, *Catálogo de los Religiosos Agustinos Recoletos de San Nicolás de Tolentino desde el Año 1606 en que Llegó la Primera Misión á Manila, hasta Nuestros Días* (Madrid: Imprenta del Asilo de Huérfanos del Sagrado Corazón de Jesús, 1906); and Orden de los Agustinos Recoletos (hereafter OAR), *Boletín de la Provincia de San Nicolas de Tolentino* 60, 629 (1970), printed in Marcilla, Navarra. The first of the *Crónicas,* or chronicles, of the Recoletos was the work of P. Fr. Andrés de San Nicolás. It is sometimes cited as the *Historia General de los Religiosos Descalzos del Orden de los Ermitaños del Gran Padre y Doctor de la Iglesia San Augustin de las Congregacion de España y de las Indias,* printed in Madrid in 1664. Volumes I–XII of the *Crónicas* refer to the Philippines, and, of these volumes, the first four refer to the first mission period (see Table 1, below). The Recoleto *Boletín* cited in this study draws exclusively, in some cases verbatim, from Volumes I–IV of the *Crónicas.* The *Crónicas* likewise draw from the original Recoleto archive, which I consulted in Marcilla, Navarra. The *Catálogo,* on the other hand, is an encyclopedia of the Recoletos who had worked in the Philippines, listed chronologically according to the specific *barcada,* or shipload, in which they arrived. Each listing consists of an abridged curriculum vitae in narrative form, in which important events or peculiar circumstances in the personal and professional lives of each Recoleto are noted. The *Boletín* is the Recoletos' evangelical journal, and for selected themes it draws from the Order's archival records for educational and informational purposes. Some of the data presented in narrative form in Peter Schreurs, *Caraga Antigua 1521–1910: The Hispanization and Christianization of Agusan, Surigao, and East Davao* (Cebu: University of San Carlos Publications, 1989), were also derived from the same sources as the *Catálogo* and the *Boletín.*

much work to be done. These were not narratives of defeat or victimization, however, as such reports were intended to spur Spaniards back home to action for the Recoleto cause, whether by contributing funds, joining the Order, or other means. This tone is in sharp contrast to, for example, that of the Jesuits, who were consistently triumphalist in their accounts—and suspiciously so, according to the Recoletos.[2]

The mission history of the Philippines is colored by political rivalries among the different orders, between the clergy and civilian authorities, and, later, between the Religious orders in general and the Church hierarchy itself over the entry of so-called Secular or Diocesan priests.[3] In the case of Mindanao, competing claims made by the Recoletos and the Jesuits, as well as the internal political battles within the colonial administrative body of Spain in the Philippines, influenced the distribution of missionaries across time and space. While the conflicts themselves lay outside the scope of this study, they serve to illustrate that, even in a relative backwater like Mindanao, missionizing was hardly a straightforward, much less isolated, affair.

I conceptualize the mission history of northeast Mindanao as consisting of four distinct periods that closely parallel the history of its colonial administration. This particular periodization reflects an attempt to reconcile the competing agendas of Recoleto, Jesuit, and indigenous historians in order to present a historical framework for Mindanao based not on Manila-centric events but on the patterns of missionization and the nature of their impact on Lumad patterns of settlement and political interaction.

The first mission period begins with the official colonization of the Philippines in 1565 and extends into the first two decades of the nineteenth century. This is what I consider the early colonial period because it precedes the intensification of both

---

[2] In fact, the Recoletos once openly accused the Jesuits of being delusional and presenting fantasy and fabrication as fact. Take, for example, P. Fr. Rafael García's biting critique of the now famous 1667 publication by the Jesuit Combés, describing this account of the victorious Jesuit missionization of Mindanao as "vainglorious," "chimeric," and downright "falsified." See OAR, *Boletín de la Provincia de San Nicolas de Tolentino*, pp. 13–17. See also Francisco Combés SJ, *Historia de las islas de Mindandao, Iolo, y sus adyacentes*, vols. 1–8 (Madrid: W. E. Retana, 1897 [1667]). The hostility of the Recoleto reaction should be understood in the context not only of the tight competition between the two orders for mission territory, but also relative to the Recoletos' apparent view that Jesuits, in general, were not widely noted for humility or self-deprecation.

[3] See Salvador Escoto, "The Ecclesiastical Controversy of 1767–1776: A Catalyst of Philippine Nationalism," *Journal of Asian History* 10,2 (1976): 99–133. Religious—*Religioso* in Spanish—are Catholic clergy who take a vow of religious obedience and follow a Rule as determined by the particular ecclesiastical order to which they belong and/or are ordained. Rules pertaining to poverty (owning no property), chastity, and the sanctity of the cloister apply to Religious but not to Secular clergy. Secular (or Diocesan) clergy, on the other hand, are clergy under the authority of a local bishop and may be assigned anywhere within that bishop's territorial jurisdiction or diocese. Secular clergy do not belong to a Religious order and therefore follow no rules of cloister and make no vows of obedience except for canonical obedience to the bishop of their diocese. In earlier Church history, Seculars were allowed to marry, but are now bound by the traditions of celibacy and chastity as part of their service to the Church. However, they make no vow of poverty, are paid a salary, and are not part of any institution or apostolic community, factors that, according to the historian and Religious priest Peter Schreurs MSC (personal communication, May 1, 2005), at times resulted in the material abuse of parishes and parishioners. Today the dividing line between Religious and Secular priests is blurring in that Secular priests have taken to forming their own apostolic communities for the purpose of religious fellowship.

colonial rule and missionization that came to Mindanao with the nineteenth century. Within this first mission period, the Recoletos had established the first fully functional, permanent missions in Butuan and Cagayán by 1622, and, as with general colonial administration, this early period was characterized by a dearth of personnel available for an area that was politically and economically marginal relative to Manila. Not surprisingly, Recoletos describe this period as a time of *escasez,* or scarcity.

Table 1. Periods of Missionization for the Island of Mindanao

Mission Periods	Duration	Characteristics
First	1600–1820	*Escasez,* or scarcity, of Recoleto personnel, with fewer than forty Religious for all of Filipinas, which then included the Marianas Islands
Second	ca. 1820–1859	Intensification of Recoleto missions in terms of personnel due to new training college in northern Spain
Third	1859–1898	Re-entry of reconstituted Jesuit Order to Mindanao and subsequent jurisdictional rivalry with the Recoletos
Fourth	1898–1946	American colonial period; introduction of English language, American Catholic missionaries, and new Protestant missions

Conversion statistics were used as ammunition in the war of words that was waged between the Recoletos and Jesuits in the late nineteenth century, and in one related newspaper article, the Recoletos state that this *escasez* of personnel was then so grave that for several years the parishes and missions of Surigáo, Cabongbongan, Higaquit (Gigaquit), Cacub, Butuan, Hingoog (Gingoôg), Maínit, Habongan (Jabonga), Talacogon, Línao, Iligan, and Inítao—all in northeast Mindanao—had no missionaries in residence. Indeed, a review of the Recoleto personnel catalogue shows that, over the course of the seventeenth century, a grand total of only seventy-six Religious were assigned to Mindanao, and not all at the same time. This *escasez* persisted into the early nineteenth century, and P. Fr. Toribio Minguella reported that, in 1820, the Recoletos were ministering to over 123 towns and annexed areas scattered over twenty-seven islands and comprising eight provinces from Manila to Mindanao to the Marianas Islands—all of which they somehow managed with only thirty-six Religious. After the first two decades of the nineteenth century, more and more Recoletos became available for ministering to Mindanao and elsewhere, thanks to the opening of a new Recoleto training college in Monteagudo, Navarra, Spain. The second mission period was therefore a time of mission intensification that started in the 1820s, when the number of Recoletos and colonial administrative personnel assigned to Mindanao began to increase exponentially. This period closes with the return of the newly reconstituted Jesuit Order to Mindanao in 1859, and its usurpation of Recoleto territory on the island.[4]

Our present-day understanding of northeast Mindanao's political and spatial geographies comes almost exclusively from the third mission period. Thanks to the Jesuits, we have bureaucratic correspondence, mission records, and economic data for this period of colonial administration. This is because, as with all Jesuit enterprises, they documented their own work in great detail. Despite the return of the Jesuits, however, Misamis province remained in the Recoletos' top five sources of Religious tribute. Table 2 shows that, towards the end of Recoleto control in 1877, the province of Misamis, which was under the bishopric (*obispado*) of Cebú, was credited with collecting just under 15,000 *tributos*, about 700 more than the tribute total for the capital island of Cebú itself. Misamis was ranked fifth among all Recoleto missions in the archipelago, ranking below only the much more densely populated and established Christian areas of Bohol, Negros, Zambales, and Cavite. In fact, two decades earlier, in 1853, Misamis had already become a sufficiently large population center to require a detailed manual explaining the different tribute requirements per population class, including how to determine tax rates in the case of mixed marriages between *naturales* ("natives"), *Sangleyes* ("Chinese"), and *mestizos* (mixed-race) *Sangleyes, españolas,* and *indios.*[5] The *indios* category would have included the increasing number of Christian Visayan migrants from Bohol.

Table 2. Top Five Recoleto Missions in Filipinas, 1877[6]

Mission	Location	Number of Tributes
Bohol	Visayas (island)	52,600 ½
Negros	Visayas (island)	43,870 ½
Zambales	Luzon	23,058 ½
Cavite	Luzon	18,525 ½
Misamis	North Mindanao	14,925 ½

Finally, the fourth mission period covers the American colonial period and the resulting change in the modus operandi of missions, including the eventual

---

[4] See Sábada, *Catálogo.* The Recoletos' ability to achieve their goals despite such limited resources was flaunted with great pride as something that, in their minds, distinguished them from Jesuits, whom they apparently regarded as overprivileged: "Conviene advertir que tantos escaseaba entonces el personal de la Orden, que no pudieron en bastantes años proveer los curatos y misiones ... En 1820—escribe el C. de la Historia Padre Minguella—la corporación de Recoletos administraba en Filipinas 123 pueblos y anejos, esparcidos en 27 islas, de la comprensión de 8 provincias, desde la de Manila (entonces Tondo) hasta la de Mindanao é islas Marianas. Para atender á tan vasta administración sólo contaba con ¡36 religiosos!" "Los Recoletos En Mindanao," *La Época* (Madrid), Num. 13.948 (June 29, 1891), p. 1.

[5] See Venancio de Abella, *Ynstruccion para el Gobierno y manejo del Subdelegado de Hacienda de la provincia de Misamis* (Ayer collection, handwritten MS., 1853), from the Newberry Library, in Chicago, IL (hereafter NL).

[6] These figures are derived from: NL Ayer 2143.A81,A8,1863, Folio Sheet 2.

replacement of Spanish-speaking missionaries with English-speaking Americans, and the beginning of sanctioned Protestant proselytizing in the islands.[7]

This study focuses on the first mission period, in particular the early days during which the encounter between island Southeast Asia and the European West was incarnated in the initial conversions of Lumad peoples, and played out in the genesis of the Augustinian Recoletos. In this period, northeast Mindanao's handful of permanent missions was statistically negligible in comparison to a Philippine total of almost two hundred individual missions, with ninety-eight in Luzon alone. At any given time, there were fewer than twenty Religious, total, in the entire northeast Mindanao region, ministering to roughly 30,000 people scattered over the second largest island in the archipelago.[8] The historian John Leddy Phelan goes so far as to state categorically that "on the island of Mindanao the Spanish conquest did not take place." Christian conversion on the island of Mindanao was, in Phelan's estimation, inconsequential, and its impact did not warrant much, if any, scholarly consideration. Though he concedes later that some churches were established in Mindanao by Spaniards, he dismisses them as mere "frontier outposts ... confined to a few strategic coastal sites."[9]

In tandem, the Jesuit historians also regularly imply, though they never openly assert, that nothing remarkable took place in northeast Mindanao until their reconstituted Order reentered the mission field in 1859.[10] Conventional history

---

[7] During the Spanish period, especially during the Carlist wars, conversion to Protestantism was considered tantamount to sedition.

[8] John Leddy Phelan, *The Hispanization of the Philippines: Spanish Aims and Filipino Responses, 1565–1700* (Madison, WI: University of Wisconsin, 1959), pp. 22, 140, 167–76. See also Appendix D in this volume.

[9] Ibid., p. 167. Despite his important contributions to our understanding of religious conversion and culture change during the Spanish colonial period in the Philippines, Phelan was an historian of the Americas and not the Philippines. It is also my understanding that he never set foot in the Philippines, relying mainly on the rich but nonetheless limited records on the Philippines archived in the Newberry Library of Chicago. We can conclude, therefore, that he saw "Hispanization" and religious conversion in the Philippines through particular Americano frames based on the impact of missionary and colonial activity on Amerindians, which, as we already know, was radically different from the conditions in the Philippine archipelago. Nor was Phelan a Southeast Asianist, as can be seen from his study, in which he attributes the apparently limited local impact of Hispanization to a "failure" of not only Spanish colonial administration, but also of the conversion efforts and spiritual administration by Iberian missionaries. In fact, I cannot think of anyone else in Philippine studies who would suggest that the missionaries of this time simply were not thorough enough. If anything, the opposite charge is leveled against the Church, and Filipinos often mourn the disappearance of our imagined true, indigenous identity. Phelan's analysis of the "Hispanization" and colonization of the Philippines was obviously not informed by the distinct technological context and social-cultural constructs through which Austronesian peoples would have received and absorbed such foreign events and phenomena, whether these be religious, political, or other cultural forms.

[10] A case in point is Bernad's "study of the exploration and evangelization of Mindanao," which, in actuality, relates the activities of Jesuits to the exclusion of almost all other parties, giving the impression that nothing else of substance took place on the island while the Jesuits were in exile. See Miguel Bernad SJ, *The Great Island: Studies in the Exploration and Evangelization of Mindanao* (Quezon City: Ateneo de Manila University Press, 2004). Not surprisingly, the Recoletos have for centuries accused the Jesuits of being creative with the truth, and even introducing outright fabrications, in relation to this matter. See OAR, *Boletín de la Provincia de San Nicolás de Tolentino*, pp. 2–21. See also Appendix D in this volume.

unfortunately follows this bias, as in, for example, the description of "Mindanao" written by Philippine historian Ricardo Jose in the first-ever comprehensive historical encyclopedia of Southeast Asia.[11] In Jose's entry, the history of Mindanao is primarily concerned with the Islamization of Mindanao, as reflected in the subtitle "The Muslim South." The Lumad warrant only a fleeting mention, and the Lumad-Recoleto interaction covered by this study is reduced to one abysmally inadequate sentence: "Jesuit missionaries began converting the people in northern Mindanao."[12] Even Ronald K. Edgerton's history of Bukidnon, more comprehensive and nuanced than any work on Bukidnon that had come before, only goes as far back as the late nineteenth century, and therefore relies almost exclusively on Jesuit sources from the third mission period.[13] Not surprisingly, historical studies to date give the distinct impression that the Recoleto missions, despite having been maintained continuously for nearly three centuries, had little notable impact on Mindanao.

The Recoletos vehemently disagree with this characterization. In fact, the birth of the Recoletos as a Religious order was tied logistically to the nascent Spanish colony of Filipinas, their first mission field. While other clerical personnel had indeed set foot on Mindanao earlier, none of them built lasting missions or assigned permanent personnel, not even the Jesuits who arrived in Butuan in 1596.[14] In an article on the first missionaries to Mindanao, entitled "Primeros evangelizadores de Mindanao," P. Fr. Rafael García argued forcefully against the rather wobbly Jesuit claim of responsibility for the Christianization of Mindanao, pointing out that, while they arrived in Butuan in 1596 as chaplains of the armada of Esteban Rodriguez de Figueroa, the Jesuits did not stay there. Instead, they administered Butuan as a mere *visita*, or annex, from the island of Bohol,

> ... whose great distance did not permit them to visit except sporadically, such that instead of making progress, it reduced [the presence of Christianity], and those few Christians who were there when [the Recoletos] arrived [in 1622] were so ignorant of all Christian ideas and as immersed in their ancient superstitions as if [these superstitions] had never been abandoned.[15]

The Filipino Jesuit Miguel Bernad insists that the Butuan mission, though short-lived, "had lasting effects" in terms of establishing Christian doctrine among the locals. However, he seems to concede that the period of actual contact was brief, explaining that the Jesuits withdrew from Butuan because "they had other commitments," and that the natives rebelled and returned to their "evil practices" after the fact.[16] Francis Madigan SJ also admits that between the Jesuit mission's

---

[11] Ricardo Trota Jose, "Mindanao: The Muslim South," *Southeast Asia: A Historical Encyclopedia from Angkor Wat to East Timor*, ed. Ooi Keat Gin (Santa Barbara, CA: ABC-CLIO, 2004), pp. 890–93.

[12] Jose, "Mindanao," p. 891.

[13] Ronald K. Edgerton, *People of the Middle Ground: A Century of Conflict and Accommodation in Central Mindanao, 1880s–1980s* (Quezon City: Ateneo de Manila University Press, 2008).

[14] OAR, *Boletín de la Provincia de San Nicolas de Tolentino*, p. 13.

[15] Ibid., p. 47 (citing Archivo Provincial de los Agustinos Recoletos, Marcilla, Spain [hereafter ARM], leg 84, num 1, doc 1).

[16] Bernad, *The Great Island*, pp. 47–57.

establishment in 1596 and its official closure two decades later, the mission in Butuan was actually staffed for only five cumulative years.[17] Peter Schreurs further adds that many of the Butuan converts were relocated to Bohol after the mission was shut down, which means the assertion that the Jesuits left a viable mission in Butuan is a nonstarter.[18] In any case, the Recoletos themselves make no claim to having been the first missionaries in Mindanao to preach the Christian Gospel successfully, instead giving that honor to the Augustinians.[19]

The Mindanao experience was unquestionably a critical component of the Recoletos' evolution as a Religious order. In my conversations with Spanish priests at the Recoleto seminary in Marcilla, Navarra, I was told that "Filipinas" remains part of the core identity of every Recoleto,[20] despite the fact that the Philippine "province" has been completely independent of Spanish administration since 1998.[21] Recoletos are also tied intimately to Mindanao because this is where some of their first missions were planted, making it the "original theater of their apostolic undertakings."[22] In addition, Mindanao is where their earliest martyrs—six alone in the first decade of mission work[23]—met with sticky ends, having been felled by various Moro and Moro-allied antagonists, including some of the Karaga Lumad discussed in chapter four. Given that general antagonism towards Islam and Muslims was part and parcel of the Spanish missionary and colonial repertoire, owing much to the legacy of the *Reconquista*, the proxy war against Islam in the southern Philippines was a factor in the perseverance of missionaries who worked

---

[17] Francis Madigan SJ, "The Early History of Cagayan de Oro," *Philippine Studies* 11,1 (1963): 81. He was citing another Jesuit, Horacio de la Costa SJ, *The Jesuits in the Philippines, 1581–1768* (Cambridge, MA: Harvard University Press, 1961), pp. 154, 165–66, 171, 319. Nor did Butuan warrant even a fleeting mention in de la Costa's later memoir on the legacy of the Jesuits in the Philippines. See Horacio de la Costa SJ, *Selected Studies in Philippine Colonial History*, ed. R. Paterno (Metro Manila: Philippine Province of the Society of Jesus/Ateneo de Manila University Press, 2002).

[18] Peter Schreurs, *Caraga Antigua 1521–1910: The Hispanization and Christianization of Agusan, Surigao, and East Davao* (Cebu: University of San Carlos Publications, 1989), p. 118.

[19] OAR, *Boletín de la Provincia de San Nicolas de Tolentino*, p. 4.

[20] This is reinforced by the seminary museum's permanent display on the history of the Recoleto order, which consists almost entirely of artifacts from the Philippine missions, especially Mindanao. Likewise, a Recoleto website announcement celebrating 2006 as the Year of the Missionary describes the significance of the early Philippines this way: "The Philippine missions were for nearly three centuries the place (and cause) into which the Recoletos poured the warm apostolic zeal that they had amassed at their training centers in Spain, [forged] in the heat of the tabernacle and the furnace of austere living." See www.agustinosrecoletos .com.co/Principal.aspx?tab_Codigo=49, accessed October 30, 2006.

[21] Until the late twentieth century, the Philippines was the core of the Recoleto *provincia* or administrative unit of *San Nicolás de Tolentino*, named after P. Fr. Nicolás de Tolentino, a French national who arrived in 1618 with the first *barcada*, or shipload, of Recoletos to the new colony of Filipinas. He served in Zambales, Cavite, and, for a time, Caraga. In 1998, the Recoletos created a separate administrative province for the Philippines, which was named after the recently canonized St. Ezekiel Moreno, who, ironically, is better known for his work in the Americas, in particular Colombia.

[22] "… *Mindanao, teatro primitivo de sus apostolicas empresas*," Sábada, *Catálogo*, p. 99.

[23] Named as P. Fr. Juan de la Madre de Dios (1623); H. Fr. Juan de S. Nicolás (1624); PP. Fr. Jacinto de Jesús y María, Alonso de S. José, Juan de Sto. Tomás, and Pedro de S. Antonio (1631, killed in the Caraga Revolt), in "Los Recoletos En Mindanao," *La Época* (Madrid), Num. 13.948 (June 29, 1891).

with the Lumad, and I believe it remains an intimate aspect of continuing Recoleto sentimentality towards their former missions in this area, missions that were described by ecclesiastic authorities in Manila as "the most laborious and dangerous of ministries in the Philippines."[24]

To live and work in Mindanao in the early colonial period was to do so in an area that "always serve[d] as the theater of war and as the object of disasters."[25] First of all, the natives being served by the Recoleto missions—and this would include those missions in the Lumad areas—were freely characterized as "among the most unconquerable and fierce people in these districts."[26] It was acknowledged, however, that their "race is not so rude that it cannot be conquered by kind acts."[27] All the same, in Mindanao, the reality in the mid-seventeenth century was such that, of all its areas that were administrated by the colonial government, or ministered to by the Recoletos, "scarcely one is reduced to obedience;[28] therefore those who live unsubdued in the mountains only wait for ... opportunities in order to foment disturbances and restlessness."[29] In addition to the constant risk of insurrection from the purported beneficiaries of mission work, the missionaries also risked being attacked while traveling in rivers or at sea, and raided by Moros from Magindanaw, Davao, and Lanao. The first half of the 1700s, in particular, were horrifying years for all coastal dwellers and travelers throughout the Philippines, due to such an intensification of Moro piracy and slave-raiding that, in 1739, "they ['already masters of the sea'] had so closed the passage from [Calamianes and Mindoro] to Manila that for more than six months nothing could be heard from the Religious living in those fields of Christendom."[30] In addition to morbidity and mortality from such human assaults, they also had to cope with assaults of an environmental nature, not just in terms of working in the tropical heat dressed in black wool cassocks,[31] but also the

---

[24] Stated as *"los ministerios mas trabajosos y peligrosos de Filipinas."* OAR, *Boletín de la Provincia de San Nicolás de Tolentino*, p. 39, citing (AHN num 294, Documentos de Indias, Sección Varios). The reputation of Mindanao as extremely hostile territory is noted by another order, the Augustinians, who in 1599 abandoned their attempts to establish permanent missions on the island after realizing that "only force could open a path to missionizing [there], the people being of extreme fierceness." OAR, *Boletín de la Provincia de San Nicolás de Tolentino*, p. 7.

[25] Emma Blair and James Robertson, *The Philippine Islands, 1493–1898*, vol. 36 (Cleveland, OH: Arthur H. Clark Company, 1903–1909), p. 177. This is a translation based on Luis de Jesus, *Historia general de los religiosos descalzos ... de San Agustín* (Madrid, 1681), Lib. II, Decada VII, Cap. II, Sec. III, Num. 739.

[26] From a 1648 letter to the king of Spain from "the most illustrious *cabildo*," or municipal council, of Manila, in support of continuing alms for the Recoletos and allowing them to import more missionaries. See Blair and Robertson, *The Philippine Islands*, vol. 36, pp. 121–12; translation based on de Jesus, *Historia general*, Lib. I, Decada VII, Cap. I, Sec. III, Num. 240.

[27] See Blair and Robertson, *The Philippine Islands*, vol. 36, p. 136; translation based on de Jesus, *Historia general*, Lib. I, Decada VII, Cap. I, Sec. VII.

[28] This means that none of them had become sworn vassals of the king of Spain. Yet.

[29] Blair and Robertson, *The Philippine Islands*, vol. 36, p. 127; translation based on de Jesus, *Historia general*, Lib. I, Decada VII, Cap. I, Sec. VI, Num. 258.

[30] Blair and Robertson, *The Philippines Islands*, vol. 36, p. 180; translation based on de Jesus, *Historia general*, Lib. II, Decada VII, Cap. II, Sec. III. Num. 741. In fact, this whole section is about how "even in carrying on missions in infidel lands, our religious could not suffer greater hardships than those which they endure in [América]."

[31] This is from remarks I overheard in the Recoleto *convento* in Marcilla, Spain, during Holy Week in March 2005. In later centuries, the Recoletos in the Philippines were allowed to wear cooler materials, such as linen.

fact that the Philippine archipelago is a magnet for natural disasters, including typhoons and earthquakes. Indeed, the Recoletos of Filipinas were of the opinion that "to suffer the inclemencies of the weather ... is a martyrdom." The constant threat of piracy and slave-raiding also meant that coastal dwellers, including the missionaries, were regularly escaping to the interior uplands, and forced at such times to "go without food, or live on herbs of the field."[32]

Considering the physical isolation and foreignness of Spanish priests in the early colonial period, and the number of Recoletos who, rendered extremely vulnerable by their geographic isolation, died violent deaths either through misadventure or homicide, we can conclude that being a missionary in Mindanao in the seventeenth century was a high-risk vocation. It was also a vocation that offered no economic or other material reward, and therefore one that might be considered viable only by those who came to it as a matter of faith. In fact, even though a majority of those who served in Mindanao did not die violent deaths, the assignment itself was a *de facto* life sentence in one way or another.

The death of the Recoleto P. Fr. Juan de la Madre de Dios in 1623 shows the level of danger those early missionaries faced, and highlights the fact that their lives were literally at the mercy of the Lumad:

> We find the blessed Father preaching to the *indios* who were living along the banks of the Tandag river, and a leader of theirs whom they called Suba— lordly and tyrannical to those under his command, of very depraved habits—unable to bear the admonishments of this Religious, sacrilegiously took his life with spears.[33]

The same Suba was later killed by native troops serving with the Spanish garrison at Tandag, led by a man named Dacsa.[34] I should note that the killing of Suba took place in the Caraga region which, until the nineteenth century, was noted primarily for the belligerence of its indigenous population.[35]

Only a year earlier, however, this particular Recoleto, P. Fr. Juan de la Madre de Dios, had had some unexpected success in converting all sorts of Karagas and "pacifying" one of their leaders, a *datu* named Inuc. According to Schreurs's version of this episode, Inuc spared Madre de Dios's life and became a Christian because he was impressed by the sheer audacity of this Recoleto who, moved by divine inspiration, entered hostile territory and approached Inuc alone and unarmed.[36] In

---

[32] Blair and Robertson, *The Philippine Islands*, vol. 36, pp. 180–81; translation based on de Jesus, *Historia general*, Lib. II, Decada VII, Cap. II, Sec. III. Num. 741. "Herbs of the field" in this usage likely refers to wild vegetation (perhaps even weeds), as it does in Genesis 2:5 (King James Version).

[33] "Hallábase el bendito Padre evangelizando a los indios que habitaban en las márgenes del río de Tandag, y un principal de ellos que llamaban Suba, soberbio y tirano con los que tenía a sus órdenes y de costumbres muy depravadas, no pudiendo sufrir las amonestaciones del Religioso, quitóle sacrílegamente la vida a lanzadas." Sábada, *Catálogo*, p. 54, citing the *Crónicas*, vol. II, p. 53.

[34] Schreurs, *Caraga Antigua*, p. 138.

[35] Joseph Montano, "Excursion al Interior ... de Mindanao," *Boletín de la Sociedad de Geografía de Madrid* 23 (1887): 40–57.

[36] Schreurs, *Caraga Antigua*, pp. 117–37. I did not find the original source of the Inuc conversion narrative, though it appears in more than one Recoleto publication.

their records, the Recoletos refer to this inspired spiritual state as being *animado de santo celo*, or "moved by holy zeal," using it to explain acts of extraordinary courage or dedication in the mission field—the same holy zeal that would fatefully bring Madre de Dios to confront *datu* Suba a year later. The story of Inuc's conversion hints that he appreciated Madre de Dios's *santo celo* as a sign of his individual "prowess." But did he really see Madre de Dios as a formidable man who warranted respect? Or was Inuc merely mellowing with old age, perhaps growing weak and needing new allies?[37] Four hundred years later, we cannot answer these questions with any certainty. However, we should consider whether, in a missionary of such "holy zeal" as P. Fr. Madre de Dios, the *datu* Inuc might have seen marks of prowess as well. Similar acts of courage could very well have allowed these early missionaries to be perceived by the Lumad as figures of authority, despite the fact that they had no social standing, having neither economic wealth nor kinship ties.

So who were these intrepid Recoletos? Madre de Dios was one of eight Recoletos who, arriving from Mexico in two separate *barcadas,* or shiploads, planted the first seeds in this mission field. They are referred to in Recoleto historical narratives as *Los Ocho,*[38] "The Eight," and as many as 20,700 recorded baptisms of indigenous people are attributed to these men in their first two years (1622–1623) of mission work in Mindanao. "The Eight" were: Miguel de Santa María, Agustín de San Pedro, Francisco de la Madre de Dios, Jacinto de San Fulgencio, Jacinto de Jesús María, Juan de la Madre de Dios, Juan de San Nicolás, and Nicolás de Tolentino. Of *Los Ocho*, two in particular stand out as critical to the conversion of the Lumad, at least in historical imagination. While every Recoleto in Mindanao was important due to the sheer lack of personnel, it is rather impossible to imagine Lumad conversion in the first mission period without the specific presence of both Agustín de San Pedro and Juan de San Nicolás.[39]

The legendary Recoleto P. Fr. Agustín de San Pedro arrived in northeast Mindanao as a newly ordained twenty-four-year-old priest in 1623, and soon became the Order's most important mission planter.[40] According to Recoleto personnel records, he arrived with P. Fr. Jacinto de San Fulgencio,[41] whose peacemaking efforts

---

[37] We return to *datu* Inuc in chapter four.

[38] These eight are not to be confused with another group of eight Recoletos who were the first dispatched from Spain to Nueva España ("New Spain," which in the early seventeenth century still included, politically, the Philippines) to initiate the Filipinas missions. Based on the names listed on the official travel request from around November 8, 1617, this particular group of eight included about half of Mindanao's *Los Ocho*, including Juan de la Madre de Dios, Juan de San Nicolás, and Nicolás de Tolentino (see Archivo General de Indias in Sevilla [hereafter AGI], Filipinas, 80, N.1/1617, which actually lists only seven people). Agustín de San Pedro is named in a separate document dated approximately one week later, listed erroneously as "Pedro de San Agustín," but he apparently did not depart Spain for Filipinas until 1622, arriving the following year (AGI, Contratación, 5350, N.40/29-10-1616).

[39] OAR, *Boletín de la Provincia de San Nicolas de Tolentino*, p. 51, citing research by P. Fr. Toribio de Minguella.

[40] Based on the official Recoleto catalogue compiled by Sábada, *Catálogo*, pp. 81–83. However, in what can only be a clerical error, immigration records listing the names of Religious headed to Filipinas in 1622 describe the Recoleto "Pedro de San Agustín" as being an experienced thirty-eight-year-old theologian, priest, and missionary (AGI, Filipinas, 80, N.74/1622).

[41]The *Boletín de la Provincia de San Nicolas de Tolentino* literary narrative of the defense of Imolagan names his partner as P Fr. Jacinto de Jesús María. Jesús María was a contemporary of San Pedro in Mindanao, having arrived in the previous *barcada*. However, the latter's personnel record as summarized in the *Catalogo de los Religiosos* does not include this episode

have already been mentioned. He served for almost forty years in northeast Mindanao, rotating as Prior of Cagayán, Butuan, and Tandag, and was directly responsible not only for conversions in these missions, but also for the construction of various fortifications (*fortalezas*), including military garrisons (*presidios*), there and in the inland settlements of Linao, as well as the Visayan island of Romblon.[42] He was reportedly instrumental in mustering the Kagayanon and other Lumad warriors in support of Spanish troops in several anti-Moro campaigns, and was the first missionary—though not the last—to introduce the *naturales* to European-style combat.[43] These *hazañas militares* (miltary exploits) earned him his moniker of "warrior-priest," and San Pedro is known today among Recoletos and Mindanao historians alike as *El Padre Capitán*.[44] Though *El Padre Capitán*'s exploits were always framed as defensive warfare against Moro incursion, he also engaged in aggression, leading military offensives that took Lumad warriors into the Moro territories in the name of defending the Recoleto mission effort. But this does not mean he shirked his priestly duties. He even gained the rare appreciation of Jesuit historians, meriting mention in Francisco Combés's account, as he was reported to have "personally baptized more than ten thousand adults" in Mindanao.[45]

In sharp contrast, P. Fr. Juan de San Nicolás is described in both the *Catálogo* and the *Boletín* as a model of Christian humility and non-violence. Like the better-known El Padre Capitán, San Nicolás was Portuguese, something that Spanish Recoletos acknowledge with patriotic hesitation.[46] However, nothing much else is known about his past, and even the details of when he officially joined the Order seem uncertain. In any case, what matters to Recoleto archivists is that he was exemplary of the Order. He was with the first small group of permanent missionaries selected for Mindanao by the Bishop of Cebu. In the next chapter, we find him, along with his much younger partner, twenty-three-year-old P. Fr. Juan de la Madre de Dios,[47]

---

or any service in Cagayán, whereas the record of San Pedro specifically mentions Jacinto de San Fulgencio. The anonymous *Boletín* writer appears to have mixed up the two Padre Jacintos while in the throes of literary realization. See Sábada, *Catálogo*, pp. 66–67, and 81–83.

[42] In 1644, he was transferred to the island of Romblon in the Visayas, where he eventually died sometime around 1653. As is true of any good legendary figure, the actual circumstances of his death, including the date, are unknown, according to Sábada, *Catálogo*, p. 83, citing the *Crónicas*.

[43] P. Fr. Carlos de Jesus, who served in the Visayas, also had his own *hazañas militares*. See Sábada, *Catálogo*, p. 5.

[44] The nickname *el Padre Capitán* literally translates to a title of "Father-Captain," but it celebrates San Pedro's contradictory role of "warrior-priest," representing God and the Catholic Church, both inherently pacific, while also fighting as a soldier for the colonial government, engaging actively in warfare and not a little self-glorification.

[45] Blair and Robertson, *The Philippine Islands*, vol. 36, p. 149; translation based on Luis de Jesús, *Historia general*, Lib. I, Decada VII, Cap. 7. See also Francisco Combés SJ, *Historia de las islas de Mindandao, Iolo, y sus adyacentes* (Madrid: W. E. Retana, 1897 [1667]), Tomo III, Cap. 69.

[46] OAR, *Boletín de la Provincia de San Nicolas de Tolentino*, pp. 43–55. References to his Portuguese (Farense) origins seem to have been made mainly to differentiate him from two additional Recoletos in the catalogue with the same name. One was born in Madrid and served on Palawan Island, from where he was kidnapped by Corralat/Kudarat in 1637 and tortured to death. See Sábada, *Catálogo*, p. 61. Another who served in Mindanao in the nineteenth century appears to have been "accidentally" drowned by locals in Gigaquit. See OAR, *Boletín de la Provincia de San Nicolas de Tolentino*, p. 746.

[47] (AGI, Filipinas 80, N.1/1617).

encountering the Kagayanon in their quest for a new mission site. Before arriving in Cagayán, however, San Nicolás served first in Gigaquit, and then in Butuan, where his converts' consanguineal ties to Kagayanon *principales* would prove critical to his later success in the mission field.

P. Fr. San Nicolás had the knack, as well as the persistence, to overcome even the most "obstinate" of natives.[48] He is also memorialized for his peaceful nature that, according to the narrative, was the linchpin of his success as a missionary:

> He was held in high esteem by all the indigenous people, both friends and enemies, all of whom he treated the same, such that even their enemies the Magindanaw would come in peace to seek his counsel, and with his presence all sides enjoyed peace and calm even though they were neighbors of the rebels, and enemies of all of them. He was loved by all and for everyone he did good things … He lived in a humble shack. All the hard work he did among barbaric and fierce people, he carried out with extreme patience because of the results he hoped for and his desire for all those peoples to prosper from it. Seeing his mildness and good character … they loved him like he was their own father. In this manner he converted and baptized many.[49]

After Cagayán, he moved on to establish a new mission in Bayug, west of Cagayán, where he was already known from previous apostolic visits or "excursions" undertaken while based in other missions. The number of these apostolic visits is unknown, as they often go unmentioned, and, in this very early period, do not appear to have been recorded for their own sake. Indeed, not much was recorded in general during this time, not even the name of the second missionary who accompanied San Nicolás to Bayug.[50] But we do know that the apostolic visit was a standard aspect of mission work, and that it remains a common practice among missionaries to this day. In the example of San Nicolás's prior contact with Bayug, however, we can see both the development of a social familiarity between missionaries and non-mission natives, and the related opening of new missions, as significant artifacts of these apostolic visits, something that I will return to later.

Thus, in Bayug, San Nicolás was welcomed by the *datu*, recorded for posterity only under his unfortunate nickname of Dolomayor (Spanish for "great malice"), who encouraged the missionaries to evangelize there. Much to the Recoletos' frustration, Dolomayor himself did not convert,[51] though he entrusted his children to

---

[48] OAR, *Boletín de la Provincia de San Nicolas de Tolentino,* p. 46, citing *Crónicas* Tomo II, p. 42.

[49] Ibid., p. 45, citing *Crónicas*, Tomo II, p. 69, and quoting the words of P. Fr. Andrés del Espíritu Santo, from volume 600 of the *Boletín de la Provincia de San Nicolas de Tolentino*, pp. 129–30: "Fue grande la estimación que de él hicieron todos los naturales, así amigos como enemigos, que con todos trataba casi igualmente pues los enemigos mindanaos venían de paz a buscarle y comunicarle, con lo cual los partidos donde estuvo gozaban de paz y quietud aunque eran vecinos de los rebeldes y enemigos de todos. Era querido y amado de todos, y a todos procuraba hacer bien … Vivía en una pobre choza. Todo lo cual y otros muchos trabajos que se pasan entre gentes bárbaras y feroces, llevaba con suma paciencia por el fruto que esperaba y el deseo de aprovechamiento de aquellas gentes. Estas, viendo su apacibilidad y buen trato, se vinieron a domeñar de suerte que le amaban y querían como a su verdadero padre. Por esto convirtió y bautizó a muchos."

[50] OAR, *Boletín de la Provincia de San Nicolas de Tolentino,* p. 49.

[51] Ibid. " … él se quedó en ceguedad …," i.e., he remained in blindness.

them for baptism, and "always helped them with everything." Despite this degree of cooperation, maintaining the mission was a struggle, for the missionaries often had to forage far and wide for their food. Eventually, San Nicolás left his partner behind and moved alone to a settlement on the nearby Lavayan river,[52] to convert the aborigines (*moradores*) there, a task at which he again succeeded through dogged persistence and hard work.[53] This hardship affected his health, as he was reported as having recurrent episodes of being covered with sores (*calenturas*). Having arrived in Mindanao as one of *Los Ocho* in 1622, he would remain on the island until his death in Cagayán in 1647, marking a quarter century as a missionary who was "totally devoted to holy ministry."[54]

CONVERTING CULTURES

Conversion was, of course, a major component in the larger "civilizing" campaign of Spanish colonialism.[55] Conversion itself was originally integral to Western ideas about cultural "improvement," which posited a unilinear continuum from a primitive state towards greater perceived rationality, modernization, and eventually "enlightenment." The "darkness" of non-Western religious traditions is still differentiated from the "light" of Christianity by missionaries today. As Peter van Rooden explains, "the modern spread of Christianity would always be accompanied by fundamental ambiguities about the relationship between civilizing and converting aspects of the mission, and about the relationship between the missionary endeavor and colonial authority."[56] No doubt the colonial-era Recoletos approached their missions in Mindanao with this imperative.

The typical missionary enterprise therefore envisions a much larger impact beyond simply changing people's religious affiliations and practices; it also aims for a "restructuring of desires."[57] The ultimate goal of the missionary is totalizing transcendence, that is, not simply to convert people but to "remake" their whole world.[58] With regard in particular to the Lumad in the first mission period, the

---

[52] Most likely a reference to what is now the Lawayan River in nearby Misamis Occidental province.

[53] It is at this point in relating the never-ending physical hardship endured by P. San Nicolás to convert the Lumadnon of Mindanao that the Recoletos are moved to remark with undisguised disdain: "De la vida sacrificada de los misioneros jesuitas en Butuán no se pueden cantar muchas alabanzas." See OAR, *Boletín de la Provincia de San Nicolas de Tolentino*, p. 50.

[54] "… residió siempre en Mindanao totalmente consagrado al sagrado ministeri." See ibid., p. 45.

[55] It was also an element of American colonialism in the Philippines.

[56] Peter van Rooden, "Nineteenth-Century Representations of Missionary Conversion and the Transformation of Western Christianity," *Conversion to Modernities: The Globalization of Christianity*, ed. Peter van der Veer (London: Routledge, 1996), p. 84. See also W. R. Hutchison, *Errand to the World: American Protestant Thought and Foreign Missions* (Chicago, IL: University of Chicago Press, 1987); and Jean Comaroff and John Comaroff, "Christianity and Colonialism in South Africa," *American Ethnologist* 13 (1986): 1–22.

[57] Margaret Jolly, "Devils, Holy Spirits, and the Swollen God: Translation, Conversion and Colonial Power in the Marist Mission, Vanuatu, 1887–1934," *Conversion to Modernities: The Globalization of Christianity*, ed. Peter van der Veer (London: Routledge, 1996), pp. 231–62.

[58] See Michael Barnett, "Remaking the World," *The Immanent Frame* (2008), at http://blogs.ssrc.org/tif/2008/03/17/ remaking-the-world/, accessed September 21, 2011. It would also be interesting to consider the missionary enterprise from a humanitarian perspective. That is,

Recoletos worked to remake their world along the lines specified by Catholic doctrine, perhaps with a few Spanish cultural values thrown in for good measure.

I would add that, just as experiencing "the field" typically transforms anthropologists and other types of field workers in many ways, we can assume that the missionary experience would likewise have engendered some degree of transformation among the Recoletos. The mission experience often transforms the missionary—emotionally, culturally, politically—and sometimes even the missionary endeavor itself.[59]

The colonial government explicitly recognized and appreciated the political importance of Religious missionaries as a civilizing influence, in particular their role in maintaining social order, and restoring it when conflicts grew out of control. This was especially important in pericolonial areas like Mindanao. Chroniclers of both the Jesuits' and the Recoletos' missionary efforts celebrated their unofficial mandate as peacekeepers, often remarking that it was their patriotic duty to protect colonial personnel and other Spaniards from the *furor,* or wrath, of the natives.[60] In part, this mandate existed because of the missionaries' predictably intense social ties to indigenous communities, but it was also due to policies for mission work that emphasized proselytization in indigenous languages. This means that, by design, the Religious had the equivalent of a linguistic monopoly in many parts of the archipelago and that, even if it wanted to, the colonial government itself would not have been able to manage such communities effectively. In other words, *santo celo* or no, the Religious were the only outsiders with any real cultural or social authority in Filipinas, especially in the outer reaches of the archipelago.[61]

As we have already seen, the caliber of a missionary's *santo celo* was the key to his success in terms of this larger civilizing mission. The Recoletos had to be more than just communicators of religious doctrine, they also had to be "men of prowess" to persuade Lumads, without the threat of force, to willingly turn their own worlds upside-down. Even given what we know, it is tricky to parse out what enables a Religious, especially a foreign one, to engage in peacemaking. Christians may claim

---

missionaries generally see themselves as performing the spiritual equivalent of what today would be termed "humanitarian assistance," in that their mission, though couched in the language of religion and conversion, is fundamentally about improving the lives of people whom they considered to be living in spiritual darkness. The various "secular" acts of the Recoletos noted in this and subsequent chapters—such as helping to secure political favors, military training and assistance, healing of the sick, general education, or advocating against tax collectors on behalf of the Lumad—have a parallel in humanitarian work in the present day, such as help with food security, medical assistance, literacy, education, and political advocacy to protect human rights. Most major religious movements today, in fact, have parallel humanitarian aid organizations that operate on an international scale, including Catholic Relief Services, Jesuit Refugee Services, and other groups engaged in what can be called "social Christianity."

[59] In chapter four, I return to the idea that missionaries were also "culturally converted" by the Lumad. On how later Protestant mission work has transformed Western Christianity, see van Rooden, "Nineteenth-Century Representations of Missionary Conversion," pp. 65–88.

[60] See Schreurs, *Caraga Antigua,* pp. 114–15. See also Sábada, *Catálogo,* pp. 48–105.

[61] According to Schreurs, this language policy was engineered by the Catholic Church to secure power for itself in the colonies (personal communication, Tilburg, Netherlands, May 1, 2005). It was also a consequence of post-de las Casas policymaking. Whether by design or coincidence, the outcome was the acquisition of extensive political power by the Catholic Church, such that today it still has the power to paralyze the Philippine government at the policy level.

that this is due to the particular qualities of their religions as opposed to the qualities of others.[62] On the other hand, perhaps the Recoletos' very foreignness lent them an air of political impartiality, and therefore fairness, which would have allowed the Religious to cultivate conflict resolution as an occupational niche.[63] Ultimately, however, when an outsider steps into an active combat area in an attempt to deescalate the situation, it is very much a demonstration of inherent prowess, which for the Recoletos was *santo celo*.

There is a clear record of colonial-era missionaries intervening in active conflicts in Lumad areas, even after open violence had already erupted. For example, the Karaga *datu* Inuc was described as giving the Spaniards "problems" until his conversion in 1622 by the aforementioned P. Fr. Juan de la Madre de Dios. In the early seventeenth century, Karaga *datus*, in general, were presumed to be belligerent troublemakers, and the Recoletos portray Inuc's conversion to Christianity as the catalyst for his transformation into a peace-loving and loyal ally. Inuc is, in fact, one of the earliest named converts to Christianity among the Karagas in Mindanao.[64]

Another example of the missionary as a peacemaker among the Lumad is P. Fr. Jacinto de San Fulgencio, who was deemed an exemplary Religious (*ejemplarísimo religioso*). In 1635, he was instrumental in bringing back to the Christian fold, and to the *pueblos* of Caraga, those who had turned *remontado*[65]—basically, "backsliders" who had removed themselves from colonial authority by fleeing the "civilization" of Christian settlements for the hinterlands—after the Caraga Revolt of 1631. As described in chapter four, the Caraga Revolt was called a *sublevación* (sedition or mutiny) rather than a mere uprising because it involved the serious apostasy of long-settled Christian converts, the premeditated murder of four Recoletos, the desecration of Catholic symbols, including a church, and an attempt to incite other settled Lumads, including non-Karaga, to take up arms against all foreigners. After the mutineers were eventually routed, their unrepentant companions fled town and went into hiding in the uplands for years. The Caraga Revolt involved fatal acts of treachery and therefore represented an extremely painful breach of trust for the Recoletos, a betrayal not easily forgotten. San Fulgencio's act is remarkable because

---

[62] For example, Christians sometimes contrast their own "peaceful" religion with Islam by linking Islam with extremism, intolerance, and violence, as voiced most recently by Pope Benedict VII, among others. The doctrinal model of Jesus Christ as "Prince of Peace" cannot be ignored. In the Philippines, most peace activists are Christians by faith or upbringing, but this is easily explained by the fact that most of the population belongs to one of the many denominations of organized (as well as disorganized) Christianity. The predominance of Christian peace activists is easily balanced out by the existence of such ultra-violent cults as Tadtad (lit. "chop" in Visayan languages), whose members also claim to practice "true" Christianity, and lower-profile movements linked to extra-judicial killings that also claim Christian affiliation, such as the so-called Philippine Benevolent Missionaries' Association. See Sheila Coronel, *Coups, Cults, and Cannibals* (Pasig City: Anvil, 1993), pp. 101–44. See also Oona T. Paredes, "Commentary: Benevolent Altruism or Ordinary Reciprocity? A Response to Austin's View of the Mindanao Hinterland," *Human Organization* 55,2 (1996): 241–44.

[63] In early modern Southeast Asia, foreigners were, in fact, routinely recruited by indigenous societies to resolve internal conflicts, following the "stranger-king" model. See David Henley, *Jealousy and Justice: The Indigenous Roots of Colonial Rule in Northern Sulawesi* (Amsterdam: VU Uitgeverij, 2002).

[64] See Sábada, *Catálogo*, p. 54. See also Schreurs, *Caraga Antigua*, pp. 117, 136–37.

[65] Those who left the *reducción*, or Christian settlement, for *el monte*, or the hinterland.

he walked into hostile territory and convinced the former mutineers to return to the *reducción*.

Another notable veteran of the Caraga Revolt was P. Fr. Lorenzo de San Facundo, who actively stemmed the revolt in Tago by convincing a key leader, Mangabo, and his men to stop the violence. In later years, San Facundo would do the same with the "Jolos" in an attempt to reduce Moro attacks. After the fact, P. Fr. José de la Anunciación was noted as having helped restore order.

> [He] rendered a very important service to the Nation, appeasing the natives of Caraga who still had not calmed down completely after the insurrection of the year 1631.[66]

Twenty years after the Caraga Revolt, another, unrelated uprising occurred in Linao, and the same P. Anunciación, still ministering in the Linao area, again helped restore order. Towards the end of his life, he played peacemaker a third time, "contributing much to the reestablishment of order"[67] during the 1660 *alzamiento* (uprising) of Pangasinan, in the northern island of Luzon, along with P. Fr. Carlos de Jesús, who likewise served the same function during yet another uprising in the Ilocos region.[68]

The uprising at Linao—during which the *naturales* apparently made an alliance to "shake loose" from Spanish power—also allowed a relatively new arrival, P. Fr. Miguel de Santo Tomás, to demonstrate the intensity of his *santo celo*:

> In the uprising of the town of Linao ... our Religious, who at the time was administering in Butuan, distinguished himself by his actions and zeal in taking measures so that the rebellion did not spread: he sent dispatches to [the nearby garrison of] Tandag and to the *Real Audiencia*; he affectionately welcomed the Spaniards who took refuge in Butuan ... he exhorted the *indios* to remain faithful to Spain, and there was no measure he did not employ to salvage such a difficult situation.[69]

The events at Linao, much like in the Caraga Revolt, showcase the great vulnerability of these missionaries. But they also show how the missionaries were held in great esteem and affection by most members of the communities they served, which gave them social and political capital that other Spaniards simply could not acquire. This special status is critical in explaining the case of P. Fr. Juan de San Agustín who, taken captive early in the Caraga Revolt and on the verge of being executed, managed to secure freedom for himself and a lay worker by appealing to one of his captors, a high-status female (*una india principal*) who "venerated" the Religious.[70]

LOCALIZING MODERNIZATION

Peter Schreurs describes the typical pattern that unfolded throughout the Lumad areas of Mindanao when Recoleto missionaries made contact with the indigenous

---

[66] See Sábada, *Catálogo*, p. 79.

[67] Ibid.

[68] Ibid., p. 105.

[69] Ibid., p. 94.

[70] Ibid., p. 65, 84.

people. Traveling unarmed into the settlements of uncivilized *monteses*, a Recoleto would seek to meet with the local *datu*. Some meetings, such as the one with *datu* Salangsang of the Kagayanon, described in the next chapter, were arranged or mediated in some way by a female relative of the *datu*. In such cases, the meeting was predictably friendly, or at least polite. More often than not, however, the reception was hostile—sometimes even deadly for the missionary—but in their narratives the Recoletos generally focused on how they managed to overcome initial Lumad resistance by impressing one *datu* or another with their humility, vulnerability, and, of course, their great zeal. In time, according to the typical scenario, the *datu* is inspired to repent his heathen ways, and, as proof, he gives up polygyny by releasing all but his favorite wife. The process is often marked by a public, often highly dramatic, submission to the missionary's religious authority, usually followed by a pledge of allegiance to the king of Spain. The *datu*'s public conversion is then followed by the conversion *en masse* of men who formed his *sacup,* or alliance group, especially other *principales*, meaning the other *datu* and their family groups, in an equally public event.[71]

After these public conversions, the missionaries then became established in the community and proceeded with adult catechism, preparation for baptism, and other religious and spiritual work, as well as work on the material dimension of the mission itself as both a sacred and everyday space. As discussed in the next section, whereas new religious teachings and rituals altered the supernatural world of Lumads, material modifications, such as the construction of a *convento*, a *presidio*, or other fortification, and other renovations of local spaces, similarly altered Lumad social reproduction, with major implications for indigenous social organization. Later in the seventeenth century, missionaries would select the children of converts, particularly from among the *principales*, for additional Catholic schooling under the supervision of the Bishop of Cebu, both to train them as future leaders of their people and to build a loyal indigenous Christian cadre.[72]

So why would the Lumad convert? In the social sciences, particularly among Southeast Asianists, studies of religious conversion generally focus on the social, political, or semiotic factors that structure conversion and religious practice, as opposed to, say, theology or doctrine.[73] Lumad conversion is analyzed here as a public phenomenon, in part because its private component is impossible to track so many centuries later. In fact, analyzing the internal rationales of conversion may not even be material to writing Lumad ethnohistory. Talal Asad pointedly asks why

---

[71] See Schreurs, *Caraga Antigua,* pp. 104–13, 136–37. See also Pedro Chirino SJ, *Relacion de las Islas Filipinas/The Philippines in 1600*, trans. Ramón Echevarria (Manila: Historical Conservation Society, 1969 [1604]), pp. 336–38. See also Bernad, *The Great Island,* pp. 51–52.

[72] For example, the son of Butuanon *datu* Silongan was sent to be schooled by Jesuits in Cebu, together with other Butuanon boys. See Schreurs, *Caraga Antigua,* p. 115.

[73] For example, see Rita Smith Kipp, "Conversion by Affiliation: The History of the Karo Batak Protestant Church," *American Ethnologist* 22,4 (1995): 868–82. Or see: Andrea Molnar, "Christianity and Traditional Religion among the Hoga Sara of West-Central Flores," *Anthropos* 92 (1997): 393–408; Robert Hefner, ed., *Conversion to Christianity: Historical and Anthropological Perspectives on a Great Transformation* (Berkeley, CA: University of California Press, 1993); or Webb Keane, "Materialism, Missionaries, and Modern Subjects in Colonial Indonesia" and Patricia Spyer, "Serial Conversion/Conversion to Seriality: Religion, State, and Number in Aru, Eastern Indonesia," both in *Conversion to Modernities: The Globalization of Christianity*, ed. Peter van der Veer (London: Routledge, 1996), pp. 137–70, 171–98, respectively.

religious conversion would even need explaining or justification, reminding us that "too often, the assumptions we bring with us when talking about the conversion of people in another epoch or society are the ideological assumptions in and about our [own] modern condition."[74]

The trend has definitely been to frame religious conversion as a quest for "modernity," particularly with regard to Christian conversion. Embracing radical religious change—perhaps to align materially, spiritually, or intellectually with a "modern" or, more precisely, a "Western" mode of existence—in fact requires a very broad, totalizing sort of transformation in itself. It is a move that involves accepting new, even radical ideas, as well as a new, superseding reality, and a significant reinterpretation of one's old identity. In this sense, religious conversion, like adapting to "modern" ways, becomes about challenging the status quo in order to nurture and express "alternate notions of self and self-worth."[75]

Another approach, one that uncouples Christian conversion from "becoming Western," analyzes conversion as a form of negotiation between contested realities, rather than the repudiation of one reality (e.g., "tradition") for another (e.g., "modernity" or "Western culture"). In the face of fundamental conflicts between tradition and modernity, conversion—when viewed in such relational terms—can provide "an intersubjective, transitional, and transactional mode of negotiation between two otherwise irreconcilable world-views."[76] Within North American contact studies, this form of negotiation is sometimes referred to as the "middle ground."[77] It is conceived simultaneously as a world view and a process, as "a means of communication or a meaningful system of symbols," and as a continuous "creative negotiation of cultural forms," through which the framework of a "common, mutually comprehensible world" is created.[78] This negotiation, or "middle ground," process is also shown clearly in studies of conversion outside of the Americas.[79] This perspective, which views conversion as negotiation, is particularly relevant in culturally stressful situations, such as an encounter with a radically different culture, the process of incorporation into a new world system, or entrenched conflict—which could also describe the Lumad situation in my period of study.

Perhaps because religion involves supernatural claims, radical transformations undertaken within a religious context—like proverbial leaps of faith—are understood and justified more readily relative to non-religious contexts. In Gauri Viswanathan's view, religious conversion became a critical accompaniment to "modernization" precisely because secular and colonially derived ideologies alone were insufficient for the proper cultural incorporation and/or expression of such

---

[74] Talal Asad, "Comments on Conversion," *Conversion to Modernities: The Globalization of Christianity*, ed. Peter van der Veer (London: Routledge, 1996), pp. 263–73.

[75] Robert Hefner, "Introduction: World Building and the Rationality of Conversion," in *Conversion to Christianity*, ed. Robert Hefner (Berkeley, CA: University of California Press, 1993), p. 26.

[76] Gauri Viswanathan, *Outside the Fold: Conversion, Modernity, and Belief* (Princeton, NJ: Princeton University Press, 1998), p. 175.

[77] Richard White, *The Middle Ground: Indians, Empires, and Republics in the Great Lakes Region, 1650–1815* (Cambridge: Cambridge University Press, 1991).

[78] White, *The Middle Ground*, p. x.

[79] For example, see Terence Ranger, "The Local and the Global in Southern African Religious History," in *Conversion to Christianity*, ed. Hefner, pp. 65–98.

radical changes in lifestyle.[80] Patricia Spyer makes a comparable case for recognizing the idiomatic relationship of "citizenship" to "religion" in Indonesia, the latter being "the very mode in which citizenship is made."[81]

In the first mission period, one tangible way in which such a "renegotiation" manifested itself among the Lumad was a deescalation of revenge raiding, a defining and fairly common Lumad practice. The case of an organizationally comparable population from the Americas shows us how this might have unfolded. In their study of Waorani warfare and peacemaking in the Amazon, Clayton Robarchek and Carole Robarchek argued that religious conversion to Evangelical Protestantism was used by the Waorani as a conscious, deliberate strategy to transcend, and therefore mitigate, intractable social and political problems. Robarchek and Robarchek showed how a small group of Waorani, exhausted by the incessant violence in their communities, decided to collaborate with Western missionaries, seizing on religious conversion as an opportunity to both transform the status quo and secure peacemaking efforts in the absence of a broader pan-tribal leadership.[82] By physically withdrawing from the cycle of revenge raiding on explicitly religious grounds, a small group of Waorani, primarily women, managed to set peacemaking in motion where all other attempts had failed.

I know of at least one Higaunon Lumad community of Christian converts who, in the 1990s, similarly refrained from revenge raiding on explicitly religious grounds. These particular families were angry about being defrauded by a relative over money and ancestral land rights. Without attempting to hide their extreme frustration, the converts explained to me that, had they not become Christians, they would have killed the offender long ago to settle the score, without hesitation, no matter the consequences. However, being devout Christians, they felt they were obligated by Biblical dictum to forgive him, because anything else would be tantamount to negating the faith that, in their view, saved them from themselves. "He is lucky," they said, "and he knows it."

No matter the framework we use to analyze conversion (and all that comes with it) we cannot ignore the penetration and incorporation of outside influences, and the replacement of old ways with new ways, because the old ways have, one way or another, proved insufficient. Agency and a degree of free will are implicit—the people choose to convert—but the specter of the colonial civilizing mission lingers, our deeply embedded (and very modern) notions of what is "indigenous" and "authentic" muddying our engagement with Lumad history.

Southeast Asians, however, are generally described by area specialists as always having been more than eager to accept new ideas from the outside and incorporate them into their traditions. Barbara Andaya argues that understanding Southeast Asian "localization"—now commonly accepted as a defining cultural and historical characteristic of the region—brings us to "modernity" without all the cultural

---

[80] Viswanathan, *Outside the Fold*. See also Susan Bayly, *Saints, Goddesses, and Kings: Muslims and Christians in South Indian Society, 1700–1900* (Cambridge: Cambridge University Press, 1989).

[81] Spyer, "Serial Conversion/Conversion to Seriality," p. 193.

[82] Clayton Robarchek and Carole Robarchek, *Waorani: The Contexts of Violence and War* (Fort Worth, TX: Harcourt Brace, 1998). For a contrasting perspective on the Waorani/Huaorani case, see Laura Rival, *Trekking through History: The Houarani of Amazonian Ecuador* (New York, NY: Columbia University Press, 2002).

baggage of European "civilization."[83] This Southeast Asian iteration of modernity—manifested in a selective localization that involves the combination of imported elements with indigenous ones"—is defined not by an "age of discovery," as with Europe, but "an intimate involvement with international trade which stretched back over hundreds of years," thanks to the region's location between two major trading powers, China and India. In historical Southeast Asia, we can see how localization was a profoundly modernizing compulsion: in the quest not just for newness but also "now"-ness, the foreign—whether in the form of people (e.g., missionaries), religion (e.g., Christianity), language, or any and all kinds of material culture—was not, as a matter of course, regarded as a threat to the social order.[84] Nor, I might add, to local perceptions of their own cultural authenticity or their sense of political and social autonomy.

In chapter five, I also point to localization as a significant aspect of the Lumad political response to colonialism and missionization. I argue that strategic political moves by indigenous Lumad leaders to increase their articulation with the colonial apparatus was not a capitulation to Spanish authority, but a conscious attempt to "harmonize"[85] a foreign tradition with local politics. We know that "the special knowledge and powers claimed by Southeast Asian rulers were frequently manifested in their possession of exotic items incorporated into the royal regalia."[86] The clear relationship of political power—specifically, of a leader's prestige and status—to material and other linkages to "the foreign" underlines the cultural significance of newness and "nowness" in the Southeast Asian cultural matrix, and within this matrix, the Lumad world. Localization, in turn, informs the logic of conversions by Lumad *datu* in a way that other approaches to conversion simply cannot.

Finally, by framing Lumad conversion within the concept of localization, we can recapture local agency in a productive way, without having to uncouple the past from the present. As Craig Reynolds argues, the "local genius" inherent in localization offers scholars a "prime mover" for regional history, and "shifts the focus onto Southeast Asians and their future, away from their suspect origins as mere borrowers and culture brokers."[87] Particularly in dealing with Southeast Asia's early modern period, localization lets us '"write back" against the foreignness—of "influences" or of evidence—that must constantly be negotiated because of the nature of the sources of early history.[88] In our case, these influences were the Recoletos of the first mission period, and the evidence the archival record of the Spanish colonial period that the Recoletos and other colonial agents left behind.

---

[83] See, for example, Barbara Watson Andaya, "Historicizing 'Modernity' in Southeast Asia," *Journal of the Economic and Social History of the Orient* 40,4 (1997). See also O. W. Wolters, "Southeast Asia as a Southeast Asian Field of Study," *Indonesia* 58 (1994): 3, 11; and Adrian Vickers, ed., *Being Modern in Bali: Image and Change*, Monograph 43 (New Haven, CT: Yale University Southeast Asia Studies, 1996), pp. 1–7.

[84] Andaya, "Historicizing 'Modernity,'" pp. 395–96.

[85] I believe that the term "harmonize," borrowed from Michael Laffan, captures most elegantly the operational side of Southeast Asian "now"-ness with regard to localization.

[86] Andaya, "Historicizing 'Modernity,'" p. 396.

[87] Craig J. Reynolds, "A New Look at Old Southeast Asia," *The Journal of Asian Studies* 54,2 (1995), p. 431.

[88] Ibid., p. 433.

From this Southeast Asian perspective, we can ultimately harmonize Lumad conversion to Christianity with the trend of converting to modernity, albeit taking the longer way around. We are also better able to historicize the Lumad and return them to the modern world of which they were already a part by the time the Recoletos arrived. Allowing them to be global and local at the same time would mediate the desegregation of regional history with Philippine history, and ultimately national history with colonial history, along the same lines. The real question, therefore, may be why we ever thought the Lumad would not convert, when conversion is such an obvious opportunity to get in touch with the "new" and the "now" on so many levels.

Living "Under the Bell"

Beyond what came to be, and what has been recognized as, the typical Lumad conversion scenario, there was more to the conversion experience—and therefore the mission experience—than the simple, personal act of declaring a new religious allegiance. Contact with the missionaries brought about significant changes in the Lumad landscape with the advent of the *convento*.[89] In the Philippine context, the generic term *convento* goes beyond the traditional meaning of a cloistered space and refers broadly to the establishment of all missionary-created spaces, including *visitas*, or outposts, in Lumad territory. This simple word, *convento*, also speaks to the reorganization of Lumad life in profound ways. These changes included the construction of military fortifications of European design, the reorganization and training of local residents into more effective militias under the direction of missionaries with prior military training or experience, the relocation of settlements to more defensible positions in terms of the terrain, and the consolidation of typically small, autonomous settlements into larger villages for the purpose of defense. Missionaries also involved converts in field service, as "apostolic helpers," throughout their large mission areas, on a regular basis.

All these changes meant that the once-scattered Lumad were now thrown together in regular patterns of social interaction unrelated to *pangayaw*, or revenge raiding. As the missions and missionaries became embedded in particular Lumad communities, an identification with Christianity in some observable form—such as participation in mission life, personal ties to missionaries, conversion—would have emerged as an important social commonality among the Lumad. The *convento* was also a site for the creation of new localities, the establishment of new routines, the weaving of new social geographies, and, consequently, the formation of new identities. Rather than undergoing a simple label-change to "Christian," Lumad

---

[89] On the local use of the term *convento*, I found the following in a report by the Weather Bureau in Manila: "This word, which means monastery, cloister, or convent, is universally used in the Philippines to designate also the habitation of the clergy attached to a parish church. Although these are, as a rule, spacious buildings and were formerly inhabited almost exclusively by friars, they cannot properly be called monasteries ... in order to avoid lengthy circumlocutions, the Spanish word 'convento' has been retained ... The reader who is not familiar with this country may find it strange that, in reporting earthquake damages, so much emphasis appears to be laid on the harm done to churches and *conventos*. This is easily explained by the fact that these buildings were often the only structures within the ... area, and built nearly everywhere in the most substantial manner." See Miguel Saderra Masó SJ, *Catalogue of Violent and Destructive Earthquakes in the Philippines, 1599–1909* (Manila: Bureau of Printing, 1910), pp. 5–7.

identities were transformed in the same way that the so-called "fluid" identities of island Southeast Asia have also changed over the centuries: they were altered by flowing through new networks with new economic, religious, political, and other practices.

What did all the changes mentioned above mean in terms of the everyday lives of the Lumad people? Writing about parallel developments in the same period in Spanish colonial New Mexico, in what was once known as New Spain, the archaeologist Mark Lycett describes a process very similar to that which took place in pericolonial, "frontier" areas like Mindanao. Here, as was the case throughout the Philippines,

> missions were the single most important setting of colonial and indigenous contact. More than simply sites of conversion … missions were the physical context in which colonialism as an historical process of disruption, incorporation, and transformation was situated.[90]

However, colonial frontier missions have a "multidimensional nature" and "may be conceived of simultaneously as place, as emergent community, and as an institutional logic or colonial project."[91] Moreover, missions should not "be characterized as either wholly indigenous or wholly colonial places," according to Lycett.[92]

> Within such settings, colonial interactions may have been asymmetrical but they were also reciprocal and mutually constitutive. Accordingly, the mission and other instruments of colonial governance are best understood not as global or ideal institutions, but as diverse and historically situated strategies, practices, and relations articulated by many agents in divergent contexts over long periods of time.[93]

Missions were, therefore, more than monolithic, prefabricated instruments of conquest. In fact, one would find varying degrees of colonial incorporation, across this colonial landscape, owing to the great diversity of cultural, environmental, logistical, and political factors at work within the Philippine archipelago. Marginal, pericolonial areas like Mindanao were certainly not subject to the same conditions that defined major population centers like Cebu and Manila, which were under the full power of colonial administration. As Lycett explains regarding the parallel case of colonial New Mexico:

> At any given point in the seventeenth century, the indigenous landscape might be made up of fully incorporated places subject to resident Spaniards, less populous and less central *visitas*, formerly missionized places, and displaced refugee communities. To the extent that these differences structure the possibilities for accommodating, adopting, challenging, negotiating, or

---

[90] Mark Lycett, "Archaeology Under the Bell: The Mission as Situated History in Seventeenth Century New Mexico," *Missionalia* 23,3 (2004): 358.

[91] Ibid.

[92] Ibid.

[93] Ibid.

appropriating colonial power relations, they are crucial to understanding variation in historical experience.[94]

Diversity and differential incorporation within the colonial Philippines also explains how the Lumad and other populations like them could have experienced the *convento* in a meaningful way for centuries, yet still emerged as culturally distinct from lowland Filipinos at the close of the Spanish colonial period.

In a direct, spatial way, the missionaries played a critical role in the reorganization of Lumad warfare, not only in terms of weaponry but also in terms of architecture, strategy, and tactics. For the Lumad, this may well have been the most immediate political consequence of converting to Christianity and allying with the missionaries. These conversions mattered as public political acts that had tangible political consequences for the rest of the population. Although the specific impact of these conversions on internal political factions is impossible to determine without more data, in chapter three we will see from the Kagayanon case that, even without conversion, the mere act of accommodating the missionary presence as a social courtesy had immediate and devastating consequences for the community in terms of warfare. The political context in which these conversions occurred was already quite complex, even in the first mission period.

The immediate goal of frontier missions such as those of the Recoletos was to bring as many non-Christians as possible *bajo la campana* or, literally, "under the bell." The church bell in this context resonates as a multidimensional referent to Spanish colonial influence, evoking an aural geography of the political, social, economic, technological, and spatial reach of the idealized colonial experience. "Idealized," that is, according to Spanish Christian fantasies of a divinely consecrated civilizing mission. The "civilizing" impulse of the missionaries themselves was embodied by an effort to bring as many of the *naturales* as possible within the reach of church bells, both aural and metaphorical. Therefore, the frontier mission's church bell also signifies the nexus of a community that was simultaneously being civilized, Christianized, and colonized.[95]

We already know that, like the parallel case of the Southwestern United States in the same period, missions in the colonial Philippines were "the physical context in which colonialism as an historical process of disruption, incorporation, and transformation was situated."[96] In convincing the Kagayanon to move from their original settlement of Imolagan to the fortification in Cagayán, as told in the next chapter, the Recoletos achieved two things: the political reorganization and management of putative and potential converts in order to better minister to them; and securing the Order's social and apostolic jurisdiction over the population. Moreover, prior to the construction of Cagayán, the pagan *diwatahan,* or altar, at Imolagan was converted into a Christian church, showing that religious conversion *per se* manifested itself spatially, where the old deity or deities were physically

---

[94] Mark Lycett, "On the Margins of Peripheries: The Consequences of Differential Incorporation in the Colonial Southwest," *The Post-classic to Spanish-Era Transition in Mesoamerica: Archaeological Perspectives*, ed. Susan Kepecs and Rani Alexander (Albuquerque, NM: University of New Mexico Press, 2005), p. 107.

[95] Tangentially, this fundamental link to social identity may be why the political issue of repatriating the Balangiga church bells stolen by American forces during the Philippine-American War resonates so strongly with Filipinos.

[96] Lycett, "Archaeology Under the Bell," p. 358.

replaced by the Kagayanon with Christian relics, and the old *diwatahan* space requisitioned and rearranged—converted—into Christian spaces. The process and impact of the common Spanish colonial practice of *reducción* is, therefore, best understood spatially, in that it restructured multiple aspects of indigenous social organization, in a very literal sense, from the ground up. The arrival of missionaries in Mindanao therefore reorganized Lumad life in several significant ways as the Recoletos planted new missions and established villages in the fashion of the existing Spanish colonial practice of *reducción*. In the Kagayanon case, there were some major developments and related consequences: (a) regularized contact—and presumably a cultural exchange—was established between the foreign missionaries and Lumadnon of multiple generations; (b) local residents were reorganized and trained into more effective militias, based on European military strategies, mainly by those Recoletos who were either combat veterans or schooled in European military history, such as Agustín de San Pedro; (c) typically small, scattered, kin-based settlements were relocated and consolidated into larger, more defensible village settlements on better, more defensible terrain; (d) military fortifications of European design were constructed alongside most of the mission outposts, especially in the coastal areas, for protection against Moro raids and/or unfriendly Lumads, leading to normalized contact between Lumadnon and Spanish troops and civil officials; (e) mission communities and other Lumad settlements were brought in contact with each other through apostolic excursions undertaken with the missionaries; and (f) political organization, architecture, agriculture, and economic organization were gradually transformed, as necessary, and behavior altered in ways as yet undetermined, to deal with the changes outlined above. As to what is still knowable about the internal beliefs of the *datu*s and other converts, "everything is buried in the tomb of the unknown."[97]

In his biography, El Padre Capitán is credited not only with founding more than one hundred villages in Mindanao and the Visayas—including Linao, Cagayán, and Romblon[98]—he is also recognized for introducing European military tactics to many of these communities as standard operating procedure for defensive purposes.[99] To appreciate the full impact of this new way of doing things, we can extrapolate the impact of this newly transferred technology of war to other Lumad communities with which missionized Lumad were in contact. Considering the significant logistical changes made apparent in the Kagayanon case (in chapter three), we can assume that similar changes took place in other, subsequently missionized Lumad areas.

We know that only a very limited number of priests and brothers were available to minister to all the missionized communities. This meant that the same missionaries would travel throughout a large geographical area, accompanied and guided by Lumad converts as their "apostolic helpers," thereby bringing together people who had not been together before. The practice of using local Lumads as apostolic helpers was in place from the very beginning, when the Recoletos, making

---

[97] OAR, *Boletín de la Provincia de San Nicolas de Tolentino*, p. 44. The original quote refers to the pre-Recoleto life of P. Fr. Juan de San Nicolás, for whom no records exist of his year of birth, date of arrival in Filipinas, his reasons for being in the colony, or his prior vocation: "Todo se halla enterrado en el sepulcro de lo desconocido."

[98] This is from the caption of an heroic painting of *El Padre Capitán* hanging in the Recoleto monastery in Marcilla, Navarra, Spain.

[99] Schreurs, *Caraga Antigua*, p. 139.

their way to Linao in the interior in 1622, brought with them native assistants from Butuan.[100] Thus the once-scattered and independent Lumad were now being thrown together in regular patterns of social interaction by their association with and allegiance to the missionaries. I use the phrase "allegiance to the missionaries" because not everyone who lived in these mission communities was a convert. Some were still in preparation for baptism. Still others were there only due to kin ties, such as those that existed between the relatively distant communities of Butuan and Cagayán, or ties of social–political alliance, as outlined in the discussion of *sacup* in chapter five.

Given all these modes of interaction, it is safe to assume two things: that these new ideas concerning religion, social organization, politics, and warfare were also disseminated to other Lumad areas for which written records do not exist; and that, in such "unwritten" areas, where the new technology of war itself did not transfer, a response of some sort to the changes implemented by one's neighbors—whether they were allies or enemies—would still have been necessary, even in areas that remained geographically or politically marginal. In other words, the impact of missionization was not limited to those who actually converted to Christianity. As Lycett explains:

> Individuals and communities differently situated within the mission system had different potentials for both exploitation by and participation in colonial society. Residence in different forms of the mission as place has implications for access to resources as well as for potential for subjugation, surveillance, and discipline. Perhaps just as importantly, residence in such places also dictates much of the daily routines and rhythms of life. From prime to vespers, new patterns of work, of ritual performance, of instruction, and of time discipline became the fabric of everyday life under the bell.[101]

CONVERTING CONFLICT

The changes in internecine relations among the Lumad, with particular reference to the deeply embedded patterns of *pangayaw* or revenge raiding, would not have required the conversion of every Lumad adult into a devout Christian. What took place in the first mission period was likely quite similar to the remarkable process documented among the Waorani in South America, wherein a deeply entrenched pattern of revenge killings quickly ceased among a few missionized Waorani, as part of their individual conversion process. This, in turn, generated a ripple effect among other Waorani groups, such that even isolated bands that had never been missionized, nor had more than sporadic contact with missionaries, eventually joined the ceasefire—albeit for pragmatic rather than moral or religious reasons.[102] This profound change did not require the conversion of all Waorani involved; in fact, the moratorium on Waorani vendettas "was not dependent on profound psychological reorganization in most members of the society ... the changes were much more superficial for most people."[103] Instead, all that was needed was "the

---

[100] Ibid., p. 138.

[101] Lycett, "Archaeology Under the Bell," p. 364.

[102] Robarchek and Robarchek, *Waorani: The Contexts of Violence and War,* p. 159.

[103] Ibid., p. 180.

formation of new reference groups that transcended the narrow interests of individuals and kindreds," a development that, among the Lumad, was made possible by their exposure to ideological and behavioral alternatives, such as those presented by the missionaries.[104]

All these changes would have subsequently rippled through the way the Lumadnon thought of themselves, an entirely predictable development as the daily lives of missionaries and Lumads became more and more intertwined through the *convento*. With children and adults "converting" at the same time, the zeal of the newly converted would also have cut across generational lines. Given this context, the natural marker of "insider" status in these reorganized communities would therefore have become a closer identification with the *convento*, with the missionaries, and, by extension, an identification with Christianity, in some observable form, whether in full conversion or, at the very least, respecting the social authority of the missionaries and reclassifying them as friends.

Beyond these immediate interactions, routinized around the *convento*, the most profound consequence of Christian proselytizing and conversion in Mindanao was the creation of new cultural norms in the Lumad world, and a new basis of commonality among the Lumad, as well as between Lumads and missionaries. Anthropologists point to the importance of common social norms in the evolution of ethnic markers, arguing that, more than any factor that may encourage social cooperation between humans—such as proximity and familiarity, shared kin ties, or economic need—the perception of shared values is most likely to lead to cooperative and altruistic behavior that, in turns, breeds the emergence of new identities.[105] As more communities were brought together in new social networks across the Lumad world, peaceful relations would have been reinforced by the development of greater political interdependence, and by the shared Christian norms promoted by the missionaries and, more importantly, by other Lumad.

Missionaries also proudly noted the easy bonds of friendship and honest affection that developed between themselves and the locals who, according to missionary accounts, were deeply impressed by the priests' spiritual devotion, which manifested itself in humility, an apparent willingness to live amongst them unarmed. This impression was particularly strong when compared to their interaction with other Europeans they may have known or heard of, such as colonial officials, troops, and *cobradores,* or tribute collectors, as well their political interaction with the Moros.[106]

It is easy for me to believe that these bonds developed in reality, having personally observed the same type of relationship develop between foreign missionaries and upland peoples. The same may also be said of anthropologists and the communities they work with for the purpose of academic research. Such bonds are comparable, and would have been reinforced by proximity, and by the perception that the missionaries brought themselves little or no material advantage

---

[104] Ibid., p. 179.

[105] See Richard McElreath, Robert Boyd, and Peter J. Richerson, "Shared Norms and the Evolution of Ethnic Markers," *Current Anthropology* 44,1 (2003): 122–29.

[106] This was all to change by the nineteenth century, which is remembered today as the time when the friar orders consolidated their political power and increased their landholdings at the expense of both the native clergy and the colonial state, deteriorating into the abuse of native converts. The increase in the number of Secular clergy, who are not accountable to any Religious order, during this period may have also been a factor.

with their fieldwork. It also would have easily engendered some feelings of protectiveness on the part of the Lumad, especially if new arrivals were perceived as alone, defenseless, and socially and culturally inept in their new surroundings.

From the very beginning, the bonds that developed between missionaries and Lumadnon were apparently so strong that the colonial government came to rely on the missionaries to protect Lumads from exploitation and abuse by unscrupulous tribute collectors and the military, and to protect the same officials from the wrath of the Lumads. The behavior of Spanish troops was always roundly criticized by Jesuits and Recoletos in reports to their superiors. Whereas the Lumadnon vastly outnumbered Spanish troops and tribute collectors all through the colonial period, the logistical isolation of Spaniards, in general, was acute in Mindanao's first mission period. Despite this logistical imbalance, the civility of Spanish troops and tribute collectors reportedly left much to be desired, as described by Recoleto witnesses on the ground in Mindanao, and by others elsewhere in the Philippines as early as the 1580s.[107] While aggressive Spanish soldiers and *cobradores* posed a seemingly widespread problem in the archipelago in the earliest decades of the colony, the missionaries were on record as being predisposed to vigilance against colonial abuses, as discussed in the previous chapter.

Ultimately, the development of any cooperation between Lumads and Spaniards was made possible primarily through the relationship of both sides to missionaries and mission life. This relationship was negotiated through a Christian lens that also promoted a reorientation of Lumad attitudes towards their former Moro allies. The preexisting relationships between different Lumad groups and their Moro neighbors, in particular the Magindanaw, changed from one involving alliance and tribute payments into one of direct conflict, with religious undertones. This antagonism grew very quickly to the extent that Lumad warriors, on their own initiative, were willing to fight actively against Moros and unfriendly Lumads in defense of their new faith, and in defense of their new allies, the missionaries. Most importantly, this change points to the development of a new group identity for those among the Lumad who valued an attachment to Christianity and to the Recoletos who represented it. The Recoletos had, in essence, become "blood brothers," a relationship understood both in terms of the blood compact that was commonly used

---

[107] (ARM, leg 61, num 1; and ARM, leg 61, num 2). The Recoleto complaint details the excesses of tribute collectors (*cobradores*) in the province of Caraga, including but not limited to abusing local hospitality, demanding more tribute than the indios were obliged to pay, and hauling away to Cebu those unable to pay their tribute in entirety, forcing them to leave behind their children and crops. Dated 1657, it resulted in the immediate issue of a *mandamiento* (order) the following year by the Governor General Manrique de Lara against the perpetuation of these specific practices. Soldier abuses are also noted elsewhere, as causing *vejaciones a indios* (the humiliation of indians), such as in (AGI, Filipinas, 331, L.9, F.4v-5v/1690) and (AGI, Filipinas, 84, N.97/12-7-1601). Regarding the shameful conduct of Spaniards in general, in (AGI, Filipinas, 34, N.62/1584), we find the Archbishop of Filipinas, Domingo Salazar admonishing Spaniards to provide restitution for the bad things they have done since their arrival (*a restituir todo el mal que hubieran hecho desde su llegada*), free their slaves, and repay the *indios* if they (the Spaniards) had collected tribute but failed to perform their spiritual and other obligations in exchange. See also *Affairs of the Philippine Islands* by Fray Domingo de Salazar OP, which covers the years 1582 to 1583, as translated in Blair and Robertson, *The Philippine Islands*, Vol. 5. It is notable that our main source on Spanish abuses are the denouncements by their compatriots. In fact, they fancied themselves protectors of the *indios* in all senses, including from other *indios*, as indicated in (AGI, Filipinas, 329, L.2, F.86r-88r/26-05-1609), which is a report on the abuses by native *caciques*.

to seal agreements and alliances in the region, as well as in the sense that "brothers" from both sides had actually spilled blood and risked their lives fighting together in battle.

This change in political alliances reframed Lumad warfare into a wider battle pitting the Spanish colonial forces against the military dominance of Moro groups, represented in this period mainly by the leadership of the Magindanaw Sultan, Kudarat. The participation of Lumads in this wider battle between Spain and the Moros may not have been critical in the larger geopolitical context. After all, Spain was unable to control Muslim piracy until the latter half of the nineteenth century. However, within the context of the eastern half of Mindanao, Lumad participation in regional military action was, in fact, decisive in securing the long-term independence of the Lumads from their tributary relationship with the Magindanaw sultanate.

As to the total impact of early Spanish missionaries and mission life on the indigenous population of northeast Mindanao, we know that they changed more than just religious affiliation. They transformed Lumad society through the introduction of concepts from European military tradition, which resulted in the reorganization of Lumad communities into reinforced settlements with higher population densities. Just as a transition from a rural to an urban setting requires major lifestyle changes, this simple defense-related change in settlement patterns would have transformed Lumad society in tangible ways, altering, among other things, the way people grew their food, how and where they built their houses, the types of political authority they recognized, and the manner in which they engaged in collective violence.

Early Lumad conversion to Christianity appears to have been a cohesive force not only in terms of solidifying relationships between Lumad converts and missionaries, but also among different settlements of Lumad converts. With the formation of political and social alliances among formerly acephalous communities, the resulting rise of a Christian identity was inevitable. The next two chapters are about the conversion of the Kagayanon and the Caraga Revolt, events from the early 1600s that tested the strength of this relatively new Christian identity, with some rather surprising results.

CHAPTER 3

BLOOD BROTHERS AND THE ENEMIES OF GOD: STORIES OF THE KAGAYANON CONVERSION

Against the backdrop of the previous chapter, we now examine the arrival in 1622 of Recoleto missionaries in coastal north Mindanao—the area that surrounds what is now Cagayan de Oro city—into Kagayanon Lumad territory, and observe how the contact scenario played out in this particular instance.

In this chapter, I review the conversion experience of the Kagayanon, focusing on the emergence of strong social ties between the Kagayanon and the Recoleto missionaries, and the consequent social and political impact of this new relationship. The title of this chapter refers to the *sandugo,* or blood oath, which, at the time, was the standard practice for creating and symbolizing such allegiances throughout the islands.[1] The chapter closes with a discussion of some of the major changes that came with missionization, including logistical adaptations related to warfare, and the ripple effects that came with the increased interaction of missionized communities with other, formerly hostile Lumad groups. The conversion experience of another Lumad group, the Karaga, explored in detail in the next chapter, is also referenced throughout this chapter.

At the time of missionary entry into Mindanao, the Kagayanon were under the *sacup,* or alliance group, of the Magindanaw, a Moro sultanate based on the west coast of the island and ruled at the time by the legendary Kudarat (known as *Corralat* to the Spaniards). Equally legendary figures, at least from the Spanish perspective, are the early seventeenth century Recoleto missionaries mentioned in chapter two: P. Fr. Agustín de San Pedro,[2] whose peculiar contribution to Lumad missionization included passing on his military aptitude to the Lumadnon, and P. Fr. Juan de San Nicolás who, along with San Pedro, was one of the eight original Recoletos who laid the groundwork for the evangelization of Mindanao. With the relatively detailed yet underutilized records of these and other Recoletos, we are able to steal brief but significant glimpses of the Lumad experience with the Christian missions. San

---

[1] As described in *Relación vreve de el alevoso levantamiento de los indios de Caraga, en las Philipinas,* MS 3828 (Biblioteca Nacional, Madrid, 1632), pp. 215r–216r. See also Pedro Chirino SJ, *Relacion de las Islas Filipinas/The Philippines in 1600,* trans. Ramón Echevarria (Manila: Historical Conservation Society, 1969 [1604]), pp. 238–39. Also, see chapter four, this volume.

[2] In popular memory, he is sometimes mistakenly called "Pedro de San Agustín," an error also found in some of the embarkation and shipping records in the Archivo General de Indias (hereafter AGI) in Sevilla, Spain. See (AGI, Contratacion, 5350, N.40/29-10-1616); and (AGI, Filipinas, 80, N.74/1622). However, the Recoleto personnel records provide the final word concerning his proper name.

Nicolás, in particular, was the key figure in converting the Kagayanon, and therefore a key figure in this chapter.

COMMENTS ON MADIGAN'S STORY OF THE KAGAYANON CONVERSION

A well-known account of the Kagayanon story is the 1963 article by Jesuit scholar Francis Madigan concerning the founding of Cagayan de Oro city in what is now Misamis Oriental province.[3] Since this version is already deeply ingrained in local historical imagination, it might be useful to begin by referencing his version and tackling straightaway how it differs in substance from the official narrative presented by the Recoletos. Given its closer connection to the primary source material related to the events in question, I would give primacy to the Recoleto narrative, which includes the accounts published in the Order's *Boletín* and their *Catálogo* that focus on the apostolic achievements of the two aforementioned key missionaries.[4] However, because Madigan's narrative is so compelling and already well-known, I think it remains valuable to reference it in this chapter, even as we move forward with the Recoleto's internal narrative of their own Mindanao missions.

Madigan, a respected Jesuit historian of Mindanao, presents an extended dramatic account of the conversion of the Kagayanon, albeit one that does not cite any specific primary sources. It is apparent from a careful reading that his account relies entirely on Emma Blair and James Robertson's English translation of the Recoleto *Crónicas*.[5] Madigan, in fact, cites the latter "as reproduced in Blair and Robertson ..."[6] While the Madigan/Blair–and–Robertson version is not completely contradicted by the Spanish-language sources I consulted, it contains quite a number

---

[3] Francis Madigan SJ, "The Early History of Cagayan de Oro," *Philippine Studies* 11,1 (1963): 76–130.

[4] Francisco Sábada del Carmen OAR, *Catálogo de los Religiosos Agustinos Recoletos de San Nicolás de Tolentino desde el Año 1606 en que Llegó la Primera Misión á Manila, hasta Nuestros Días* (Madrid: Imprenta del Asilo de Huérfanos del Sagrado Corazón de Jesús, 1906); and Orden de los Agustinos Recoletos (hereafter OAR), *Boletín de la Provincia de San Nicolas de Tolentino* 60, 629 (Marcilla, Navarra, Spain, 1970).

[5] Emma Blair and James Robertson, *The Philippine Islands, 1493–1898*, vols. 21 and 35 (Cleveland, OH: Arthur H. Clark Company, 1903–1909). Excerpts from the Recoleto *Crónicas* are spread out, as part of a national chronology, over several different volumes of Blair and Robertson. To commemorate the "Year of the Missionary," the Recoletos recently reconsolidated these disparate pieces into one digital document, available online at www.agustinosrecoletos.org/docs/9184_Chronicles_EN.doc, accessed September 2, 2007. They are pieced together from the following portions of Blair and Robertson, *The Philippine Islands*: Volume 21, pp. 111–259, which contains a text by P. Fr. Andrés de San Nicolás, plus part of the *Historia* by P. Fr. Luis de Jesus; Volume 35, pp. 59–101, which is taken from the *Historia* by P. Fr. Luis de Jesus; Volume 36, pp. 109–88; and Volume 41, pp. 57–231, which, according to Blair and Robertson, was translated from an *Historia* by P. Fr. Pedro de San Francisco de Assis, printed in 1756 in Zaragoza, Spain, by Francisco Moreno. The translated title Blair and Robertson provide is "General history of the discalced religious of the Order of the hermits of the great father and doctor of the Church, San Agustin, of the congregation of España and of the Indias." See Luis de Jesus OAR, *Historia general de los religiosos descalzos del orden de los hermitaños del gran padre ... San Augustin, de la Congregacion de España y de las Indias* (Madrid: Lucas Antonio de Bedmar, 1681).

[6] See Madigan, "The Early History of Cagayan de Oro," p. 82, fn. 10. As previously explained, the Blair and Robertson translations have far too many errors to be considered reliable "reproductions" of these Spanish-language sources.

of minor deviations that, taken together, do alter our understanding of the Kagayanon conversion in a significant way.[7]

For one thing, the Recoleto version renders the *datu* Salangsang's defection from Sultan Kudarat's *sacup*—in my view the single most crucial development in the Kagayanon conversion story—in a much more plausible manner. Rather than presenting Salangsang's defection as the intentional and defiant act of someone who had seen the light of Christianity (as in Madigan's version), the Recoleto narrative shows that the *datu* really had no other realistic options after the Magindanaw Moros carried out their scorched-earth strategy in response to the polite hospitality Salangsang had shown towards the Recoletos. It also revealed how undesirably tyrannical an ally the Moros could be. Another important discrepancy is that the Madigan version centers around the heroism and military brilliance of Fray Agustín de San Pedro, whereas the Recoleto account focuses on the relationship between Salangsang and Fray Juan de San Nicolás, with San Pedro playing a relatively minor role. The overall tones of the accounts are also radically different: Madigan, in Jesuit style, gives us a highly triumphant rendering of the events, in which the Recoletos and the Kagayanon build an impenetrable fort and are well-armed with mortars, arquebuses, and reinforcements from Caraga, laying in wait for the Moros to mount an attack. The Recoleto narrative, on the other hand, gives one the distinct feeling that Salangsang's followers and their allies managed to survive the whole affair by the skin of their teeth and only through God's divine mercy.

Madigan's particular narrative also includes quite a bit of ethnographic detail that was drawn not from firsthand Recoleto descriptions or even from Blair and Robertson but, in his words, were instead "derived (often deductively) from present-day survivals,"[8] as well as from commonly circulated historical descriptions of the Tagalogs and other groups that the author presumed to be interchangeable with the Kagayanon in regard to custom, culture, and social organization. Thus he gives us an unusually strong and definite picture of the Kagayanons' purported dress, habits, marital practices, system of slavery, and other detailed ethnographic information that may not be applicable to the Kagayanon case at all. This creative ethnographic description introduced by Madigan is highly suspect and, when considered along with his reliance on the Blair and Robertson version of events, it means that, at the end of the day, the divergence between the well-known Madigan story and the Recoleto narrative is quite substantial. Privileging the Recoleto narrative requires us to adjust our understanding of the way in which the historical encounter between the Kagayanon, the Spaniards, and the Magindanaw unfolded in the coastal hills of the Misamis region. It is indeed remarkable how even a few details can change the way we interpret particular moments in history. Despite these differences, however, I do

---

[7] This includes Madigan's statement that a large swath of northern Mindanao (almost half of what is now Misamis Oriental province) was granted as an *encomienda* to "a certain Juan Griego" in 1571 by Miguel Lopez de Legazpi. See Madigan, "The Early History of Cagayan de Oro," pp. 80–81. This has been routinely repeated as fact, verbatim, even making its way into the Wikipedia entry on Cagayan de Oro City. I searched repeatedly in both the AGI and the ARM (Archivo Provincial de los Agustinos Recoletos, Marcilla, Spain) for the details of this alleged order and find no evidence of either the *encomienda* or any "Juan Griego," certain or uncertain. Moreover, this particular area was never, at any point in time, assigned as one single *encomienda* to just one person. The same archives, however, contain a worthwhile documentary history of colonial-era *encomiendas* in northern and eastern Mindanao, going as far back as the late sixteenth century, and awaiting proper study.

[8] Madigan, "The Early History of Cagayan de Oro," p. 90, fn. 16.

note that the larger outcomes in both stories were the same, for, ultimately, the Kagayanon converted on a large scale, the Magindanaw lost influence in the area as a result, and what is now Cagayan de Oro city was established in the seventeenth century, giving the Catholic religion and Spanish colonial administration a solid foothold in northern Mindanao that would last through the centuries in the face of local revolts, Moro attacks, foreign occupation, and, much later, a national revolution.

The Kagayanon were a Lumad population living in the Cagayán river area, and their primary settlement was a hilltop fortification somewhere in the interior called "Himologàn" in Madigan's version, but more likely to have been phonetically closer to "Imolagan."[9] Madigan estimates a Kagayanon population of "more than five hundred, according to the Chronicler."[10] Kagayanon territory was located in the hills within the vicinity of what is now Cagayan de Oro city, Misamis Oriental province. Madigan describes "Himologàn" as the main town of the territory called Cagayán, explaining that, in the past, "its Malay [sic] settlers of the Cagayan River area had gained control over the Misamis coastline and the adjacent mountains."[11] In contrast, the Recoleto version gives the impression that Imolagan was simply another settlement in the area, albeit a relatively large one, and that its residents, including Salangsang, did not have any hold on the surrounding settlements.

Imolagan was located at the very doorstep of the Moro territories—it was less than a day's trek from the main Maranaw settlement of Marawi on Lake Lanao. A roundtrip over land from Imolagan to Magindanaw territory could be completed by foot in a week, but it was much faster by sea. While Moro piracy and raiding had a real impact on Christian identification among Lumads, for the moment I would like the reader to focus simply on the tense geopolitical context of the Kagayanon Lumad world. In this way, we can recognize the political as well as the social gravity of the Kagayanon decision to defy Magindanaw power in the early 1600s. As noted above, the Kagayanon were paying tribute to the Sultan of Magindanaw at the time, and, as they were non-Muslims, they were at a great disadvantage in this relationship not

---

[9] The original spelling is Himolagan, but given the voiceless initial /h/ in Spanish, spelling it as Imolagan would, in my opinion, express the original pronunciation more accurately, with the accent probably on the second-to-last syllable. Spaniards generally wrote the voiced initial /h/ sound as a J, therefore it would have been "Jimolagan," not Himolagan. It is written as Himologàn by Madigan, who also speculates for no specified reason that there was a glottal stop in the last syllable. See Madigan, "The Early History of Cagayan de Oro," p. 77, fn. 1. Local historians consistently use the name "Himologan" to refer to this episode, likely because they rely exclusively on Madigan's version for their information. I do not know which name is more true to the original Kagayanon name, but given that Madigan relies on the poorly translated Blair and Robertson version of this story, which also uses "Himologàn" throughout, the disparity in spelling may very easily be a basic transcription error by Blair and Robertson. In contrast, the Recoleto versions consistently spell it "Himolagan" with no diacritics of any sort. See Blair and Robertson, *The Philippine Islands,* vol. 21.

[10] Madigan, "The Early History of Cagayan de Oro," p. 88. Madigan is referring here to the Recoleto chronicler, Luis de Jesus, although it is quite clear to me that he relied on the translation by Blair and Robertson, rather than the actual Recoleto *Crónicas.*

[11] Ibid., pp. 79, 85–86. Madigan further specifies that, like the Cagayan de Oro city of today, there were already two ethnically distinct peoples there, with the Kagayanon people being "Visayan" and the interior people being "Bukidnon," each supposedly speaking distinct languages. There is no evidence of such an ethnic and linguistic delineation this early in the colonial period. It is true that, in many places, there were "interior" and "coastal" populations, but they would have been, in this case, Kagayanon as well.

only socially—for they were relegated by the Magindanaw to the inferior outsider category of *alfoores*[12]—but also politically, because of the demographic, material, and military superiority of the Magindanaw.

According to Madigan's version, Salangsang, whom he portrays as the chief of all the Kagayanons, was initially unreceptive to a request made by the two Recoleto missionaries that he travel to Imolagan. Salangsang was reluctant for several possible reasons. Madigan mentions in passing the strong influence exerted by *baylans,* or shamans, on the local populations, though he ultimately concludes that the primary reason for Salangsang's hesitation was due to his people's fear of reprisal from the Magindanaw Moros, to whom they paid tribute. As a result, the Recoletos, who at that time were waiting in Camiguin, were summarily barred from entering Kagayanon territory. This was in 1622. But all was not lost, according to Madigan, because "someone remembered … that Salangsang's grandmother had been baptized sometime before—perhaps by the Jesuits—and at the time was living in Butuan. Perhaps she could help."[13] The Recoletos then summoned an elderly female convert named Magdalena Bacuyo[14] in order to deploy her in their quest to evangelize Imolagan. The possible grandparent relationship[15] between Salangsang and Magdalena Bacuyo indicates that they belonged to the regional power elite in Mindanao and the Visayas, and therefore the Recoletos were able to use social pressure on Salangsang and the Kagayanon to gain admittance to their territory. Salangsang is thus on the record as having revised his attitude and welcomed the missionaries as friends, allowing them to stay in his own house for an extended period. They were also allowed to construct a chapel and hold Mass outside of the Imolagan fortification. From Madigan's account, one can easily imagine Salangsang squirming with discomfort and dread as he was obliged to be hospitable in his grandmother's presence.

Not surprisingly, the arrival of the missionaries drew an immediate negative reaction from the Magindanaw sultanate, then led by Sultan Kudarat, who had already been forced to deal with troublesome Spanish incursions into his home territory. Kudarat reportedly sent messengers to order Salangsang to kill the two missionaries. Although "more than a thousand warriors accompanied the

---

[12] *Alfoores* and *haraforas* were terms used by Moro groups at the time in reference to their non-Muslim neighbors. See Thomas McKenna, *Muslim Rulers and Rebels: Everyday Politics and Armed Separatism in the Southern Philippines* (Berkeley, CA: University of California Press, 1998), p. 308, n. 11.

[13] Madigan, "The Early History of Cagayan de Oro," p. 86.

[14] Madigan gives Magdalena's surname as Bacuya, not Bacuyo, again following the Blair and Robertson version of this story. Again, the name in the Recoleto record is more likely closer to the original indigenous name. "Bacuyo" is, in fact, still used as a surname in northern Mindanao today, but not Bacuya.

[15] Note that Philippine groups, including the Lumad groups, and indeed most of island Southeast Asia, are generally ambilineal in character and use what is called the "Hawaiian" or generational kinship system, in which all relatives of the same generation are classified as the same kind of relative. This leads to the real possibility that Salangsang may have referred to Magdalena Bacuyo as his grandmother (and she called him her grandson) because she was a relative from the same generational cohort as the mother of one of his parents. He was not necessarily her direct descendant, though at the very least he was certainly someone from two generations younger than her within the same extended family group. It is not clear whether the Spaniards noted the genealogical difference, and it's possible they may not have noticed at all if the locals did not make an obvious distinction in their terminology.

messenger," Salangsang refused to carry out the order.[16] This is because, by the time Kudarat's order came, more than a year had passed since the missionaries' arrival, and the Recoletos had, by this time, managed to endear themselves to many of the Kagayanon who, in the spirit of friendship, allowed their children to receive catechism and, in some cases, baptism. Salangsang's resistance resulted in a brief détente lasting several months, during which the Kagayanon engaged in a combination of deception and diplomacy to evade Magindanaw demands and searches. Salangsang himself "sent the Fathers to a small and secluded village in the mountains while Cagayan awaited the reaction of the Maguindanao prince."[17] At one point, the Kagayanon were continually shuttling the missionaries from place to place to convince the Magindanaw that the missionaries had left their territory entirely and returned to Butuan for good.

When Salangsang's deception was eventually uncovered, it was interpreted by Kudarat as evidence of an open revolt: his politically worthless subjects were now consorting with his sworn enemy. Things turned from bad to worse after Salangsang, deliberating with his "council," decided to "throw off the yoke of the Maguindanao once and for all" and to seek assistance from the Spaniards in doing so. According to Madigan, this nearly suicidal decision was due to the fact that some of Salangsang's "chiefs"—perhaps fellow *datu*—were personally inclined towards Christianity, and that Salangsang never liked the Magindanaw to begin with:

> He had no love for the predatory Maguindanaos whose sole interest in his people seemed to be the exaction of a yearly tribute. Nor did he like their religion, which forbade the eating of pork and the drinking of liquor, two ancient customs of his people.[18]

The Recoletos therefore departed for the Caraga region, to secure armed support from Spanish troops stationed in Tandag. They returned within two weeks, this time leaving Madre de Dios behind and bringing a twenty-three-year-old Fray Agustín de San Pedro, who "had been appointed by the Recollect superior to be Prior of Cagayan and to assist in its defense."[19] From this point on, according to Madigan's version, San Pedro, who would come to be known as *El Padre Capitán*, basically takes command of the whole situation, telling Salangsang what to do, deciding on all the major strategic changes required to fight the Magindanaw, including the construction of a new stronghold, and drilling the Kagayanon men in the use of Spanish arquebuses. The clergymen were followed by one hundred native troops from Caraga and half a dozen Spanish soldiers.

Meanwhile, a Magindanaw "fleet" of thirty boats, "each with its full complement of well-equipped warriors," arrived to attack Imolagan from the sea.[20] The new, fortified settlement, San Pedro's superior planning, plus Spanish arquebuses and mortars, allowed San Pedro, the Spanish reinforcements, and the Kagayanon to hold back this force of approximately two thousand warriors.

---

[16] Madigan, "The Early History of Cagayan de Oro," p. 101.

[17] Ibid., p. 103.

[18] Ibid., p. 104.

[19] Ibid. San Pedro indeed became Prior of Cagayán, but not until 1626, several years after these particular events took place.

[20] Ibid., p. 109.

> Although they made many assaults on different parts of the wall [of the fortification], they found the same vigilance and stout defense everywhere. In addition, Fray Agustin led several sallies from the fort, wielding a sword mightily over his head and trampling enemy stragglers under the feet of the horse he had brought with him to Cagayan.[21]

A siege of several weeks was also unsuccessful, thanks to San Pedro's advanced planning. With their supplies exhausted, the Magindanaw were forced to retreat, and as they were breaking camp, they were attacked by San Pedro, Salangsang, and a light force of Kagayanon men: "Bursting in upon the Maguindanaos unexpectedly, he turned their retreat into an utter rout. Few of the enemy escaped. Cagayan had won a complete victory."[22]

This fantastic success apparently broke whatever remaining influence the *baylans* had on the Kagayanon, because after this victory Salangsang and his family converted to Christianity, followed by a large proportion of the Kagayanon population. And so it came to pass that Cagayán became a stronghold of Catholicism and loyalty to Spain, and remained so even up to the time of the Philippine Revolution. To avenge his surprise defeat at Imolagan, Kudarat launched a series of punitive raids from Lanao against the newly Christianized Kagayanon. In response, a rapid return raid was led by the newly converted Salangsang and his new brother in Christ, *El Padre Capitán*, during which the Maranaw settlement of Marawi on Lake Lanao was thoroughly sacked. According to Madigan, this counterattack kept the Muslims away from Cagayán for almost a decade.[23] So goes Madigan's rendition of these events.

THE RECOLETOS AND THE ROCK OF IMOLAGAN

The Recoleto version, told in storybook form under the title *La Roca de Himolagan*, or "the rock of Imolagan,"[24] is much more detailed than Madigan's narrative, and comparatively subdued, as its focal point is the apostolic work of Fray Juan de San Nicolás rather than *El Padre Capitán*'s prowess in battle. In fact, *El Padre Capitán* is barely mentioned at all, except for the fact that he turns up towards the end of the story. This and other nuances make the much less triumphalist Recoleto version of this encounter somewhat more interesting because the actions of the Kagayanon appear more down-to-earth and culturally comprehensible, in terms of their polite and cautious treatment of the Recoletos and their pragmatic reasons for finally going

---

[21] Ibid.

[22] Ibid., p. 110.

[23] Ibid., pp. 111–13.

[24] This story first appeared under anonymous authorship on September 19, 1886, in the *Boletín Eclesiástico del Arzobispado de Manila*, vol. 11, no. 38. The *Boletín Eclesiástico* related news about all the Orders, not just the Recoletos. This item was then reprinted verbatim in the retrospective issue of the Recoletos' *Boletín de la Provincia de San Nicolas de Tolentino*, citing the *Crónicas*, Tomo II, Cap. II, and claiming that the story agreed with the *Crónicas* and was an entirely historical account. According to the *Boletín de la Provincia de San Nicolas de Tolentino,* the only difference between the *La Roca* and the *Crónicas* versions was that the former incorporates imagined dialogue between the different characters involved. See OAR, *Boletín de la Provincia de San Nicolas de Tolentino*, pp. 48–61.

to battle against their politically more powerful former allies, the Magindanaw. In the remainder of this section, I work from my translation of this account, with a few of my own comments and observations.

First and foremost, in the Recoleto account, there were no powerful *baylans* to contend with among the Kagayanon, though the missionaries were certainly familiar with indigenous shamans by then. Complaints about demonic idols and influential *hechiceros*, or sorcerers, who often figured as major cultural hurdles to native conversion have been a regular trope in missionary accounts from the very beginning of Spanish colonial expansion in the Americas.[25] They were certainly a hurdle for Fray Juan San Nicolás during his first mission in Gigaquit, located at the northeastern tip of Mindanao. Gigaquit back then was described as a "totally pagan region where, as our historians would say, the evangelical trumpet had not been sounded." Moreover, its inhabitants were

> basically prisoners of the coarsest idolatry, victims of the deceits and tricks of the *babaylanes*, priests of their ridiculous idols. And as a consequence, their customs were barbaric, perpetual [were] their wars for frivolous causes, justice was absent, and their greed insatiable. In other words, what is already known and very common among the nomadic pagans of the Far East.[26]

There, and also in Butuan, San Nicolás was the one who had somehow "made a breach in the wall" of pagan hostility, enabling missionary work to proceed in both places.[27] After placing P. Fr. Jacinto de San Fulgencio (who reappears later in the story with *El Padre Capitán*) in charge of Butuan, San Nicolás set out for the river of Cagayán in 1622, accompanied by P. Fr. Francisco de la Madre de Dios. They made the journey by boat, with a stopover on the island of Camiguin that lasted much longer than they had anticipated, prepared for, or wanted. While stuck on Camiguin, they were visited by an elderly female convert from among the *principales* of Butuan, a woman named Magdalena Bacuyo, who had already taken the initiative to have a long talk with her grandson Salangsang, a *datu* of the Kagayanon people, about the Recoletos. It was she who wanted the Recoletos to go to Cagayán, and she ultimately coaxed her extremely reluctant grandson into receiving the Recoletos, pressuring him with a tale of woe that depicted the missionaries as helpless foreigners trapped on Camiguin without friends to help or feed them.

In this version, it is notable that Magdalena Bacuyo is portrayed not merely as a cultural mediator, but as the main instigator of the excursion to Cagayán. She was, in fact, the one who encouraged San Nicolás to go there, insisting that Salangsang and his people "will become good Christians if they listen to your advice and your words."[28] Her apparent devotion is further explained by the fact that she was converted and baptized by San Nicolás himself, and not "perhaps by the Jesuits," as Madigan so coyly suggested. Schreurs, in *Caraga Antigua*, asserts that Magdalena Bacuyo was, in fact, the same woman known as "Magdalena Baluyot," who some twenty years earlier had similarly intervened in the Jesuits' conversion of *datu*

---

[25] Nicholas Cushner, *Why Have You Come Here? The Jesuits and the First Evangelization of Native America* (New York, NY: Oxford University Press, 2006), pp. 75–78.

[26] OAR, *Boletín de la Provincia de San Nicolas de Tolentino*, p. 46.

[27] Ibid., p. 48

[28] Ibid., pp. 56–61.

Silongan in Butuan at the turn of that century.[29] Given that both Baluyot and Bacuyo are common surnames, and Magdalena was a very common baptismal name for female converts, it is difficult to judge the accuracy of this particular claim without further documentation. If it is true, then this Magdalena certainly deserves as much recognition as any of the Recoleto men with regard to the larger story of successful Lumad missionization. On the other hand, if San Nicolás is the one who had baptized her, then she cannot have been the same Magdalena who had earlier helped the Jesuits turn Silongan into a Christian and Spanish subject.

Returning to our narrative—which from this point closely matches Madigan's until the moment when the Magindanaw enter the story—Salangsang makes his reservations about the whole arrangement crystal clear to his persistent grandmother, explaining specifically that his fearsome political overlord, Sultan Kudarat, would be very annoyed by the presence of Spaniards within his *sacup*. Hoping to discourage the Recoletos, Salangsang tells Magdalena Bacuyo that, because of his people's poverty, all they can give the missionaries is a room to sleep in and nothing more. But San Nicolás and Madre de Dios heartily accept this "generous offer" and look forward to being able to "work spiritually on such fertile ground among the most gentle spirits of all the island."[30] Magdalena prepares everything for their voyage across the Camiguin channel to the mainland of Mindanao, some forty nautical miles away. Her preparations include the provision of an armed escort, consisting of her sons and some of their friends, to the mouth of the Cagayán River, the point at which these escorts would secure guides to bring the missionaries safely to the rock promontory called Imolagan, where her grandson lived. After an arduous boat trip on seas that are still rough today, the party reaches Imolagan, and upon their arrival are greeted by the "prince" Salangsang and surrounded by five hundred[31] of his men, all armed with spears and native swords, called *campilanes*. Salangsang was said to have received them "in a somewhat mild [*benigno*] manner, due to the fact that said Religious allowed them to give each [missionary] a light slap on the face," explained by the Recoleto chronicle as "a sign among those barbarians that they were being admitted [to the settlement] as beloved friends."[32]

The Imolagan settlement described in the Recoleto account was located on a naturally fortified cliff, totally inaccessible except by climbing a rope of braided *liana* (young rattan) vine, and therefore ideal for defense. On the rock itself was one large, extended dwelling constructed as a barracks, and also capable of housing the

---

[29] Peter Schreurs MSC, *Caraga Antigua 1521–1910: The Hispanization and Christianization of Agusan, Surigao, and East Davao* (Cebu: University of San Carlos Publications, 1989), pp. 111–15. See also Peter Schreurs MSC, "The Beatas of Butuan," *Kinaadman* 3 (1981): 176–83.

[30] OAR, *Boletín de la Provincia de San Nicolas de Tolentino*, p. 56

[31] With regard to the five hundred warriors of Imolagan, as well as the one thousand Moro warriors sent later by Kudarat, I assume these numbers are exaggerated, or, at the very least, rounded off rather high. If the solitary "longhouse" in Imolagan housed five hundred warriors and their extended families, the population of Imolagan would have to be upwards of three thousand individuals, assuming there were six individuals or so in each family unit. The level of food production necessary to sustain such a large non-riverine settlement for an extended period, not to mention the architectural features required to house several hundred families in one structure, suggest that it is unlikely so many people were settled in this inaccessible location, as described. As to the likelihood of Kudarat sending a thousand warriors just to intimidate a minor Kagayanon *datu*, I would leave that answer to Magindanaw historians.

[32] OAR, *Boletín de la Provincia de San Nicolas de Tolentino*, p. 58.

numerous relatives of Salangsang and his men.[33] It was organized like a well-insulated cloister that could be opened only from the inside. In the midst of this cloister, on a sort of patio, was a temple dedicated to the local guardian spirit, referred to in the narrative as *Diwatahan*, whose idol occupied a small, filthy, "miserable" alcove of sorts.[34] There are no images from this period, but one can imagine a fortified, elevated longhouse with the *diwatahan* at the center.

The Recoletos made an indelible impression on Salangsang and his people for daring to come with neither reinforcements nor arms "like those of the Spaniards of Cebú." The two Recoletos also refused to carry the native arms offered to them and attempted to put the Kagayanon at ease by declaring that they "have never been men of war."[35] They endeared themselves further by not being burdensome guests: they procured their own food, helped the community collect water and firewood, and behaved as generally helpful and amiable individuals. After some time, they were granted permission to build a chapel by the river, on the outskirts of Imolagan. They would work by themselves on their chapel during the day, and in the evening climb back up to Imolagan. The two Recoletos would shut themselves together in their room, coming out primarily to talk about their God to the local *principales*. Although—or perhaps because—the older people and other adults resisted their teachings "for fear of having to give up their own bad habits," they brought their young children to the Recoletos in order to learn about Christianity.[36] In any case, the narrative says, San Nicolás and Madre de Dios were more than happy to convert the children, all of whom later received the Catholic sacrament of baptism "with great joy."

Into this setting arrived representatives of Kudarat, the "pirate king of Mindanao," to collect the annual tributes from Imolagan and the surrounding Lumad settlements. Upon hearing that the Recoletos were being accommodated along that part of the Cagayán River, Kudarat ordered Salangsang to kill the missionaries straightaway, sending along a thousand armed men to ensure that this order was carried out. But despite his political loyalties and very real fears, Salangsang could not even contemplate executing the missionaries. The Kagayanons had, by then, become very fond of them, and this fondness was proven by numerous efforts at hiding and later defending these Recoletos. In an attempt to negotiate a peaceful resolution to this crisis, Salangsang ultimately persuaded Kudarat's tribute collectors to settle for collecting tribute from the Recoletos, to which the completely defenseless Recoletos regretfully agreed. But this compromise proved totally unacceptable to Kudarat, who resolved to turn the Kagayanon people against the

---

[33] Ibid., p. 57.

[34] We do not know which particular *diwata* it is, because in almost any Philippine language the term *diwata* (from Sanskrit, *devata*) is merely a generic word for guardian spirits, and *diwatahan* can mean either the place where the *diwata* is worshipped or the actual practice of worshiping a *diwata*. Modern Lumadnon count dozens of supernatural beings in their cosmology, including evil spirits, and various *diwata* often represented as carved wooden idols.

[35] OAR, *Boletín de la Provincia de San Nicolas de Tolentino*, p. 57.

[36] Ibid., p. 59. "Para que les enseñasan los sagrados misterios y la doctrina cristiana, los indios traían sus niños a los Padres ... pues los viejos y adultos se resistían grandemente a admitir dogmas y moral del cristianismo por temor de tener que abandonar sus vicios." It is not clear to me whether this refers only to the actions of *principales* or to those of other Kagayanon as well.

Recoletos by systematically attacking their neighboring settlements. And from this point on, the Recoleto narrative departs completely from Madigan's version.

Declaring "holy war," in the Recoletos' words, against the settlements on that part of the river, Kudarat reportedly assembled his most war-hardened warriors, and "subjected to blood and fire some of Himolagan's neighboring settlements, killing without mercy the few who fell into their hands."[37] Fleeing for their lives, San Nicolás and Madre de Dios escaped by sea "in dangerous conditions using rickety boats," and in desperation hid in dense forests, caves, and other hazardous (*mortiferos*) places, always carrying with them their sacred objects from the chapel they had constructed. In the wilderness, probably somewhere to the east, they encountered two other Recoletos, P. Fr. Agustín de San Pedro and P. Fr. Jacinto de Jesús María, who had fled from other settlements on northern Mindanao that had fallen under attack from Kudarat's forces.

Eventually, Kudarat's brutal extermination campaign turned Salangsang completely against his former overlord. He really had no choice by this point, given the unforgiving nature of the Magindanaw war ultimately directed against him and his people at Imolagan. Begging the Recoletos to stay put, Salangsang himself took up arms to defend them at Imolagan, also dispatching two native sailboats (*vintas*) to deliver to the garrisons in Caraga and Cebú letters from the two missionaries urgently requesting aid. We do not know much about the response itself, such as how long the reinforcements took to arrive, or how many Spanish troops were involved. We only know that the reinforcements "could not have come at a more opportune moment."[38]

Encouraged and inspired by this turn of events, the indigenous people reportedly saw the error of their ways and dismantled their *diwatahan*, turning it into a "church" where those who wanted to convert to Christianity could be baptized. We are not told the exact numbers of converts, but many of the Kagayanon did get baptized, including Salangsang. Salangsang's conversion was dramatized by the Recoleto imagination very much in line with the typical contact scenario: Salangsang first acknowledged that the Recoleto God was a god of peace, mercy, and compassion, and begged for baptism exclaiming: "I do not want to die in the next battle without your God's grace!" P. Fr. Juan de San Nicolás then baptized Salangsang and his wife after ensuring that the *datu*'s intentions were sincere, and "after becoming Christian, he spontaneously swore allegiance, freely and for always, to the monarchs of Castille."[39] The conversion of the *datu* and his family was immediately followed by that of the rest of the natives of Imolagan.

As Kudarat and his army slowly approached, intending "to exterminate once and for all those who had disobeyed him," Salangsang gave orders to build a new fortification with bulwarks. Once this was done, the "piety of the natives caused them to erect a *convento*" for their beloved Recoletos, which they named "Cagayán," and around which they built their own dwellings.[40] While the popular history of Cagayán holds that this new fortification-plus-*convento* formed the core of what is now the lowland, coastal city of Cagayan de Oro, the Recoleto narrative does not

---

[37] Ibid.

[38] Ibid., p. 60.

[39] Ibid., p. 59.

[40] Ibid.

actually specify where these early structures were located, only that they were in a different—and presumably more defensible—place than Imolagan.[41]

The Recoleto story culminates with the assault by Kudarat's army, which, aided by several of Salangsang's neighbors, entered Cagayán before dawn one day with the intention of getting rid of the Recoletos for good. The attack came without warning, and the village was overcome, house by house, through hand-to-hand combat.[42] The Moros soon penetrated the monastery where, at last, they were repelled by the Kagayanon, who were gathered there in force under the leadership of *El Padre Capitán*'s partner, Fray Jacinto de Jesús María. After losing a number of men in the scuffle, the Moros recovered quickly and, aided by fresh reinforcements, renewed their attack with even greater determination. The battle was tenacious and brutal (*tenaz y ruda*), and rendered rather cinematically in the Recoleto publication, which reported that Salangsang, leading his men, "fought like a lion," cutting down their enemies "with every swing of his *kris*."[43] But ultimately, the defensive forces were overwhelmed, and the Moros pushed them back from the *convento* gate, forcing Salangsang to leave behind eight of his most loyal warriors, who were mortally wounded. Having taken the gate, the Moros then took the rest of the convent easily, making their way through the whole structure by daybreak. When they arrived at Fray Jacinto's cell, they did not find him, but they ransacked it anyway, "just in case he and the other Religious were hiding." The account then states that Fray Jacinto suddenly emerged, "boldly and serenely" repelling the intruders "without taking a single scratch" as he made his escape. He then fled to a nearby wood to wait for the fury to subside.[44]

Seeing that the convent had fallen into the hands of the Moros, Salangsang, his men, and the Religious regrouped in the original settlement site of Imolagan to await the impending arrival of Spanish and native reinforcements, and to plan their attack for the following day. In this, they were met "with such good luck that before the sun came up, they had retaken the convent and settlement [of Cagayán]," aided in part by the protective fire of Spanish arquebusiers. Subsequently, they pressed forward, "cutting the throats of all the Moros they found in their path." It is said that the Moros fled in fear at the force of this attack, in the process leaving behind "a number of their companions, who were then put to the sword and lance by the native peoples."[45]

The Recoletos attributed this decisive victory not to *El Padre Capitán*, but to their strong relationship with the Kagayanon people; specifically, the latter's religious devotion that, from the Recoleto perspective, was proven by their willingness to fight to protect the Recoletos and the *convento*. Thanks to this experience, their *datus* also permitted the permanent placement of Spanish troops on the banks of the river, establishing a garrison that would later become the Presidio de Cagayán and serve as

---

[41] See OAR, *Boletín de la Provincia de San Nicolas de Tolentino*, p. 107. Madigan claims that it was located "between Carmen St. and the estuary south of the Cathedral and between Rizal St. and the river" in present-day Cagayan de Oro city.

[42] Ibid., p. 60.

[43] A *kris*, or *kalis*, is a double-edged sword indigenous to Mindanao, distinguished by the undulating design of its blade.

[44] Ibid., p. 61.

[45] Ibid.

the headquarters of Spanish colonial administration in northern Mindanao for the remainder of the first mission period.

BLOOD BROTHERS

According to these narratives, specific developments related to the arrival of the Recoletos appear to have turned the Kagayanon decisively against the Magindanaw, and perhaps against the Moros in general, and moved them to fight. What made these foreign missionaries worth fighting for? Though Spain's prior assaults on the Magindanaw warranted only a fleeting mention in the above narratives, it may have been politically significant that the Spaniards had very recently made serious inroads against Kudarat in his own territory. These Spanish victories against the Moros would have shown Salangsang and his fellow *datu* that an alliance with Spain could bring the Kagayanon an advantage in terms of security. The fact that, by then, the Spanish presence had been growing across the strait in Cebú for almost half a century also would have told Salangsang that these foreigners were not temporary interlopers but a stable, long-term force to be reckoned with in his political universe. Finally, Spanish military successes in the region would explain why Kudarat had reacted so strongly to the presence of Spaniards among the Kagayanon. Likewise, the later victories won by the Magindanaw against Spanish troops, pointing to possible Spanish weaknesses, appear to have precipitated the Karaga revolt against the Spaniards, which is discussed in the next chapter. It is not surprising, however, that in their narrative, the Recoletos emphasize the spiritual impact of their righteousness on the animist Kagayanon, rather than the strategic impact of rising Spanish political and military dominance on their attractiveness as potential allies.

Fray Juan de San Nicolás, in particular, is shown as modeling idealized Christian behavior through *bondad y mansedumbre*—goodness and meekness—to demonstrate the purity of the missionaries' intentions and the strength of their faith. The willingness of the missionaries to engage in highly risky behavior, such as entering hostile territory without a military escort or sidearms, was also used to demonstrate the power of the Christian deity to protect his servants from danger. It may sound melodramatic and hackneyed, but it is not far-fetched at all. I have, in fact, heard modern-day Lumadnon explain more than once, in exactly this manner, that they allowed specific foreign missionaries to take up residence in their settlement because they were deeply impressed by their behavior, such that they were convinced the foreigners truly cared about them and were there for purely altruistic purposes.[46] More importantly, however, it was also mentioned to me time and again that they had been genuinely curious about whether the new foreign deity might indeed be more powerful than their own ancestral spirits. Lumadnon are routinely characterized as culturally conservative and extremely resistant to change, but the Lumad in the archival record—as well as the Lumad I know in the present day—are really quite like most Southeast Asians: keenly and pragmatically interested in novelty, and more than ready to acquaint themselves with the foreign, even if only to

---

[46] See Oona T. Paredes, "True Believers: Higaunon and Manobo Evangelical Protestant Conversion in Historical and Anthropological Perspective," *Philippine Studies* 54,4 (2006): 546–49. I should add that, in my experience, not only the Lumadnon make this observation. Lowlanders in Mindanao have also remarked to me in the past that foreigners in general, missionaries included, seem to genuinely care for the company and well-being of the Lumadnon, and treat them much better than they (the lowlanders) generally do.

satisfy their curiosity. In other words, contrary to the stereotypes, Lumad people have always been rather "modern" in outlook.

One additional factor mentioned by Madigan, but not noted in the Recoleto narrative, is the supposed cultural incompatibility between Lumad and Moro practices, which, in turn, attracted the Kagayanon to the Spanish religion. Islamic rules against eating pork and consuming liquor meant that the Kagayanons' liberty to engage in these activities, culturally important to them as well as to most Lumad today, would have been threatened.[47] Yet the historical record, outside Madigan's account, provides little evidence that the Kagayanon felt their traditions to be threatened in the way Madigan describes, for although Moro elites may have been observant Muslims, the average Moro of this period, not just in Mindanao but elsewhere in Island Southeast Asia, was routinely described by foreigners as having a "lack of apparent religious devotion."[48] Therefore, the relevance of this supposed cultural incompatibility to the Christian conversion of the Kagayanon—or for that matter, in their refusal to convert to Islam— appears weak at best, and deserves to be questioned.

Last but not least, one of the most interesting elements of the Recoleto account is the report that the Magindanaw had intentionally struck Salangsang's neighbors first, slowly increasing the threat to Cagayán by moving closer and closer until the Moros were finally upon them and there was no avenue open for the Kagayanon and their allies to escape. According to the narrative, Salangsang and his people were shocked and appalled by Kudarat's cruelty, not only demonstrated by his brutal attacks on neighboring peoples, who had nothing to do with the missionaries, but also in the way he targeted so tenaciously a pair of defenseless and harmless visitors who had done the Moros no wrong. The Recoleto account focuses on how this so affected Salangsang's moral conscience that he was moved in his soul to accept the Christian faith. Of course, it could also be that Salangsang saw the need to defend his own interests. If anything, these punitive actions, carried out by Kudarat's forces, made it obvious to Salangsang and his *sacup* allies that the Moros, so quick to destroy their own vassals, were not dependable as allies.

THE ASSAULT ON MARAWI

Madigan adds a postscript to his account of the events outlined above that provides us with a second, equally interesting episode of Lumad–Spaniard collaboration, which again demonstrates the willingness of the Lumads to fight their neighbors under the command of a Christian authority figure. In 1639, according to Madigan, five hundred Lumad volunteers from the Caraga region joined Spanish troops in a major raid into hostile Moro territory. They were led by *Capitán* Francisco Atienza, then the *alcalde mayor* (chief magistrate) of Caraga province, who, along with fifty Spanish troops, had been ordered by the governor general, Sebastián Hurado de Corcuera, to attempt the military pacification and subsequent conversion of the Maranaws living around Lake Lanao. Despite the fact that the Lanao missions would be given to the Recoletos' rivals, the Jesuits, the Recoleto Fray Agustín de San

---

[47] See Madigan, "The Early History of Cagayan de Oro," p. 104. See also Schreurs, *Caraga Antigua*, p. 131.

[48] McKenna, *Muslim Rulers and Rebels*, p. 82.

Pedro was reportedly recruited by Atienza to help him conquer the Lake Lanao area for the Crown and for the Holy Faith.

The joint Spanish–Lumad expedition successfully captured Marawi and the surrounding towns. Their advantage was due to the speed with which they were able to travel to Lanao. *El Padre Capitán* had apparently designed a boat that could be disassembled, to make it easier to carry when traveling over land, and reassembled very quickly at the water. The use of six such boats allowed the expedition to make a swift and unexpected assault from the lake and move their artillery efficiently, so that they essentially fought a one-sided inland naval battle. Madigan's summary says that the native participants were all Karagas, who are the subjects of the next chapter. The presence of the *alcalde mayor* of Caraga likewise suggests the participation of Karaga warriors, who by this time were known for their enthusiastic participation in Spanish military expeditions into Moro areas. An equally significant aspect of this expedition is that it was under the joint command of San Pedro and *Capitán* Atienza, a partnership that strongly suggests the Lumads might have agreed to participate only if they were under the command of the young Recoleto. According to Madigan, San Pedro and his volunteers came along on their own initiative, paying for their own expenses and taking care of their own needs, such as food and weaponry, during the expedition, which in itself is noteworthy.[49]

I did not find any direct reference to this assault on Marawi in the Recoleto archives. However, Peter Schreurs, citing Jesuit sources, does mention such a joint expedition to the Lanao area carried out by *El Padre Capitán* and Francisco de Atienza, which took place sometime between 1638 and 1641, and which also featured this highly creative strategy of disassembling and reassembling boats. Schreurs, however, cites the Jesuit chronicler Francisco Colín in noting that the volunteers were from Butuan, not Caraga.[50] He further cites from the account of the Jesuit Pablo Pastells a 1654 letter from the Recoleto Provincial to the king of Spain that describes the expedition as one of pacification, intended to "subdue" peacefully the Lake Lanao and Iligan areas.[51] The boats were carried by the Lumad volunteers over land, and the expedition's success was measured not by the number of Moros killed but by the marked increase in the number of tribute payers, which rose from almost none to over twelve thousand tributes for the Crown. P. Fr. Agustín de San Pedro, who was the Prior of Butuan at the time, had reportedly brought along with him the aforementioned modular boats, as well as "a great number" of Butuanon men, and apparently paid for their food and other expenses out of his own pocket. I might add that I find it unlikely that the Kagayanon warriors would have stayed away from this expedition, given their ties to the Recoletos and the fact that they were the ones living on the frontier with the Maranaw. In fact, the expedition, if traveling over land, would have had to travel straight through Kagayanon territory to reach Marawi itself. In contrast to the Madigan version, there is no mention in the account offered by Schreurs that this effort to subdue Marawi was being specifically undertaken to "open up" the area for the Jesuits. This was, in fact, already Jesuit

---

[49] Madigan, "The Early History of Cagayan de Oro," pp. 118–20.

[50] Schreurs, *Caraga Antigua*, pp. 141–42.

[51] Peter Schreurs, *Mission to Mindanao 1859–1900, from the Spanish of Pablo Pastells SJ*, vol. 3 (Quezon City: Claretian Publications, 1998), quoting from III: 714 in the original Pastells series. See Pablo Pastells SJ, *Misión de la Compañía de Jesús de Filipinas en el siglo XIX, Tome III* (Barcelona: Tip. y Lib. Editorial Barcelonesa S. A., 1917).

territory, taken away from the Recoletos just a few years earlier. Given the rivalries among the orders at the time, *El Padre Capitán* was more likely to have participated in the name of Christendom generally, and not to aid the Jesuits.

In the Madigan and Schreurs narratives, therefore, we find two versions of the same story, told differently. The devil, as they say, is in the details, but the important underlying truth revealed by either version is that, in both cases, the Lumad warriors—whether they were Butuanon, Karaga, Kagayanon, or anyone else— participated as *El Padre Capitán*'s men, serving the Church's agenda and not the Crown's. This underlines once again the primacy of the missionary relationship in the colonial-era encounters between the Lumad and the Spanish.

Finally, the Recoleto *Crónicas* relate at least one more similarly interesting expedition, involving Fray Juan de San Nicolás. As with the earlier stories, this episode, though missing many details, also provides evidence of the development of strong social bonds between the Recoletos and the Lumad. This time, however, the expedition ended in an embarrassing defeat for the Spaniards. According to the *Crónicas*,[52] *Capitán General* Juan Niño de Tabora had ordered the *Maestre de Campo* of Manila,[53] a Spaniard named Lorenzo de Olaso,[54] described as quite a valiant soldier overall (*muy bizarro militar*), to punish the Moros for their frequent raiding (*fechorías*). Niño de Tabora had also asked the local Recoletos to join the multiethnic raiding party—composed of both Spaniards and Lumads—as military chaplains, and they obliged. Accompanying Olaso as chaplains were our P. San Nicolás and P. Fr. Miguel de la Concepción, who had fortuitously brought along a party of Karaga *flecheros*, or archers, whom the missionaries had recruited and trained themselves.

The Moros in question had apparently entrenched themselves in an unnamed, inaccessible mountaintop, and were armed with "many projectile weapons." We are not told where this encounter took place, except that it was in a Moro area within striking distance of Caraga. The location could easily have been Cateel, to the south of Caraga proper, which was widely recognized as *de facto* Magindanaw territory in those days. I also assume this confrontation must have taken place long before the aforementioned Marawi assault, even before the Caraga Revolt of 1631, given that Niño de Tabora died in 1632. Returning to the action, as the joint party of mixed Spanish–Lumad troops, Recoletos, and Karagas made their approach, Olaso was reportedly hit in the head with a rock, presumably one thrown by the Moros, and was thrown far to the ground by the impact. Olaso lived, but the accident caused most of the troops to desert, leaving mainly the Recoletos and their own Lumad recruits to carry on. The fighters who remained endeavored to recover Olaso before retreating in the absence of sufficient military backup. Again, as with the previously mentioned expeditions, the important point here is that the Lumads who came

---

[52] OAR, *Boletín de la Provincia de San Nicolas de Tolentino*, pp. 54–55, citing Tomo III, p. 303 *passim*.

[53] Olaso is listed as such in a 1636 letter by Governor General Sebastián Hurtado de Corcuera. See Blair and Robertson, *The Philippine Islands*, vol. 26, p. 305. The online *Diccionario de la Real Academia Española* (DRAE; http://www.rae.es/) defines the *Maestre de Campo* as the rank of a superior military officer who had command responsibility over several *tercios*, or Spanish infantry regiments, in the sixteenth and seventeenth centuries. I write more on the *maestre de campo* in chapter six.

[54] Curiously, the same Lorenzo de Olaso (or Olazo) appears a decade later in a government investigation into witchcraft (*hechizos*), in which he was apparently the target of other Spaniards (AGI, Filipinas, 85, N.93/25-7-1642).

along—and stayed—were attached and loyal to the missionaries, not to the Spanish troops. Despite being outnumbered, abandoned, and outmaneuvered, they stayed because the missionaries stayed, an act of allegiance that again underlines the close ties and the trust that had already developed between the Lumads and the Recoletos.

CHAPTER 4

TREACHERY MOST FOUL:
MARÍA CAMPAN AND THE
CARAGA REVOLT OF 1631

The inhabitants of Caraga revolted, as I stated in my last dispatch, after killing the captain and commander, with twenty soldiers, in an expedition that he made. Thinking that they could gain the fort with that force, they came to it, but it did not fall out as they imagined. The greater part of the province rose, and killed four discalced Recollect religious. A severe punishment was inflicted on them in the month of September; and recently, in the month of May just passed, another fleet went there to punish and reduce them. I trust, our Lord helping, that they will remain quiet, although they are not Christians; for there is little confidence to be placed in them.

> —Report by Governor General Juan Niño de Tabora, in Manila,
> to Philip IV of Spain, dated July 1632[1]

Early in the first mission period in Mindanao, specifically in early July of 1631, a year before the above letter was dispatched, a little appreciated Lumad "insurrection" erupted among a group of disgruntled Karaga[2] converts in the eastern coastal region of Mindanao. Its flashpoint was the Spanish fort of Tandag, where approximately one hundred Spanish soldiers were garrisoned. Four Recoletos, the *alcalde mayor* (chief magistrate), and a score of Spanish troops were killed as the rebels attempted to rally fellow Lumads to their side. The rumored arrival of Magindanaw warriors on a fleet of *prahus* on the coast, waiting to massacre any Christian loyalists, further fueled the drama as it unfolded over two uncertain, agonizing weeks. All the main conspirators were elite male converts who had fought against the Moros under the banner of Spain, and they set off an unprecedented series of events by manipulating the familiarity and extensive social relationships that had developed between Lumads and Spaniards over a decade of continuous mission work by the Recoletos. As noted previously, there had already been smaller incidents of individual resistance among the Lumad, not least among the Karaga; this revolt would not be the last. But the Caraga Revolt is notable for being the first

---

[1] Emma Blair and James Robertson, *The Philippine Islands, 1493–1898*, vol. 24 (Cleveland, OH: Arthur H. Clark Company, 1903–1909), pp. 216–17. This constitutes the official report to the king of Spain about the revolt in Caraga.

[2] I use the term "Karaga" in reference to ethnicity, and "Caraga" as the place name. The spelling variations themselves have no inherent significance, although the latter has been consistently used as a place name for the same general region from the Spanish colonial period to the present.

large-scale, and therefore the bloodiest, anti-Spanish uprising on record initiated by Lumad peoples. Contrary to the characterization in the governor general's letter, this was also the first to be organized and led by indigenous converts to Christianity.

In this chapter, I review reports about the revolt for glimpses into Karaga life during this period, and into the uneven but nonetheless socially intimate relationship between the Lumads and the missionaries. I discuss the ways in which the revolt was framed in the archival record, arguing that, despite the Recoleto obsession with the anti-Christian elements of the revolt, the response of the Karaga and natives is compelling proof of the early evolution of a significant missionary-centered—and therefore Christian, even if only nominally—identity among the Lumads. I also explore the impact of gender on this complex relationship through the reported actions during the revolt of a Lumad Christian woman named María Campan, and the Iberian hysteria that followed in response.

The daughter of long-term converts and one of the local elites, or *principales*, María Campan was one of only a handful of Lumad individuals—and the solitary woman—mentioned by name in the official inquest that was conducted a year later. Though she was a minor participant in the revolt, her crimes were allotted their own special hearing, given separate consideration, and assigned the same gravity as the homicidal acts of the men who actually instigated the revolt. Her supposedly heinous crime amounted to wearing the vestments of a murdered priest in the course of a mock Mass that was staged by the revolt's primary conspirator, her cousin the *datu* Mangabo. When framed within the context of more widespread and undeniably bloodier acts by other, male Karaga converts, the Spanish, and Religious, obsession with María Campan's acts appears to be entirely disproportionate. Upon closer analysis, however, it becomes clear that the Iberian response grew out of profoundly gendered expectations regarding piety and propriety. From this perspective, María Campan's actions would have been a shocking transgression of deeply entrenched Spanish sexual and religious boundaries, boundaries that were, in all likelihood, culturally invisible to the Lumad.

María Campan's later reentry into the Christian fold, following the ultimately unsuccessful revolt, along with Mangabo and others, also speaks to the complex intimacy of the missionary-convert relationship, revealing a relationship held in constant tension by the risk of betrayal and the promise of forgiveness. This relationship reflects the dual nature of conversion, in terms of how the missionaries were, in turn, converted culturally and socially by the Lumad, to the extent that the Spanish missionaries, troops, and other *colonialistas* had come to see the Lumad converts as trusted allies around whom one could lower one's defenses.

FLASHPOINTS

The Spanish fortification at Tandag, named after Saint Joseph, also referred to as the *presidio* of Caraga, was first built on the eastern coastline of Mindanao in 1609. It would undergo several incarnations as it was destroyed and rebuilt over the course of the Spanish colonial period. Its original function was reportedly "not to curtail the Moros, but the very coastal tribes who were fierce and warlike and could ill endure to be subjected to Spain,"[3] and, most likely, to curb Karaga piracy as well. In its

---

[3] Peter Schreurs MSC, *Caraga Antigua 1521–1910: The Hispanization and Christianization of Agusan, Surigao, and East Davao* (Cebu: University of San Carlos Publications, 1989), p. 97,

original form, the fort was most likely built of wood, and then, later, coral "stone."[4] By the time the Recoletos arrived in the 1620s, it was expressly maintained as a deterrent against Moro raiding, and for this purpose was garrisoned with two companies—one of Spanish infantry, and a second one of Kapampangans from southern Luzon island. An accounting undertaken by Governor General Sebastián Hurtado de Corcuera tells us that, in 1635, the Spanish company consisted of a captain, an ensign, a sergeant, four more noncommissioned officers, and forty-five infantry soldiers.[5] Presumably the Kapampangan company comprised a similar number. This would mean that Spain's strategic interests in Caraga, including the Recoleto mission and its converts, were protected by a little over one hundred men, all of whom had to be provisioned with food and lodging. These same troops spent every single day in what were no doubt rough, isolated conditions, far from home and surrounded by culturally incomprehensible *indios*—a thankless job performed for very little pay. Far more than racism, this daily social friction was, I believe, the primary cause of the abuses and other misbehavior routinely attributed to Spanish troops in the outer reaches of the colony. This was the military context of Caraga, through which the Karaga world articulated with the Spanish.

For a reportedly hostile area, the number of Spanish troops garrisoned at Tandag seems rather small when compared to manned fortifications elsewhere in Filipinas. According to the same report by Corcuera, the Spanish company in the port of Cavite had seventy soldiers, while the four infantry companies of Manila had an

---

citing Luis de Jesus OAR, *Historia general de los religiosos descalzos* (Madrid, 1681), and pp. 117–19.

[4] Such "stone" buildings were actually made from coral lime construction, which used coral lime, made from burned coral, to bind large coral blocks (i.e., the "stones") together. Unlike typical stone, dead coral is soft enough to be shaped with a machete or similar implement. A variation of this method, for solid wall construction, involved mixing the lime with sand. I do not know where this technology originated, but by the nineteenth century, it was the method preferred by European missionaries in the eastern Pacific islands for the construction of churches. See Maretu and Marjorie Tuainekore Crocombe, *Cannibals and Converts: Radical Change in the Cook Islands* (Suva, Fiji: Institute of Pacific Studies, University of the South Pacific, 1983), pp. 92–93; R. G. Crocombe and Marjorie Crocombe, eds., *The Works of Ta'unga: Records of a Polynesian Traveller in the South Seas, 1833–1896* (Honolulu, HI: University of Hawaii Press, 1968), p. 120, n. 14; and John L. Fischer, *The Eastern Carolines* (New Haven, CT: Human Relations Area Files, 1970), pp. 104–05.

[5] These numbers are from Blair and Robertson, *The Philippine Islands*, vol. 26, pp. 304–13. It is part of a detailed 1636 report by Corcuera to the Spanish king about the collection of alms from the troops to help maintain the military hospitals in Manila, as the treasury office was experiencing funding difficulties due to the Crown's own financial constraints. The original document is not identified except by the notation that it is a manuscript in the Archivo General de Indias in Sevilla, Spain (p. 314). In the report on Tandag (p. 309), the infantry is explicitly listed as "Spanish infantry," and no accounting made for the Kapampangans, presumably because the alms were collected only from Spaniards in this particular situation. However, the importance of providing proper accommodations in Manila for ailing soldiers "of the Pampanga nation" was raised as an issue in the letter, indicating the importance of Kapampangans as supplemental colonial forces very early on in the Spanish colonial period. The translated report also uses the term *alférez*, which is translated into English as "ensign" in the Spanish dictionaries, though I have also seen the term "second-lieutenant" used. I use the term "noncommissioned officers" in place of "minor posts" because in earlier parts of the same document, the phrase "posts below the commissioned officers" is used, yet these soldiers were obviously not ranked as privates. Coincidentally, also mentioned in this report is Lorenzo de Olaso, *maestre de campo* of Manila, who is mentioned in chapter three of this volume. On p. 305 of *The Philippine Islands*, he is listed as heading a company of 107 soldiers.

average of one hundred soldiers each. The *presidio* of Zamboanga was manned by three companies totaling two hundred and ten soldiers, and Terrenate had six companies with about eighty soldiers each.[6] Only the *presidio* of Zibu (Cebu), being the oldest Spanish settlement in the islands and colonial Spain's center of commerce and administration in the central and southern parts of the archipelago, had troop numbers comparable to Caraga's: one company with "about" fifty soldiers.[7] The main contrast between Caraga and Zibu, of course, is that Zibu, with its long history of colonial accommodation and a highly incorporated and therefore more Hispanized native population, was quite possibly the most politically subdued spot in the whole of the colony, especially with regard to the potential for unrest.

The Tandag fort was finally destroyed a century and a half after the Caraga revolt, after a four-month siege in 1754 mounted by the Magindanaw, which ended in a near-total massacre of the fort's occupants, with the few survivors, including one Recoleto missionary, taken into slavery. It was rebuilt a year later under the auspices of the Jesuit Father Ducós. Whereas the fort was previously staffed by a company of Spaniards and one of Kapampangans from southern Luzon, the rebuilt Tandag fort was staffed by "a garrison of one hundred Boholanos" from the central Visayas region. Again, this number implies that one hundred was the traditional number of soldiers assigned to Tandag, but the record implies that the Boholano troops were more skilled and disciplined than the Kapampangans, or even the Spaniards. The Jesuits reported that, after the Boholanos took over, "in subsequent years, the Moros returned and attacked the fort ... but each time, the Boholano garrison sent them away."[8]

Even more significant to our story are the *convento* (residence) of the Recoletos in Tandag, located about half a *legua* from the garrison, and their *capilla* (chapel) located in Tago, two *leguas* from Tandag.[9] These Recoleto buildings were secondary flashpoints in the revolt, the targets to which Mangabo and his men turned their attention after the initial attack on the fort. Proceeding to Tago, the revolt grew in momentum and, for a brief period, appeared on the verge of spilling over into other Lumad population groups.

The *capillas* and the *convento* were, like the fort, constructed primarily of coral "stone," with additional wood and *nipa* palm leaves, and like the fort, they were built and rebuilt over the centuries. What is notable here is that the Recoleto buildings were located not inside the walls of the fortification but far outside them. They were strategically placed not only to be closer to where the Karaga, converts and non-

---

[6] See Blair and Robertson, *The Philippine Islands*, vol. 26, pp. 291–313.

[7] Ibid., p. 307.

[8] Miguel Bernad SJ, *The Great Island: Studies in the Exploration and Evangelization of Mindanao* (Quezon City: Ateneo de Manila University Press, 2004), pp. 76–77. Bohol was also the island to which, a century and a half earlier, the Jesuit missionaries relocated the very first Lumad converts after they closed their mission in Butuan. The migration of Boholano Christians to northern Mindanao continued all through the remainder of the Spanish period and well into the twentieth century, and the majority of northeast Mindanao's lowland settler population came from this small Visayan island prior to World War II.

[9] At that time, a *legua* was the equivalent of approximately 2.6 miles, or a little over four kilometers. According to the official testimonies quoted below, the church in Tago was two *leguas* away (Archivo Provincial de los Agustinos Recoletos in Marcilla [ARM] leg 1, num 2, doc 2, f4r). For the record, there was also a *capilla* at Tandag, but it was located within the fortification. Unlike the *capilla* in Tago and the *convento* in Tandag, it does not figure prominently in the events in question, except that it was also duly sacked.

converts alike, lived, but also to remain separate from the intimidating atmosphere of an occupying army, so that the Recoletos and their Lumad parishioners could live in relative tranquility, in the manner of a *reducción*.[10] As explained in chapter two, the local mission system was not as integrated as its contemporary in the Spanish Americas, but the looser mission network in Mindanao was nevertheless effective. Even frontier outposts like Tandag and Tago were important sites not just of religious conversion but of social reproduction, places where the Spanish, colonial, Catholic, and indigenous Lumad worlds converged and were defined and renegotiated on a daily basis through social interaction.

While we do not have statistics specifically for 1631, we know that in the subsequent decade there were approximately three thousand "souls" counted by the mission and served through the *cabecera,* or mission center, in Tandag proper, and an additional five *visitas* or annexed villages.[11] That is, there were three thousand adults recognized and "served" by the mission, and who were presumably subject to tribute. With children and other individuals factored in, the total population would have been considerably larger, perhaps almost five times as large, though not all of them would have been Lumad. The revolt narratives reveal that there were non-Lumad people living in Tandag as well, including *indios* from other parts of Filipinas and Chinese immigrants. We can presume quite safely that this population size would have been more or less constant over the decades, because recurring troubles with Moro raiders, tribute collection, and misbehaving Spanish troops meant that people within a lowland *reducción* were likely to flee for the hills time and again for refuge. The normally anticipated "natural" growth of a stable population, and its accompanying increases in terms of food production, trade, construction, and local administration, would not have materialized under such unpredictable circumstances.

The figure of three thousand "souls" being served in the Tandag area a decade after the revolt of 1631 may well have represented a population still in recovery. In fact, the Spaniards had to deal with the revolt's aftermath for several more years, with pockets of resistance flaring up until as late as 1636. Over a decade later, in 1646, the Caraga Revolt was apparently still so fresh in local memory that it was cited in correspondence to the king in a political feud between the Recoletos and the standing *alcalde mayor*. The feud culminated in demolition of both the *capilla* and the *convento* of Tandag in 1647, for the reason that they were nearly impossible to protect due to their considerable distance from the *presidio*, making them an easy target for potential Dutch invaders,[12] Moros, and Lumad malcontents, and therefore a major

---

[10] See Schreurs, *Caraga Antigua*, p. 133. As previously mentioned in chapters one and two, a *reducción* was simply a settlement of Christianized *indios.* Contrary to popular Philippine imagination, it was not a sort of concentration camp in which natives were policed and forced to live against their will. It appears to be regularly confused with the highly unpopular American colonial practice of forced resettlement known locally as "hamletting," which was used against *insurrectos* in the Philippine-American War (or the "Philippine Insurrection" to Americans). "Hamletting" was also employed postcolonially—with equal unpopularity—by the Philippine military as a counterinsurgency tactic.

[11] Blair and Robertson, *The Philippine Islands*, vol. 36, pp. 114–18, "The convent of Tándag, in the province of Carágha of the Philipinas Islands, is demolished," which is based on de Jesus, *Historia General*, Decada VII, Lib. 1, Cap. 1, Sec. II, Num. 232.

[12] Spain and the Netherlands were in the midst of the Eighty Years' War (1568–1648) at this time. Peter Schreurs also suggests that the Dutch in Batavia (now Jakarta) had seriously

security risk. The details of this feud are not so relevant here as are its consequences some years later. The demolition of the Recoleto buildings was opposed, naturally, by the *prior* of Tandag, the Philippine-born P. Fr. Pedro de San Joseph, who argued that the missionaries' presence, symbolized by *capilla* and *convento*, was the only thing preventing the Karagas from backsliding (going *remontado*) and therefore the key to keeping them in vassalage to Spain. In fact, fears of another general uprising like the Caraga Revolt persisted for decades, and some years after the politically motivated demolition of the *capilla* and *convento*, the Recoletos themselves were mistakenly censured by the Crown for reportedly inciting, through their protestations, the 1651 uprising in Linao led by a Manobo *datu* named Dabaw.[13] Though the Recoletos were later vindicated, the controversy surrounding the demolition orders underlines both the traumatic impression left by the Caraga Revolt, and the intimacy of the Lumad–Recoleto bond, such that the Crown thought it reasonable, however mistaken in the end, that the protestations of one would incite unrest against Spain in the other.

Within the context of the Caraga revolt, this social intimacy between the Lumad and the Recoletos meant that, despite the relatively short period of contact and the glaring deficiency of Spanish military power in this pericolonial area, Lumad identification with Christianity was ultimately proven to be strong enough to withstand a real crisis. While the revolt was successful in its initial stages, it was stopped cold by the refusal of the majority of Lumads to make a definitive break with the Religious. Neither the grave threat of a massive Moro attack, in which no Christian would be spared, nor filial piety or social obligation were enough to turn the majority of Karagas against the missionaries. Far from confirming our image of the Lumadnon as steadfastly non-Christian tribes that resisted foreign influence, this series of events shows how strongly their ancestors were connected to Christianity, through its missionaries, centuries before the islands would become a Catholic majority state.

A Fierce People

Spanish contact with the Karaga of eastern Mindanao began quite early, perhaps as early as the ill-fated Loaisa expedition in 1526, survivors of which were found two years later by the Saavedra expedition to be living among the *mandaya*, or upriver-dwellers, there.[14] In 1609, the construction of the Tandag fort gave Spain a toehold in the eastern side of the island. The Karaga were well-known to the Spaniards by then, and were for a long time lumped together with the Magindanaw: as "Caragas Moros," they were attacked by Spanish troops in retaliation for the 1603 kidnapping of the Jesuit missionary Melchor Hurtado from the nearby island of Leyte. Despite

---

considered aiding the Moros in various plots to remove the Spaniards from Mindanao. See Schreurs, *Caraga Antigua*, p. 147.

[13] Blair and Robertson, *The Philippine Islands*, vol. 36, pp. 114–26, taken from de Jesus, *Historia General*, Decada VII, Lib. 1, Cap. 1, Sec. II-III, Num. 233–242. Fray Pedro de San Joseph is reported on p. 126 as having been born in Manila in 1621, and was therefore classified as a *Filipino*, according to the original definition of the word, by the Spanish colonial government. He was only in his early thirties during the events in question, and died from illness a few years later. Such a short life was typical of Recoleto missionaries in the first mission period. The Linao uprising is mentioned in greater detail in chapter two, this volume.

[14] See Schreurs, *Caraga Antigua*, p. 46.

their reputation for bellicosity, however, the Karaga "avoided all battle and absconded in the jungle," which was the standard defensive procedure among the Lumad of Mindanao for most of known history.[15] In 1613, several hundred Karagas—who at the time regularly engaged in the same raiding behavior as the Moros—attacked the Spanish fort at Tandag, which remained standing thanks only to the timely arrival of Spanish reinforcements by sea.[16] A retaliatory raid against the Karaga was conducted the following year, during which Spanish forces liberated several Visayan slaves and, it seems, crushed the prospect of further attacks by the Karaga.[17]

Just one generation later, by the time of the revolt in 1631, the Recoletos had formed relationships with and converted many of the Karaga *datus*. The conversion of the Karaga is a significant development because, in sharp contrast to the relatively painless conversion of the Kagayanon discussed in the previous chapter, *datus* among the Karaga initially reacted to the missionary presence with both violence and avoidance, some instances of which were reviewed in chapter two. The Caraga revolt was, in the minds of the Recoletos, simply a major blip in that already bloody history. It is remarkable, therefore, that by the middle of the seventeenth century, the Recoleto chronicler Diego de Santa Theresa would state that, like their other success story, the mission in the Cagayán district of Misamis, the Caraga mission area "ought to be considered as the rose among the thorns."[18]

Still, the beginning of this relationship was nothing if not inauspicious. There are many possible reasons why the Karaga responded so violently to the missionary presence at first, including the lack of any strategic security interest for the Karagas in forming an alliance with what surely appeared to be disorganized and powerless interlopers. After all, they already had powerful, if sometimes troublesome, allies in the Magindanaw. Unlike the Kagayanon, the Karaga had a very different relationship with the Magindanaw: they were more involved as political allies, and were routinely involved in Moro raiding on the Visayas islands. The Karaga were geographically divided from Magindanaw proper by the greater half of Mindanao's land mass, and by a buffer zone of mountain ranges populated by other, mutually hostile Lumad groups. The Magindanaw and other Moros were nevertheless highly mobile, especially by sea, and they could communicate with their Karaga allies as effectively as they could pilot their boats.

The Karaga were characterized by a deeply ingrained suspicion and mistrust of outsiders, which is not surprising among people engaged in frequent raiding. While there may be some debate about whether such an attitude is the cause or the end result of frequent aggression, it is undeniable that war and mistrust feed on each other.[19] Frequent warfare and the socialization of mistrust both characterized Karaga

---

[15] Ibid., p. 110. See also Horacio de la Costa SJ, *The Jesuits in the Philippines* (Cambridge, MA: Harvard University Press, 1961), pp. 294 *passim*.

[16] Francis Madigan SJ, "The Early History of Cagayan de Oro," *Philippine Studies* 11,1 (1963): 82.

[17] Schreurs, *Caraga Antigua*, p. 118.

[18] Blair and Robertson, *The Philippine Islands*, vol. 36, p. 174–75, which is based on de Jesus, *Historia General*, Decada VII, Lib. 1, Cap. 2, Sec. III, Num. 738.

[19] See Reed L. Wadley, "Lethal Treachery and the Imbalance of Power in Warfare and Feuding," *Journal of Anthropological Research* 59,4, (2003): 531–54. See also Azar Gat, "The Pattern of Fighting in Simple, Small-Scale, Prestate Societies," *Journal of Anthropological Research* 55 (1999): 563–83; Jonathan Haas, ed., *The Anthropology of War* (New York, NY:

society. In his account of the conversion of the Kagayanon, Madigan distinguishes them from the Karaga on the basis of character, drawing from the Recoleto *Crónicas*, which describes the Karaga as having a propensity for violence:

> Intertribal relations [among the Kagayanon] were not characterized by the frequent wars typical, according to the Recollect chronicler, of Caragan societies, where the same sources relate that waging war on the slightest pretext was "the chief interest and concern," and where family feuding was also rife. The beheading of captives, which the Recollects describe as almost a popular sport in Caraga, was relatively rare in Cagayan. There is no evidence that the [Kagayanon] made use of poisoned food and drink against associates and enemies, although the Recollects state this was common in Caraga because the women were even more passionate and vengeful than their fierce spouses and quick to have recourse to this weapon in their anger.[20]

This impression of the Karaga propensity for violence was enhanced by the fact that, as mentioned in the previous chapters, at least two Recoleto missionaries and numerous soldiers were murdered by Karagas during early Spanish attempts at contact. The use of treachery in some of these murders further fed the stereotype of the Karagas as being pathologically "fierce." In one case from 1624, a group of "friendly" Karagas reportedly lured P. Fr. Juan de San Nicolás, featured in the previous chapter, and attempted to drown him.[21] Such was their reputation that the Karagas were feared by Lumad warriors and Spanish troops alike. But like other groups historically or ethnographically notorious for "fierceness," the Karagas no doubt relied primarily on their reputation—more than actual violence—to intimidate and hold back their enemies.[22]

But the Karaga were eventually won over. In 1622, *datu* Inuc of Marihatag—then regarded as the "foremost problem" of the Caraga mission—made a surprise move, on his own initiative, to make peace with the missionaries.[23] According to the

---

Cambridge University Press, 1990); Jonathan Haas and Winifred Creamer, "Warfare among the Pueblos: Myth, History, and Ethnography," *Ethnohistory* 44,2 (1997): 235–62; and Steven Leblanc, *Prehistoric Warfare in the American Southwest* (Salt Lake City, UT: University of Utah Press, 1999).

[20] Madigan, "The Early History of Cagayan de Oro," pp. 94–95.

[21] Schreurs, *Caraga Antigua*, p. 138, wrote that in 1624 Fray Juan de San Nicolás was drowned by the natives of Gigaquit. Yet from the previous chapter, we know that this particular Recoleto lived until 1647 and died in Cagayán. The Recoleto catalogue mentions another missionary with an identical name who served in Mindanao two centuries later, in the nineteenth century, who was, indeed, successfully drowned by locals in Gigaquit. Schreurs appears to have confused the two men in his book. Francisco Sábada del Carmen OAR, *Catálogo de los Religiosos Agustinos Recoletos de San Nicolás de Tolentino desde el Año 1606 en que Llegó la Primera Misión á Manila, hasta Nuestros Días* (Madrid: Imprenta del Asilo de Huérfanos del Sagrado Corazón de Jesús, 1906), pp. 79, 746.

[22] Schreurs, *Caraga Antigua*, pp. 117, 132.

[23] Ibid., p. 117, following Colín, spells it Hinoc (with a silent initial /h/). Francisco Colín SJ, *Labor Evangélica, Ministerios Apostólicos de Obreros de la Compañia de Jesús, Fundación, y Progresos de su Provincia en las Islas Filipinas* (Madrid: Joseph Fernandez Buendia, 1663). Readers struck by the resemblance of Inuc/Inuk to the biblical name Enoch may think that this indicates an even more far-reaching Christian/Western influence. But as the late Fr. Schreurs was fond of saying, it would be "more pious than historically probable." Schreurs, *Caraga Antigua*, p. 136.

mission history compiled by P. Fr. Luis de Jesus, the turn of events was nothing short of miraculous:

> Fray Juan de la Madre de Dios [newly arrived in Tandag], after preparing himself by fasting and praying, decided to subdue [Inuc] with no other help than his confidence in God. He went to see him, all alone. Even Inuc himself was astonished at the boldness of this Religious who dared to come in his presence. Fray Juan talked to him so beautifully and with such fervor ... that the tyrant started to like him very much.[24]

This event seems truly remarkable until we recall that the terrible Inuc was first mentioned joining Moro attacks on the Visayas in the first decade of the seventeenth century. By the time the Recoletos arrived in Caraga, therefore, Inuc was now twenty years older, and likely past his prime as a fierce warrior and sea-raider. After Inuc's conversion, a public affair that took place in the church of Tandag,[25] the Karagas slowly became allies of Spain in a general sense, though the Caraga Revolt would prove that their sense of loyalty revolved mainly around the missionaries.

This unlikely alliance manifested itself in the involvement of Karaga warriors in pre-emptive Spanish raids against their former friends the Magindanaw Moros. Spanish troops, Karaga men, and Recoleto missionaries thus regularly worked side by side on these missions.

> Here the Spaniards are accustomed to carrying out sorties from the fort [in Tandag] with the *principales indios* of Karaga, and capturing those they can, thus scaring them and keeping them at bay. And many of the captives are baptized and receive our Holy Faith. On these expeditions a Religious always goes as chaplain, so that nothing illicit takes place, and also to determine along the way whether any of those barbaric people might be disposed to letting us preach the Gospel and teach the Christian doctrines ... [26]

It was in the course of this type of regular military cooperation that Lumad warriors—including the Karagas who organized the Caraga Revolt—witnessed signs of incompetence and lack of discipline among Spanish troops, and their repeated losses at the hands of the Magindanaw Moros. If Lumad warriors had ever been under any illusions of Iberian superiority, those illusions would have been permanently shattered by events such as the embarrassing retreat of Lorenzo Olaso's raiding party, described in the previous chapter. According to the Recoletos, it was

---

In the colonial period, there once was also a Magindanaw named "Inok, a war leader of Datu Piang," which suggests strongly that the name was not only fashionable for a warrior but also indigenous to Mindanao. Carmen A. Abubakar, "Wither the Roses of Yesteryears: An Exploratory Look into the Lives of Moro Women During the Colonial Period," in *More Pinay Than We Admit: The Social Construction of the Filipina*, ed. Ma. Luisa Camagay (Quezon City: Vibal, 2010), p. 12.

[24] Schreurs, *Caraga Antigua*, p. 136, citing de Jesus, *Historia*, p. 33.

[25] Schreurs, *Caraga Antigua*, p. 137.

[26] *Relación vreve de el alevoso levantamiento de los indios de Caraga, en las Philipinas*, MS 3828 (Biblioteca Nacional, Madrid, 1632), p. 213r. Cited hereafter as "BN 3828."

this type of disappointment with the weakness of their colonial masters that fostered discontent among the Karaga warriors.[27]

To be precise, the more socially dominant Karaga *datus*, like Mangabo, had apparently grown deeply dissatisfied by their experiences with Spanish troops, which were characterized by such frustrating and unprofitable failures as the Olaso debacle, that they could no longer see the point of participating in Spanish warfare. Up to this point, they had been treated like professional paramilitary troops and were expected to follow orders from the Spanish chain of command, like good European soldiers. However, given that Mangabo and his peers were warriors whose sense of identity was linked to supernatural ideas about male prowess, and given that their own relatively conditional leadership positions would have relied on the satisfaction and allegiance of other warriors within their own *sacups*, the embarrassing conditions that typified their collaboration with the Spanish military would have become unworkable before too long.

ON SEVERAL SERIOUS CRIMES COMMITTED IN CARAGA

Almost four centuries later, there are few contemporary primary sources remaining that describe the Caraga Revolt in detail.[28] One valuable source is a compilation of different eyewitness narratives centering on a first-person account written by Siargao-based P. Fr. Lorenzo de San Facundo, who was taken prisoner by the rebels and later released, unharmed, by Mangabo.[29] This compelling narrative, which can be found in the Biblioteca Nacional in Madrid, Spain, has already been extensively used, nearly verbatim, by the historian Peter Schreurs, who translated large sections of the document for his evangelical history of eastern Mindanao.[30] I do not wish to duplicate his efforts here except to focus on what some of the secondary details in this narrative do tell us regarding the Karaga world in the first mission period, as seen through William Henry Scott's proverbial cracks in the parchment curtain.[31]

---

[27] See also Schreurs, *Caraga Antigua*, p. 146.

[28] In this section, I draw on two of only three known primary—and contemporary—sources that deal with what is generally referred to in the archival record as "*la sublevación de Caraga*." The third document, which is closely comparable to BN 3828, is in the Archivo Histórico Nacional under the title *Informe sobre varios crimenes cometidos en [la] provincia de Caraga*, and filed as <AHN Diversos-colecciones,26,N.62>, and available online via PARES (*Portal de los Archivos Españoles*) at http://pares.mcu.es, under the reference code ES.28079.AHN/5.1.11/ /DIVERSOS-COLECCIONES,26,N.62. The original *signatura* of this AHN document was <Diversos-documentos_Indias,N.320>.

[29] See BN 3828. This account, *Relación vreve de el alevoso levantamiento de los indios de Caraga, en las Philipinas*, or "Brief account of the treacherous uprising of the indians of Caraga, in the Philippines," also includes an introduction and a concluding section synthesized from the accounts of other eyewitnesses. My copy of the document is of uneven quality, and for my own translation I relied heavily on the transcription by the Spanish historian Fernando Palanca Aguado, which was provided to me by the Recoleto archivist P. Fr. José Manuel Bengoa at the ARM, in Marcilla. There is no author designated for BN 3828. Given that there are no signatures or other authenticating marks, it is definitely a duplicate prepared by a copyist, and not the original report written by San Facundo and/or the other witnesses.

[30] See Schreurs, *Caraga Antigua*, pp. 145–63.

[31] Schreurs's translation of BN 3828 is excellent, but unless otherwise indicated I am working primarily from my own translation. See also William Henry Scott, *Cracks in the Parchment Curtain and Other Essays in Philippine History* (Quezon City: New Day Publishers, 1982).

The prelude to Fray Lorenzo de San Facundo's account was written separately, and appears to be based on information compiled from five sworn witnesses who had traveled from Caraga to Manila to be deposed, one year after the events in question.[32] In the document, the underlying cause of the revolt is identified as Spanish military incompetence, particularly the soldiers' failure to suppress the Moros, as witnessed with dismay by the Karaga and other Lumad warriors who joined Spanish troops on the sorts of expeditions described in the previous chapter. A specific reference is made to a fruitless expedition involving three hundred Karagas fighting alongside Spaniards in Jolo in 1629 that, from the Karaga perspective, must have seemed pointless. After this incident, a group of disgruntled Karaga *principales* reportedly sent a representative, a *datu* from the Tago river area named Manaral, to coordinate with Sultan Kudarat on a plot to remove the Spaniards, including the missionaries, from Caraga. And so in Caraga the Lumads began to prepare by taking note of security at the fort of Tandag, amassing weapons, building *caracoas* or war boats, and covertly "working on the feelings" of the local people. They were also visited during that time by a *kachil* (Moro nobleman) who read the Qur'an, verses from which were "written on the trees and on the sterns of the ships." Spanish attention was aroused by an unusual amount of boat-building, and suspicions grew especially after "all the people along the Tago river suddenly disappeared for no apparent reason." Spain thus began to undertake preemptive raids on several trouble spots all across the region, headed by a newly assigned commanding officer, *Capitán* Pedro Bautista,[33] who was apparently so cruel that he only made things worse. Little did the Spaniards know that their own Lumad troops were part of the larger conspiracy, and that these troops often warned their co-conspirators ahead of time that the Spanish were coming.[34]

On July 4, 1631, Bautista and nine Spaniards from the infantry of Tandag set off by boat from Tandag to make "*mangayao*," or conduct a raid, on Baganga to the south, in what is now Davao Oriental province, bordering on territory then recognized as belonging to the Magindanaw. The use of the indigenous term *mangayao* in the Spanish document indicates to me that the Spaniards had accommodated at least a few local, Lumad ideas about small-scale warfare, probably to enhance the recruitment of local warriors. They likely understood what motivated these men to engage in battle, and thus were able to attract skilled fighters to fight under the banner of Spain. The *mangayao* party that day included Fray Jacinto de Jesús María, from the church in Tago, and several high-status local Karaga men, all of whom are named in the record: Mangabo, Opan, Adia, Osor, Pixin, Dumblag, Balintos, Samal, Dana, Dolocan, Bicoy, Gumban, and Banuy, "the grandson of Ynu."[35] The journey to Baganga took over a week, and afterwards Dumblag, one of the Karaga *datu*, surreptitiously released the few Baganga men they had captured in the raid. On July 13, as the raiding party made its way back to Tandag, *Capitán* Bautista placed *datu* Dumblag under arrest for disobeying orders, and had him shackled, treating him like a common captive. Dumblag's humiliation caused

---

[32] BN 3828, p. 216v.

[33] His name is spelled "Baptista" in BN 3828.

[34] BN3828, p. 213v.

[35] This is most likely a reference to the *datu* Inuc mentioned in chapter two and the previous section of this chapter.

Balintos and the other Karaga warriors to turn on the Spaniards, killing every last one, including Fray Jacinto. The revolt had then begun in earnest.[36]

The next day Balintos, Mangabo, and the other Karagas quietly made their way back to Tago, and proceeded to engage in three days of "drunkenness and foolishness,"[37] during which Mangabo invited the people of Tago to a Mass in the *capilla* by "*Padre* Mangabo." On July 18, the people gathered at Fray Jacinto's church, and they saw a Karaga woman known as María Campan wearing the dead priest's vestments, sprinkling holy water on the crowd, declaring "I am Father Jacinto." They also saw Mangabo tear the arms off a figure of the crucified Jesus, taunting it to "make yourself brave like me."[38] With a *valarao*,[39] Mangabo then sliced the statue's face in half. Other Christ figures were also defaced and desecrated, and the church itself completely looted and vandalized. A boy from Abucay named Diego Salingat, Fray Jacinto's *criado*, or domestic servant, was also murdered.

Those who had taken part in the attack returned the next day to their respective communities, intending to pillage the whole of the Caraga coast and kill every Spaniard they managed to get their hands on. They also agreed to spread the word that they had been sent by Kudarat, and to say that he was already waiting offshore with three hundred *prahus*, and "if they wanted to be [Kudarat's] friends, they could prove it by killing all the Spaniards and the Religious. If not, then they would see how harsh he could be." A Christian boy named Thomasillo, who had apparently run all the way from Tago, alerted the Tandag garrison that Mangabo was coming to make *mangayao*, and reported on what had befallen Capitán Bautista's party after Baganga. With part of its infantry lying dead many miles away to the south, the garrison was ill-equipped to respond to the assault, so the soldiers fired off a mortar round in a vain attempt to warn the *convento*, which was about a mile away. Mangabo himself entered *convento* of Tandag in the middle of the night and murdered the two Religious there, P. Fr. Juan de Santo Tomás and P. Fr. Alonso de San Joseph, and their *criado*, a boy named Ventura, in their sleep. Others were taken hostage, and the *convento* set on fire. The troops still remaining at the fort of Tandag locked themselves in for their own protection.[40]

Meanwhile, Balintos and other high-status Karaga men set out for the island of Siargao, off the northeastern tip of Mindanao, in eleven boats. Siargao then had three main settlements. The first, Cabontog, had five hundred tribute payers, and Balintos's crew took many of them captive, killing the one man who dared to fight them. But at the next settlement, the *maestre de campo*, Diego Tirres, who also happened to be the brother-in-law of Mangabo, refused to let the rebels pass. To obtain the title of *maestre de campo*, Diego Tirres, probably a native of Mindanao or Siargao who had taken a Spanish name, would have had to distinguish himself in service to the Spanish crown. Clearly Tirres' title was well-deserved, considering the potentially serious consequences of refusing to join his relatives in the revolt.

---

[36] BN 3828, pp. 213v–214r.

[37] Ibid., "*borracheras y magaduras*," p. 214r.

[38] Ibid., "*Hazte baliente como yo*," p. 214r.

[39] The *valarao*, or *balaraw*, is a style of dagger indigenous to the Philippines.

[40] BN 3828, p. 214r–214v.

Balintos learned that the parish priest, Fray Lorenzo de San Facundo, had departed for Bacuag just two days before in a *barangay*[41] "that had been built by Tagpito," so the rebels went off to Bacuag to find him. Another *datu* named Manangalan intercepted the parish priest of Abucay,[42] Fray Pedro de San Antonio, who was preparing to leave for Cebu, killing him and taking all his clothes. Meanwhile, Mangabo's son, Zancalan, went to what is now Cantilan, where he and his forces killed four more Spanish soldiers, bringing the death toll at this point to eighteen Spaniards, including the four Recoletos. We also know of two *indio* servants who were slaughtered, with an untold number of other *indios* either killed, injured, or taken captive.[43]

Looking past the violence for a moment, we can see that Caraga was already quite an interesting world at the time. Men from the *principalia* of different Karaga communities interacted regularly with one another on Spanish military expeditions, with the Tandag garrison as their common ground. With the Tandag fort's official expeditions framed as *mangayao*, many *principales* from all over the Karaga area were, for a time, successfully motivated to fight for a Spanish military agenda that none of them may have really cared about. There are also quite a few indigenous residents mentioned by name, occupation, origin, and, in some cases, by kinship ties, in the San Facundo narrative, indicating a considerable degree of social familiarity between the Recoletos and the Lumads involved in the events. The casual use of indigenous terminology in the report (*barangay, valarao, mangayao, ylaya,* and so forth) is also notable, as is the communication between Karagas and Spaniards. While we know that the missionaries would have had to learn the local language as a matter of church policy, it seems some of the Karagas also gained a working knowledge of Spanish.

The relationship shown here between the Magindanaw and the Karaga, both feared for bellicosity and raiding, is also quite interesting. Though the Karaga were not Muslim as far as we know, they had apparently been exposed to Islam and had absorbed it to the extent that it was culturally relevant in some way—meaningful enough for them to write verses from the Qur'an, presumably carved, into trees and the sterns of their ships. Indeed, this may have been why the Spaniards originally thought them to be another Moro group. Yet, despite their extensive political and cultural ties with the Magindanaw, they somehow fell in with the Spaniards. Far from the Lumad being isolated from outside influences, their world was already caught between Europe and Islam, even in early colonial Mindanao.

Fray Lorenzo de San Facundo begins his own eyewitness account on July 22, 1631, the day Mangabo's son Zancalan and his wife, Geronima Moag, arrived in Bacuag on the pretense of visiting their relatives. There were at least seven Spaniards in Bacuag, including two Recoletos—our author, Fray Lorenzo, and a Recoleto named Brother Francisco de San Fulgencio—and two civilians—the *cobrador*, or tribute collector, Gaspar de los Reyes, and his son, plus three soldiers. The rebels saw fit to kill them quietly, one by one, which they did so that, by the time they attacked

---

[41] A native longboat, much larger than a *banca* or canoe. The mention of the boat-builder, Tagpito, by name makes this narrative much more personal than all the other known accounts of the revolt.

[42] Schreurs has deduced that the place name Abucay refers to the present-day Placer. See Schreurs, *Caraga Antigua*, p. 151, n. 23.

[43] BN 3828, p. 214v. The report does not tally the native dead, only the Spaniards.

the two friars, the other Spaniards were already dead.[44] The final tally of Spanish fatalities is thus twenty-three men, including two civilians and four Religious. Again, there was no accounting of the number of *indios* and others killed, injured, or taken captive.

The scene Fray Lorenzo describes before the first attack exemplifies the routine of life for a missionary in an early sixteenth-century *reducción* in the outer reaches of the Spanish colony. Fray Lorenzo said Mass in the morning, and later the *cantores* (choir singers) brought him a body to prepare for burial. Having done this, he sat underneath his house where *pandais* (carpenters) were working, eleven of them. At this point, Zancalan came along with seven of his men, kissed the priest's hand, and made small talk, asking to see the house, to which Fray Lorenzo welcomed them. The *pandais* grew suspicious, asking the priest what Zancalan could possibly want. Fray Lorenzo's response—"He just wants to see the house"—betrays the degree to which the Spaniards trusted that they were among friends. After offering this explanation, the priest joined Zancalan's party upstairs, asking, "So what do you think, *datu*?" The *datu* commented that the house was *"bien,"* then, without warning, the men turned on Fray Lorenzo, grabbing him from behind. A young boy who was present, Nicolás, probably his *criado*, cried out in shock, "You lowlifes! You will kill the priest?!," after which the rebels disemboweled him.[45] His outrage, commemorated in the second-person familiar plural *vosotros* form, hints at his familiarity with the aforementioned "lowlifes," opening up the possibility that he was aware of the larger revolt, and thus the murders of the other Spaniards earlier in the day, and did nothing. The idea that they would kill the Recoletos, in any case, was obviously beyond his comprehension.[46]

From this point on, the account turns action-packed, recounting Fray Lorenzo's nearly successful escape attempt, during which he and Brother Francisco managed to dodge spears and hold off Zancalan's men until the pair realized they were woefully outnumbered. Manangalan and his men had arrived by then, joined by two *principales* the friars knew, Alindahao and Cagaom. Fray Lorenzo expressed the deep betrayal he felt when he realized that the whole village knew what had been taking place all that day, yet no one had come to warn him. Along the way, he encountered one of the *pandais*—a *sangley*, or Chinese migrant worker, named Aingo, who tried to hold off the attackers, and an *indio* from the Jolo archipelago, to the west of Mindanao, who handed him a machete so he could defend himself. In the end, the two Recoletos were trapped with Reyes, who was their Bajau[47] houseboy, and a very young choirboy from Siargao named Olandos. Zancalan had lured them out by promising to put them on a boat to leave Bacuag, but instead they were taken captive. In the meantime, the rebels once again went on a rampage, destroying and looting church property, and defacing images and statues, while challenging the "gods of the Castilles" to fight back. They also took the "1,200 baskets of rice and

---

[44] Ibid.

[45] Ibid., p. 215r.

[46] "Al punto dijo el muchaco (que se llamaba Nicolás): 'vellacos, al padre matáis.' Y diéronle dos por la barriga, que le arrastraron las tripas."

[47] The term used in the text is *lutao*, which was once a common epithet for the sea-based Sama Bajau, who are traditionally from the Sulu archipelago. See Gusni Saat, "The Identity and Social Mobility of Sama-Bajau," *Sari* 21 (2003): 2–11.

more than 600 *pesos* in gold and silver" that were stored in the *cobrador*'s house, as well as other property.[48]

Again, we see interesting snippets of life in a pericolonial *reducción*. The population was surprisingly multicultural, given the presence of at least one *sangley* and several *indios* from the other side of Mindanao, not to mention seven resident Spaniards. There were also interactions between indigenous people from different parts of northeastern Mindanao. We can note, in addition, the level of local wealth collected in tribute, stored at the *cobrador*'s house in Bacuag. Even though we have no idea what portion of the tribute for the Caraga region this amount represented, we do know that Bacuag was not a very large *reducción*, even for this peripheral part of the colony, which hints at the level of productivity and commerce taking place on the ground in Mindanao during the early seventeenth century. Last but not least, while the locals obviously cooperated with the rebels to a large extent, it is clear that, to some of them at least, there was a categorical difference between the Spaniards, in general, and the priests.

After the looting of the *cobrador*'s house, the story takes a rather interesting turn. Without going into great detail, Zancalan and his father, Mangabo, soon revealed to the captive Recoletos that they had had a change of heart, much to the anger and consternation of their fellow rebels. Only a great deal of subterfuge and overt shows of force carried out by both Mangabo and Zancalan prevented the others, in particular Dumblag, from killing the Recoletos. Mangabo added to the rebels' vexation by bowing before the Recoletos, kissing their feet and hands, then proceeding to take a blood oath, swearing to protect the two friars with his life. The *sandugo* blood oath, "which they consider inviolable here," was described by Fray Lorenzo this way:

> He took a *valarao* and, lowering his trousers, which were made from some of the dyed and embroidered damask they had stolen from [the church in] Tago, [he] made two cuts below the navel, drawing blood. And he had his son place the blood in a vessel with wine. He began to swear and invoke his *diwatas* [guardian spirits] "with such exaggerated shouting that even the river trembled in fear." Having drunk the wine, he placed the vessel on his head in a grand gesture, shouting something,[49] then he embraced me and placed his headdress on me ...[50]

After a series of escalating confrontations with Mangabo and Zancalan, the other *datus* finally left in disgust. Following their departure, María Campan, among others, presented to the Recoletos the relics, chalices, and other items the attackers had earlier stolen from the church at Tago. Eventually, Fray Lorenzo was released, and Brother Francisco ransomed soon after. Thus, the two Recoletos survived the Caraga Revolt.[51]

---

[48] BN 3828, p. 214v–215v.

[49] What Mangabo shouts here remains uncertain. Scheurs writes it as *"tigbabagna,"* which I am guessing might be the name of a *diwata*. On the actual manuscript, however, it appears to be *"viva bagna"* (or *liva bagna* or *tiva bagna*). Neither version has any significance to me, and the words are not explained any further in BN3828, nor by Schreurs. See Peter Schreurs, *Caraga Antigua*, p. 156.

[50] Ibid.

[51] BN 3828, p. 215r–216r.

The Recoletos, unsurprisingly, make great hay of this: that God had changed Mangabo's hatred into love.[52] Looking past the Recoleto spin, however, we see something of indigenous Lumad political organization in action. All the leading men in the revolt were *principales,* each one a *datu* from this part of Mindanao, and while there was a hierarchy vis-à-vis each *datu* and the men in his *sacup,* no single *datu* seemed to have held real authority or other power over his fellow *datus.* The various verbal confrontations between them, not to mention the agreements they made as a group (in planning different stages of the revolt), reveal the level of consensus that was required between allies, as well as the leaders' willingness to struggle and negotiate to achieve that consensus. As is shown below in the narrative about the Butuanon *datus,* these negotiations may be a reflection not of the *ad hoc* organization of disgruntled Karaga troops, but what may be the typical *modus operandi* of Lumad political leaders.

Mangabo and Zancalan and the men of their *sacup* may have abandoned the revolt, but the other *datus* were still moving forward with their plans. While all this was happening, the *datu* Balintos made his way out of Caraga province, traveling over land with "a hundred *indios,*" towards the Agusan River and Butuan, intending to persuade the Butuanons and Agusanons to kill their Spaniards and join the revolt. The narrative says that Balintos brought along with him many *cartas,* or letters, for the various *principales* in the Agusan River settlements. The letters carried news of what had already happened in Tandag and Tago, informing the intended recipients that Sultan Kudarat's navy was waiting offshore to deal with anyone who refused to join his side. When one such letter arrived in Butuan proper it was read out in public.[53]

The larger significance of this episode is that it tells us in no uncertain terms that the Butuanons and Karagas were able to read and write in the early seventeenth century, and that they sometimes relayed messages by letter, a practice that most of us would no doubt find very surprising, not least because it is often assumed that cultures that develop around oral traditions do so in the absence of literacy. The Recoleto account, however, leaves us with no doubt. This prompts us to ask how their literacy might have originated: Was it a consequence of missionization? Or were the Lumad already literate when the Spaniards arrived? Whether it was only the *principales* who could read and write, whether only some of them could, and what language they used in such communications, we do not know, leaving us with questions the sources cannot answer. However, knowing that at least some of the Lumad *principales* were literate nearly four hundred years ago certainly forces us to reconsider what else we may have overlooked in our presumptions about the indigenous cultures of Mindanao.

As for the revolt, the tide finally turned when Balintos arrived in the land of the Butuanons, who could not be persuaded or threatened into surrendering or killing the Recoletos they had come to know. Balintos first traveled to the *ylaya,* or the upriver/interior portion of the Agusan River, towards the *convento* in Linao, where he was planning to kill the resident priest, Fray Juan de San Agustín, himself. He seemed to gather momentum, attracting people along his way, but, when he arrived in Linao, he was forced to debate with the local *datus* for two days, trying in vain to secure their cooperation, before realizing he was at a dead end. Again, we see here

---

[52] Ibid.

[53] Ibid., p. 216r.

the importance of achieving consensus among *datus* prior to acting, as well as their autonomy and equal status relative to each other, such that Balintos was willing to argue with them for two whole days before finally giving up. In this particular instance, Balintos left "very displeased," and on the way out, he and his men intercepted a boat with supplies for the *convento*, which they looted, taking four of the priest's servants as captives. Soon after this incident, the *datus* of Linao moved their resident priest, Fray Juan, down to Butuan proper because they felt they could not protect him properly in the *ylaya*. Meanwhile, downriver in Butuan, all the *principales* "speaking as one, said that they would have to be dead before they would allow the priests to be harmed in any way." A mob then formed at the *convento* as the friars there were presented with the threatening letter from Balintos, and the messengers who had delivered it. After reading the letters and understanding them,[54] the priests told the mob, "Children, here we are, do what you wish to us, because, well, it is the will of the Lord." To which the Butuanons reportedly responded, "Cheer up, because all of us would rather die than let anyone hurt you," followed by what the Recoletos describe as "so many vows and declarations that, really, you would not believe it if you had not seen it yourself." One of the Recoletos was dispatched to Cebu to alert the authorities there, while those who remained were protected by the *principales* who, along with their women, children, and others, stayed in the *convento*, preparing to hold the rebels off.[55]

Not every Butuanon was immune to the rebel call, however. A local official[56] was reported to have attacked the *convento* without warning, stabbing the guard at the door and another *indio* before he was accosted by others. Fray Lorenzo de San Facundo, the writer of this dramatic account, reckoned that "if they had not come to the rescue so quickly, he would not have stopped until killing the priest." Several more attempts were made to turn the Butuanons against the remaining Religious, including a plot hatched by *datu* Manangalan, mentioned above, who sent a man from Jabonga named Sumalay to do the deed. Sumalay was chosen because he was already well-acquainted with the Religious, and stood a better chance of getting close enough to kill them. The Butuanons, however, had taken their Recoletos to a safe location far away from the town, and they arrested Sumalay before he could complete his task. Still, the revolt threatened to spread throughout the land, and in this account, at least, the loyalty of the Butuanons was the only thing protecting the Recoletos from the rebels.[57]

It was only at the beginning of August, about three weeks after the Caraga Revolt began, that four ships finally arrived from Cebu to respond to the crisis. They were spotted off the coast of Leyte Island by some rebels who had initially gone there to make *mangayao*, but decided to return to their respective rivers posthaste. The revolt quickly disintegrated as news of the Spanish ships spread, with rebels and non-combatants alike fleeing to the wilderness of the interior. Those who did not surrender to the Spaniards are believed to have starved to death in the interior. The

---

[54] This implies to me that the letters were not in Spanish and therefore still needed to be "understood" separately by the priests.

[55] BN 3828, p. 216r.

[56] He is identified only as the *fiscal mayor* of Butuan, which means he was the municipal attorney. He therefore must have been a high-ranking *indio* to have attained such office.

[57] BN 3828, pp. 261r–216v.

account ends by stating that "the main offenders were punished, others distributed as slaves, and the rest were given a general pardon."[58]

As mentioned earlier in this chapter, the Spaniards had to deal with leftover pockets of resistance for several more years, such that the surviving Recoleto brother from Baganga, Jacinto de San Fulgencio, upon returning to the region, described the situation on the ground as being in such "tumultuous disorder" that everyone had absconded to the hinterlands. In 1635, Lumad warriors from Baganga attacked Tandag, killing yet another unfortunate commanding officer of the fort. Then the Baganga attempted to lure his replacement into an ambush by asking him to join a punitive expedition against the *mandayas,* or upriver people,[59] of Hinatuan, Bislig, and Lingig, who they claimed had been responsible for the previous attack.[60] When the Baganga plot was uncovered and suppressed—thanks to help from an old native ally named Dacsa[61]—the violence only escalated. The climate of fear initiated by the Caraga Revolt in 1631 did not effectively end until 1636, when the very last of the revolt's conspirators, namely Dumblag and Balintos, were killed and captured, respectively, in a raid on the Baganga area carried out by troops from Tandag. One hundred and twenty of their men were taken prisoner.[62]

SUCH WICKED AND SACRILEGIOUS THINGS

Another primary source dealing with the Caraga revolt is a series of affidavits from five individuals—four Spaniards and one *indio* with knowledge of the uprising—produced as part of a 1632 inquest into the alleged anti-Christian elements of the revolt. The focus of the inquest appeared to be the formalization of the martyrdom of the four Recoleto missionaries who were killed by the Karagas, namely Jacinto de Jesús y María, Alonso de San José, Juan de Santo Tomás, and Pedro de San Antonio.[63] The affidavits, sworn and notarized in the faraway colonial capital of Manila, are valuable not only for their provenance as historical objects but

---

[58] Ibid., p. 216v. The type of punishment is not stated here, but based on the aftermath of other revolts, this could mean they were either hanged or imprisoned in Manila.

[59] Today, of course, this name represents a distinct ethnic group, one of several widely recognized Lumad groups. However, four centuries ago in Caraga, it no doubt referred to people living in the interior. Back then, the word *mandaya*—a cognate of *dayak* and *ilaya*—was a general reference to upriver dwellers, rather than to any particular ethnic group. Writing in the early twentieth century, the American ethnologist John Garvan classified the Karaga as one of four subtypes of "Mandaya." See J. Garvan, *The Manobos of Mindanao* (Washington, DC: US Government Printing Office, 1941), pp. 6–7. Today, the ethnonym "Mandaya" is recognized by linguists as interchangeable with "Karaga." See M. Paul Lewis, ed., *Ethnologue: Languages of the World* (Dallas, TX: SIL, 2009).

[60] Coincidentally, Baganga, in the southern part of Caraga, was the place that had been raided by Mangabo, Balintos, Dumblag, and other conspirators, together with Tandag troops, on the eve of the revolt. Schreurs identifies the people of Baganga as "Mandayas," but he does not explain whether the capitalization of the name was found in his original source.

[61] Dacsa is the same native soldier who had killed *datu* Suba a decade earlier, as mentioned in chapter two.

[62] Schreurs, *Caraga Antigua*, pp. 162–63.

[63] The affidavits are part of a larger document from the Recoleto archive in Marcilla, Navarra, Spain, dated 1632, entitled *Traslado autentico de la Informazion hecha en Manila sobre el Martirio de nros quatro VVs Ms de Caraga*, or "Authenticated transcript of the proceedings held in Manila regarding the martyrdom of our four missionaries of Caraga" (ARM leg 1, num 2, doc 2).

also for the fact that they provide an authenticated transcript of legal testimony given at an internal Recoleto hearing, rather than an official account or *relación* intended for public or Crown consumption. We can therefore see these affidavits as expressing, and ultimately codifying, the immediate concerns of the Recoletos with regard to the momentous upheaval that had just transpired in one of their longest-running missions; a mission that, until that point, had been a testament to their copacetic partnership with the Karagas, many of whom, like the Kagayanon before them, had either voluntarily converted to Christianity or allowed their children to be schooled by the missionaries. The specific purpose of the inquest was to establish the factual sequence of events that resulted in the death of the aforementioned Recoletos, and provide evidence that the Karaga acted out of hatred (*odio*) towards Christianity itself. Such evidence would be significant to the long and drawn-out process of canonization, the path to official sainthood, a process that sometimes takes centuries. In fact, the victims' mere candidacy for sainthood would have lent considerable prestige to the Recoletos, who, at the time, were still a very new order. In other words, the inquest was an ideal opportunity for a little self-promotion, and we can presume a political undertone is embedded in these particular narratives. Given the relative newness of the events in question, which had taken place just one year before the inquest, these proceedings would have made an emotionally powerful case for recognizing these four missionaries as martyrs of the Catholic faith.[64]

The testimonies reviewed below were sworn before a notary on June 28, 1632, by the Spanish sergeants Juan Alonso (age thirty-six), Francisco de Beas (age thirty), Miguel Bautista (age twenty-five), and Simon Pasqua (age forty, "more or less"). A fifth individual, a civilian approximately twenty-four years old, also gave his testimony. While his name is not recorded in this particular document, for he was illiterate and unable to sign it, he is identified in another source as Thomas Dongon, a native of Camarines, who could not write but was "*ladino en lengua castellana*," that is, competent in speaking Spanish as a second language.[65] All the witnesses were asked to verify the details presented by responding to seven questions outlining the official Recoleto narrative of the revolt. While it appears that those who testified were not necessarily eyewitnesses to the actual murders of the Spanish priests, civilians, and soldiers, the witnesses in question claimed to have been close enough to the action to confirm the veracity of specific details in the revolt narrative—including the congregation of Karaga warriors that immediately preceded the first murders, the actual desecration of the church of Tandag, and the initial aftermath. I frame the individual responses using the text of the official narrative that opens the document.[66]

---

[64] However, it appears this bid for sainthood was unsuccessful, because the four Religious killed in the Caraga Revolt do not appear in the *Causas de los Santos*, which lists members of the Recoleto family who have been either canonized, beatified, recognized as martyrs, or declared serious candidates for the process. In fact, none of the Recoletos mentioned in this study appear on the list at all. See http://www.agustinosrecoletos.com/estaticos/view/27, accessed May 3, 2011. Schreurs was likewise unable to find their names in the *Martyrologium Romanum*. See Schreurs, *Caraga Antigua*, p. 146, n. 20.

[65] Orden de los Agustinos Recoletos (hereafter OAR), *Boletín de la Provincia de San Nicolas de Tolentino* 60, 629 (Marcilla, Navarra, 1970), p. 29. Camarines is located on the peninsula in the southwest portion of Luzon island.

[66] ARM leg 1, num 2, doc 2, f1r–f1v. This is my own translation; original Spanish terms are shown in italics, with my in-text clarifications in brackets.

Fray Pedro de San Nicolás, Solicitor General of the discalced order of our father San Agustín of these islands, states: (a) that in the province of Caraga where my Order administers the teaching of the Holy Gospel to the native *indios* of the towns that have been conquered because they were pacified by the Religious, who turned them to the doctrines through lives of exemplary fervor, spirit, and zeal to serving the Lord, procuring the conversion of those souls, and undergoing many difficulties and travails, for the *indios* of that province are prideful and bellicose, as they have demonstrated on many occasions, and in particular during the previous year of 1630[67] in the month of July; (b) that the *alcalde* [magistrate] exited the garrison in the town of Tandag accompanied by ten soldiers and some *indios* who were *principales* from among those who had the most courage and strength, and of those one was named Balintos and another Mangabo,[68] who approached their enemy *indios* of Baganga and on that occasion plotted to murder the *alcalde*, soldiers, and all the Religious of the Order out of the abhorrence they had for our holy Catholic faith; (c) how in fact they stabbed to death the *alcalde*, soldiers, and P. Fr. Jacinto de Jesus María, Deputy Prior of the Tago River who went as chaplain, going along with them with their guard down, as they had determined that they were among friends, such that not a single Spaniard was able to escape, nor could anyone reach the garrison to alert the army about what had transpired except for a *tagalo*[69] boy who had been raised by one of the Religious, a native of the town of Dilao, *extramuros* [outside the walls] of this city where they had been [i.e., Tandag]; and came to the garrison to alert them to the events; (d) how the aforementioned *principal* Mangabo came with his men, feigning peace in order to take over the garrison and kill all the soldiers, so that in the garrison that morning, when the gate was opened, they gave no hint of their murderous intentions; (e) that in the town of Tanda[g], which is almost a half league from the garrison where they entered, they murdered the Prior and his companion and robbed the *convento* and sacristy, profaned the church, and committed much insult and thievery in the rest of the *conventos* where they went from here, and they killed two other Religious priests with spears, and captured another and a lay brother, and later in the town of Tago they destroyed the sacred images and even broke the arms off a crucifix and smashed another to pieces. The aforementioned Mangabo, challenging them and speaking terrible and ugly words, ordered a Mass to be conducted, saying that Father Mangabo would conduct it. All the people being gathered in the church, an *india* named María Campana [*sic*], whom the priests had considered a very good Christian woman, dressed herself in the alb, stole, and cope [a priest's clothing for religious rituals] and got hold of the aspergillum,[70] and as she

---

[67] The correct year is 1631. Despite this error, the signed testimonies, all dated 1632, refer to the uprising as having taken place in *el año passado*—the previous year—throughout.

[68] In the document their names are alternately spelled as Mangavo and Valintos, but the pronunciation would have been identical.

[69] He was an *indio* believed to be ethnically a Tagalog, originally from Luzon Island to the north, in what is now the Metro Manila capital region. From the San Facundo narrative, we know his name was Thomasillo and that he was actually Kapampangan.

[70] The original word in the text is *asperges*, which refers to the ritual sprinkling of holy water, from the Latin *aspergere*, to wash or sprinkle. Elsewhere in the same document it is clarified

threw holy water around said "I am Father Jacinto"; (f) and thus they continued, proceeding through the towns and murdering all the Spaniards they found, and the Religious who were there—being four of them, and two who were captured, since the rest of the people had hidden in the hills and escaped however they could with a great many difficulties and deprivations; (g) and that after this, with the aid of new help that arrived at the garrison in the form of Spanish soldiers, the Religious, who are willing to adapt and assist without complaint in the propagation of the Faith despite having little or no sense of personal security, have returned to work on the conversion of the *indios*. Once again, the Order sends out Religious because there is no lack of ministries available, being that this is a rugged and poor land, and the most isolated of these islands is where, if my Order were to quit ministering to those *indios*, they would be like barbarians in their idolatry and worship of false gods … [T]hat it may be evident to His Majesty and the Royal Council of the Indies that the Religious suffer many trials, including losing their lives, for the sake of preaching the Holy Gospel, and that it would help to send [more] Religious to carry on what was already started in this sacred work, it is important to collect information since there are eyewitnesses in this city [Manila] who know about this case with certainty.

The inquest posed the following seven questions, whose details the witnesses were asked to verify in order to establish what took place during the Caraga Revolt, with an eye towards recognizing the martyrdom of the four murdered Recoletos:[71]

1. First and foremost, if they are acquainted with the aforementioned priest, Solicitor General Fray Pedro de San Nicolás; and P. Fr. Juan de Sancto Thomas [Santo Tomás], theologian and Prior of the *convento* of San Nicolás in the town of Tanda[g], native of the town of Sant Pablo de los Montes in the Kingdom of Toledo; and P. Fr. Alonso de Sant Joseph [San José], his companion and a native of Villanueva in La Mancha; and Fray Jacinto de Jesus María, Prior of the *convento* of Salagan in Tago, native of Cadiz; and Fray Pedro de Sant Antonio [San Antonio], Prior of the *convento* of Sant Joseph [San José] in Bacua [Bacuag], native of Granada; and Fray Lorenço de Sant Facundo [Lorenzo de San Facundo], theologian; and his companion the brother Fray Francisco de Sant Fulgencio [San Fulgencio]; and if they have any news about this case, say so.

2. Moreover, if they know that, on the occasion of the previous year on the 30th[72] of the month of July, *Capitán* Pedro Bautista, who left the garrison of Caraga with ten soldiers and friendly *indios*, in particular Mangabo and Balintos having stabbed to death the aforementioned captain, then turning their attentions to the aforementioned priest, that they killed him and the rest of the Spaniards, say so.

---

that María Campan was using an *hisopo*, which is a Catholic liturgical implement called an aspergillum in English. It is a sort of stick with an encased sponge used to sprinkle holy water, which is contained in a vessel called an aspersorium, into which the aspergillum is dipped.

[71] ARM leg 1, num 2, doc 2, f2r–f3r.

[72] As previously explained, this date is erroneous; it should be the thirteenth of July.

3. Moreover, if they know that, these *indios* having risen up and killed in a premeditated and sacrilegious manner the aforementioned priests Fray Juan de Santo Tomas, cutting him into pieces with a *catana*[73] in the province of Tanda[g], and his companion Fray Alonso de Sant Joseph, whom they skewered with a spear, and the priest Fray Jacinto de Jesus María and the priest Fray Pedro de Sant Antonio, whom likewise they speared, and taking prisoner P. Fr. Lorenço de Sant Facundo[74] and Brother Fray Francisco de Sant Fulgencio, who arrived as his companion—engaged, as were all the aforementioned priests, in their *conventos* administering the Holy Gospel and sacred sacraments, living good exemplary lives—that the key to their deaths was first and foremost the abhorrence that [the *indios*] had towards our holy Catholic faith and the things of Christianity, therefore their intention was none other than to finish off all the Religious who were there in those ministries, so that there would be no one to teach and indoctrinate them, say so.

4. Moreover, if they know that, in the hatred that [the *indios*] have towards our holy faith, they burned the churches and *conventos* of the aforementioned towns, having sacked and robbed and made clothes out of the vestments and showing much disrespect to the saints on the altars of Christ our Lord, and of his holy mother, cutting and burning them, especially the aforementioned Mangabo, who, in the church of the town of Tandag,[75] broke the crucified Christ between both arms, blasphemously saying "make yourself brave like me" and took out a *valarao* or *cris*[76] from his belt and hit [the statue] in the face and split it, and later turned to another, even taller Christ figure, and striking with an axe he ground it up, challenging and scorning the faith that he had professed and the holy Baptism that he had received, say so.

5. Moreover, if they know that, on this occasion, there came out of the sacristy an *india* named Canpan [*sic*] whom the priests had once regarded as a very good Christian woman, fearful of God and her conscience, dressed with the alb, stole, and cope, and with the aspergillum, throwing the holy water and saying, "I am Father Jacinto," in disrespect and scorn for the divine worship and rituals of the sacred Church, say so.

6. Moreover, if they know that not only were the *indios* content to do such wicked and sacrilegious things in the aforementioned priests' *conventos* and churches, but they also conspired and agreed among themselves to go throughout the rest of the province, putting to the blade the Religious who were in their ministries, and this they undertook by dividing themselves into troops and into armed *caracoas*[77] with leaders who acted as Captains and Chiefs; and that they would have succeeded with their harmful intentions if

---

[73] From *katana*, a slightly curved Japanese long sword, with which Spaniards would already have been familiar in the 1600s.

[74] One of the authors of BN 3828.

[75] According to the San Facundo narrative, the church in question was actually the one in Tago, five miles from Tandag town, where the garrison was located.

[76] The *kris* is a type of bladed weapon indigenous to island Southeast Asia. It is easily distinguished by its wavy metal blade.

[77] Small boats.

my Lord God almost miraculously had not impeded their way and saved the Religious and the rest of the churches through warnings from the *indios* of Butuan, who did not wish to betray [the Religious] nor join up with the mutineers even though [the mutineers] had threatened that they would cut off their heads if they did not rise up with them and kill the priests—a threat they disregarded—and [the *indios* of Butuan] responded bravely that they had to maintain the faith and defend and protect the priests even if they should die in the attempt, as they had done in the case of their Prior P. Fr. Jacinto de Sant Fulgencio,[78] and his companion Fray Diego de Sancta Ana, who were left with the *indios* in the town in a garrison of poles that they had built, and sending the aforementioned Prior to the city of Zibú[79] to alert the head officer of those provinces to send a rescue party like the one that was sent later; that until that point they [in Cebu] had not known about the situation, and because of the help that was sent, the *indios* who had the Spaniards in a tight fix did not complete their task of laying to waste all of Caraga, nor did they take the garrison, say so.

7. Moreover, if they know that, even with all those travails and calamities, the Order has not stopped sending Religious to administer the holy sacraments and subdue to the faith the *indios* who mutinied, and has preserved in the faith those whom had left it; in this way, they are exposed to the rest of the travails referred to above because of little or no personal security from the *indios*, because [the *indios*] are an indomitable and bellicose people and neighbors of the [sultans] of [Magindanaw] and Jolo, sworn enemies of ours and of our holy Catholic faith, say so.

The individual witness affidavits then follow, for the most part simply affirming the details word for word. But at moments they provide interesting details.

From Juan Alonso, we learn that the *tagalo* boy in the story, Thomasillo, was actually a native of Pampanga, like half of the soldiers stationed at the fort.[80] Was he a brother, son, or nephew of one of the Kapampangan soldiers? And were the Kapampangan men housed with their families in Tandag? And if so, did this in some way contribute to conflicts with the Karaga? We don't know.

Francisco de Beas reports seeing "with my own eyes" the bodies of three dead Spaniards who had been chopped up into pieces, and he also saw that the Tago church had been burned to the ground.[81] He saw these things presumably in the aftermath of the attack, once the rebels had moved on.

Sergeant Miguel Bautista states that the captain, Pedro Bautista (no relation noted), initially left the garrison with only eight men, not ten, and that:

> … many other *indios* were there to make an assault upon our enemies, the *indios* of Baganga, and after they were done with the aforementioned assault,

---

[78] This should read "*Francisco* de Sant Fulgencio."

[79] Cebu served as administrative headquarters for colonial officials and missionaries serving in the southern Philippines. At the time, the Bishopric of Cebu was the most powerful Catholic office in the archipelago, and Bishop Pedro Arce, in particular, was instrumental in expanding the Recoleto mandate over northern and eastern Mindanao.

[80] ARM leg 1, num 2, doc 2, f3v.

[81] ARM leg 1, num 2, doc 2, f7r.

the same *indios* who were in the company of the captain killed him and those Spaniards with whom they went, together with P. Fr. Jacinto de Jesus María, who was in the company of the aforementioned captain. And in this manner, they also went on and killed the three other Religious, and the aforementioned Spaniards.[82]

However, Simon Pasqua reiterates that, in the massacre that signaled the start of the revolt, there were ten Spanish soldiers killed, and that they were traveling in the company of "two *principales* who were heads of their *barangays*, named Mangabo and Balintos," along with another four hundred *indios* who were "Christians and friends of the Spaniards."[83] This tells us very clearly that, despite the garrison's troops being outnumbered four to one by Karagas armed with lethal native weaponry, the Spaniards felt no fear, as they believed themselves to be among friends.

This brings home the many layers of betrayal involved in the Caraga Revolt. Not only did key people among the Karaga break a preexisting military alliance between Lumads and Spaniards, they also a destroyed a more meaningful kinship: the Karagas involved were not only thought of as friends by the Spaniards and trusted with their security; they were, more importantly, fellow Christians. The feeling of betrayal is keenly expressed in both primary sources: the two *principales*, Mangabo and Balintos, came to the fort of Tandag along with four hundred of their men, "feigning peace" and giving "no hint of their murderous intentions," such that the Spaniards were caught "with their guard down, as they had determined that they were among friends, such that not a single Spaniard was able to escape, nor could anyone reach the garrison to alert the army about what had transpired."

In a study of lethal treachery in small-scale warfare, the anthropologist Reed Wadley identified the Caraga Revolt as a classic case, characterized by

> ... the deliberate betrayal of another person's trust, trust being the expectation of reciprocal, cooperative relations. Under a scenario of lethal treachery, aggressors make deliberate plans to attack opponents during peacemaking ceremonies or fall opportunistically upon noncombatants during moments of seeming friendliness. What distinguishes treacherous ambush is the necessity of deceptively peaceful social interaction between attacker and victim immediately prior to the assault, or at least the expectation of peaceful interaction. The attackers thus must be on outwardly good terms with the victims.[84]

The totality of betrayal in this form of tactical surprise is underlined by how highly it is regarded among groups that, like the Karaga, have carefully cultivated their reputation for "fierceness." For example, among the Yanomami of South America—who have gained notoriety in anthropological literature for their aggression and cycles of small-scale warfare—lethal treachery is regarded as "the ultimate form of violence,"[85] in light of

---

[82] ARM leg 1, num 2, doc 2, f8r.

[83] ARM leg 1, num 2, doc 2, f10r.

[84] Wadley, "Lethal Treachery and the Imbalance of Power," p. 533.

[85] Napoleon Chagnon, *Yanomamo: The Fierce People*, fifth ed. (Fort Worth, TX: Harcourt College, 1997), p. 190.

... the calculated advantage that aggressors take of human sociality, rendering what is normally life-giving and life-sustaining into a weapon against the victims. The tactical aim appears to be the same as with concealment and ruse, increasing victim vulnerability while reducing risk to the attackers.[86]

Wadley explains the advantage that "perpetrators of treacherous ambushes may gain by establishing a reputation for bellicosity." Bellicosity becomes both the result of the "socialization of mistrust" and also its fundamental cause, such that it feeds a cycle of violence.[87] In other words,

> ... one intractable problem with such asymmetrical attacks ... is their regular rotation; that is, "the helpless victim of today's raid [becomes] himself the raider tomorrow."[88]

Given this environment of mistrust and treachery, perhaps the Caraga Revolt should also be understood as a continuation of deeply entrenched raiding practices among the Karaga, especially among men like Mangabo and Balintos, and the warriors within their respective *sacups*. The underlying cause of the revolt could easily have been a lull in what the Karaga would have considered to be "real" warfare. That is, the Caraga Revolt may have been the unfortunate outcome of boredom and frustration with Spanish military conventions, rather than a revolt against Spanish "rule," or a sudden, profoundly negative reaction to mission life, in which most of the Lumads concerned, including the main conspirators, were already involved.

THE BLASPHEMY OF MARÍA CAMPAN

Taking into account the lethality of the treachery discussed above, it is quite striking that the Recoletos gave almost equal weight in their inquest to another kind of betrayal: that of a female Karaga convert named María Campan. While she was not accused of committing murder or engaging in conspiracy, her act was assigned its own special question—number 5—in the affidavits:

> Moreover, if they know that on this occasion, there came out of the sacristy an *india* named Canpan [*sic*] whom the priests had once regarded as a very good Christian woman, fearful of God and her conscience, dressed with the alb, stole, and cope, and with the aspergillum, throwing the holy water and saying, "I am Father Jacinto," in disrespect and scorn for the divine worship and rituals of the sacred Church, say so.[89]

---

[86] Wadley, "Lethal Treachery and the Imbalance of Power," pp. 531–32.

[87] Ibid., pp. 538–39, 547.

[88] Ibid., p. 548, citing Gat, "The Pattern of Fighting in Simple, Small-Scale, Prestate Societies," p. 573.

[89] ARM leg 1, num 2, doc 2, f2r–f3v.

The priest referred to above was the recently murdered parish priest of Tandag, Fray Jacinto de Jesús María, who had, only days before, been speared to death by Mangabo and his associates. To this particular question the witnesses give the following responses:

> *Juan Alonso:* "… I can say with certainty that an *india* named María Campan, a *principal* of the town of Tago where the aforementioned priests have a *convento* about two leagues from the garrison, came out of the sacristy dressed in the alb, stole, and cope, sprinkling holy water, and saying 'I am Father Jacinto' in desecration of the holy faith and the divine worship … "[90]
>
> *Francisco de Beas:* "This was public knowledge."[91]
>
> *Miguel Bautista:* "He knew it to be true as stated."[92]
>
> *Simon Pasqua:* "It is public knowledge that the aforementioned *india* did those things referred to in the question."[93]

What we know directly about María Campan is limited to the testimony presented in the inquest described above, but there are still a few potentially relevant snippets of information that we can deduce from the record. First, she is identified by Juan Alonso, quoted above, as being a *principal* of Tago—like Mangabo, the main architect of the revolt. This means that she was from a family with social influence in Tago, the kind of people whose men would have become *datu*. In Lumad communities of any size, but especially so in smaller communities like those of the first mission period, this would mean she was almost certainly related in some way to everyone in the community, either affinally or consanguineally. Such close genealogical ties, whether by blood or marriage, would have been especially true among the *principales*, including Mangabo and María Campan. The witnesses would likely have noted if she had been Mangabo's sister, because the San Facundo narrative mentions Mangabo's wife and mother by name, so we can safely deduce that she was a slightly more distant relation—perhaps a cousin or an in-law. She was likely related to the other conspirators as well.

Second, María Campan was specifically referred to as a *mujer*, or woman, and not a *doncella*, or girl.[94] This means she had to be beyond her late teens during the events of 1631. No husband is mentioned at all, which could mean that she was either widowed or otherwise unmarried, or married to a man of no political or social consequence. Third, given that her parents were converts, and the Recoletos had known her since she was a child, her maximum age, given the twenty-two years of missionary presence in Tandag, would have been around thirty-two years old if she had been on the very cusp of adolescence when her parents converted. But, in reality, she could have been anywhere between fifteen and thirty-two.[95] Finally, we know that María Campan had been "once regarded as a very good Christian woman,

---

[90] ARM leg 1, num 2, doc 2, f4r.

[91] ARM leg 1, num 2, doc 2, f7r.

[92] ARM leg 1, num 2, doc 2, f8v.

[93] ARM leg 1, num 2, doc 2, f11r.

[94] More precisely, a virgin.

[95] Thanks to Arlene Garces Ozanne for pointing out to me the possible significance of María Campan's age.

fearful of God and her conscience," and therefore someone whose family was quite familiar to, if not intimately known by, the Recoletos from their regular participation in Christian practices such as the Mass, confession, and other sacraments. The elements of the Recoleto narrative, as well as the sense of betrayal that pervades it, very clearly place the events of the Caraga Revolt within the context of an already established mission and an already Christianized population.

As to María Campan's motives, the record is silent. I am of the opinion, however, that it is untenable for several reasons to attribute the events in question—whether the uprising itself or María Campan's cross-dressing episode—to an assertion of indigenous religion, or, more specifically, to the assertion of a type of "sacred feminine" within Lumad indigenous religions. First of all, María Campan's acts were described by the Recoletos as a straightforward case of blasphemy, as opposed to apostasy. In other words, she was accused of mocking her own religion—in this case, Christianity—but not of abandoning it for another, or of returning to the ancestral religion of the Karaga, which would have been a locale-specific form of ancestor worship. In fact, there is not a single reference or allusion in the accounts of the Caraga Revolt to an indigenous religious movement, nor any mention whatsoever of the influence or involvement of any *baylan* (shaman).[96] This is notable in itself because the Recoletos certainly considered indigenous practices to be repellent, crude, and dangerously "pagan." Moreover, as noted in the previous chapter, they were indeed acutely aware of indigenous idolatry and the Lumads' ritual worship of "filthy" *diwata* idols, as well as the considerable influence of indigenous "priests" in other areas. These elements featured regularly, and were often played up, in their narratives of the endless difficulties they faced in the field.[97] In fact, the Christian battle against demonic idols and *hechiceros*, or sorcerers, has been a regular trope in missionary accounts since the beginning of Spanish colonial expansion in the Americas.[98] Given their deeply entrenched views of women as a dangerous, corrupting influence on decent civilization in general, and men in particular, we can be sure that they would have jumped at the chance of blaming it all on the work of a female *baylan*, or any other possible manifestation of witchcraft, especially if these evil influences could easily be blamed on outrageous women who offended their patriarchal sensibilities. Yet this otherwise convenient explanation is absent from accounts of the Caraga Revolt. It is therefore rather unlikely that María Campan was

---

[96] It is also notable that the Recoletos always wrote of shamans using masculine articles. This does not mean that all shamans were men, but it means that the Recoletos did not recognize shamanism as a predominantly "female" role. Among the Lumad at present, authority figures in indigenous religious practices are also more likely, statistically speaking, to be men rather than women. Nor have I seen anything in the relevant ethnographic record that shows a connection between Lumad shamanism and dressing as the opposite sex. Even if the revolt had, indeed, been about returning to indigenous religious practices, it would have been more likely for one of the Karaga men to emerge as the *baylan* in charge. And if so, this *baylan* would be wearing special accoutrements with supernatural significance that are specific to *baylanic* practices, and not women's clothing *per se*. (Nor, I might add, would the inverse be likely—a female *baylan* would not be cross-dressing in so-called men's clothes.) Rather than a call to a "sacred feminine," shamanism all over the world involves a multi-dimensional existential and material ambiguity not only in terms of gender (i.e., one shaman embodying all the genders, not only the feminine), but also of animal species, geography, and divinity. See Thomas A. DuBois, *An Introduction to Shamanism* (Cambridge: Cambridge University Press, 2009).

[97] See, for example, OAR, *Boletín de la Provincia de San Nicolas de Tolentino*, p. 46.

[98] Nicholas Cushner, *Why Have You Come Here? The Jesuits and the First Evangelization of Native America* (New York, NY: Oxford University Press, 2006), pp. 75–78.

a participant in indigenous shamanic practices, much less a *baylan* herself. Instead, the Recoletos explicitly framed this revolt as an anti-Christian movement instigated by known converts.

It is more likely that María Campan was, like many of the other, unnamed participants in the revolt, simply caught up in the runaway mob dynamics that had erupted all around her. It is also more than likely that María Campan, along with Mangabo and his men—who, we should not forget, were all inside the church, conducting the mock Mass and headlining the events in question—were doing what many a subjugated people have done throughout human history: performing a parody of higher authority. Pulling back for a moment from María Campan as an individual, if we were to regard her acts as just one element of the larger "mock Mass" itself, the whole event was clearly a parody of both colonial and missionary authority. If we interpret the event in this way, we can see how their acts rendered the reality of the missionized Lumad world in Bakhtinian carnivalesque. In mocking the sacredness of the Catholic Mass and the centrality of the male Spanish priest by staging a parody that featured a civilian Karaga woman performing mock sacraments for a mob of armed vandals, María Campan, along with her cousin Mangabo, his rebels, and all those Lumad who found themselves inside that church, were overturning, symbolically and physically, the established order of missionized Caraga on a multitude of levels.[99] If this particular phenomenon was understood by the Recoletos as akin to the more familiar phenomenon of, say, peasant uprisings in feudal Europe, or Indian revolts in New World, it would certainly explain why the Spaniards did not express any concern in the record that the Karaga were acting under the influence of a *baylan* this time. It is, in fact, notable in both primary sources that neither the root causes of the revolt nor its larger political objectives, if any, appear to be very well defined. Nor did the Recoletos seem specifically concerned with understanding *why* the revolt happened, except for the possible role of hated Muslims in inciting the Karaga to violence. Overall, primary sources leave the distinct impression that the Recoletos believed that such *indio* upheavals and acts of resistance were simply bound to happen among any population subject to colonial authority, especially among "treacherous" and historically bellicose people like the Karaga.

Returning to the affidavits, we find that the Spanish sergeants quoted above did not necessarily witness the events in question first-hand, given that they testified only to the fact that María Campan's blasphemous cross-dressing act was widespread public knowledge, using a Spanish legal term, *público y notorio*, that places widely known, publicly acknowledged "facts," including an individual's reputation and personal history, into the category of legal evidence, regardless of documentation or other physical proof. Only the Spanish-speaking *indio* from Camarines, in the Bicol region of southern Luzon, Thomas Dongon, testified, "Yes, I saw it,"[100] which makes him the only eyewitness to the incident. I note that, as an *indio*, he was also the only one who could have possibly blended into the mob.

---

[99] Or, alternately worded, this was one of those moments when the hidden transcript of resistance erupted onto the main text. See Mikhail Bakhtin, *Rabelais and His World*, trans. Helene Iswolsky (Bloomington, IN: Indiana University Press, 1984). See also James C. Scott, *Domination and the Arts of Resistance: Hidden Transcripts* (New Haven, CT: Yale University Press, 1990).

[100] ARM leg 1, num 2, doc 2, f6r.

According to the eyewitness testimony, María Campan's role in the revolt was quite limited: it appears that the highlight of her participation was her impersonation of the murdered parish priest of Tandag, Fray Jacinto de Jesús María. She did this primarily by putting on the late priest's alb, stole, and cope—or, as stated in the affidavits, she "made clothes out of vestments."[101] If she had been a co-conspirator, I think the witnesses and scribes would have noted it. In fact, all we know is that she was never accused of either conspiracy or murder. Yet this episode was given the same degree of attention as the more violent acts of the revolt.

Her actions were certainly blasphemous, in the sense that she showed "disrespect and scorn for the divine worship and rituals of the sacred Church," and disrespected the memory of the recently murdered Father Jacinto. It is likely, therefore, that her actions were emphasized during the inquest in an attempt to establish that the revolt was essentially an act of hate against Christianity and its representatives, the missionaries. As previously mentioned, this interpretation would have supported claims of martyrdom for the four dead Recoletos. Therefore, we can argue that María Campan's actions would have represented a straightforward form of treachery to the Recoletos, for she violated a sacred trust, and abused the social privileges she was granted as a convert. While she seems to have committed no actual physical violence, her acts might be considered a form of religious or cultural violence rendered especially heinous because, as with the lethal treachery discussed in the previous section, the victims had been lulled into a false sense of security, believing they were among friends, only to have this trust violated in so cold and calculating a manner. Moreover, this violation was primarily an outrage of material and spatial aspects: the priest's vestments and other paraphernalia—all sacred objects used in Catholic religious rituals—were desecrated when they were "made clothes," and the church at Tago itself defiled as a consecrated space when María Campan joined in with Mangabo and others. In this sense, the Spanish interpretation of this particular offense may have had nothing at all to do with the fact that it was committed by a woman.

Nevertheless, the fuller cultural significance of María Campan may be visible only through a gendered lens. Her acts were a compound violation of racial and patriarchal European boundaries on at least four distinct levels: (1) she was fundamentally othered as an *india* or "indian" woman who (2) had mocked and impersonated a man who was not only (3) a Spaniard but also (4) a respected religious authority figure within Spain's Holy Faith. The Spanish obsession with María Campan's acts, particularly when framed within the context of a wider and unquestionably bloodier treachery by other trusted *indio* converts, appeared to have been influenced by profoundly gendered expectations regarding piety and propriety. This means that her actions likely were perceived as a shocking transgression of deeply entrenched Spanish sexual and religious boundaries—boundaries that, in all likelihood, were culturally invisible to the Lumad. It is perhaps only through the lens of gender that we can even begin to comprehend how her limited actions would be considered somehow equally offensive as the widespread acts of physical violence committed by her male relatives against other men. In this sense, the Spanish response to María Campan can only be about gender, or more specifically, how Iberians gendered the world.

---

[101] From the full text of Question Number 4.

THE WORLD IS HER CLOISTER

In the early modern period, indigenous Southeast Asian ideas about gender were distinctive, characterized by a remarkably high degree of female autonomy, extending to family matters, marriage contracts, sexual relations, agriculture and food production, manufacturing, trade, politics, and direct dealings with foreigners. It seems almost redundant to state that women of this period were quite visible and consequential as far as public life in Southeast Asia was concerned.[102]

In sharp contrast, Spain at this time was "a patriarchal society with laws and institutions designed to exclude women from public life."[103] As part of the edited volume *More Pinay Than We Admit*, Marya Svetlana Camacho[104] explores the significance of *recogimiento*—a word that ties religious devotion to being "removed" from vulgar society—as a key moral and social value in the highly patriarchal Spanish colonial milieu. To be a *mujer recogida,* or modest woman, involved living a secluded and quiet life as a "proper" woman. The word *recogida* itself carries broad connotations of being "collected" as a person, like a crop that is harvested and processed, as opposed to an untended garden with plants allowed to grow wild and be overrun by weeds.[105] Notions of civility and being civilized are therefore intimately woven into its meaning. Camacho explains that *recogimiento* aligns women with a specifically Christian cosmic order, one in which the regulation of an individual's conduct through a sense of duty and propriety, as part of the pursuit of virtue, promotes harmonious relationships, which in turn preserves and promotes the social order. In the Spanish world of the early modern period, the concept of virtue was itself gendered, following "the centuries-old idea (not exclusive to Christian societies) of female imperfections both corporeal and moral." The discourse on "the contaminating nature of women" was, in fact, closely related to "fears of gender transgression and thus, the destabilization of the social order."[106] Both were part and parcel of Iberian culture at the time, and might even be considered the underlying axis of social reproduction throughout the Spanish colonial world.

Recogimiento therefore "configure[d] the central features of the feminine ideal ... as a conglomerate moral virtue encompassing modesty, chastity, interior quiescence fostered by piety, and the cultural practice and value of domesticity (and relative to that, a guarded public presence)."[107] Stress was placed on modesty (*recato*), along

---

[102] Anthony Reid, *Southeast Asia in the Age of Commerce 1450–1680, vol. I* (New Haven, CT: Yale University Press, 1988), pp. 146–72.

[103] Helen Nader, "Introduction: The World of the Mendozas," in *Power and Gender in Renaissance Spain: Eight Women of the Mendoza Family, 1450–1650*, ed. Helen Nader (Urbana, IL: University of Illinois Press, 2003), p. 3.

[104] Marya Svetlana Camacho, "The Public Transcendence of Intimacy: The Social Value of Recogimiento in *Urbana at Feliza,*" in *More Pinay Than We Admit: The Social Construction of the Filipina*, ed. Maria Luisa T. Camagay (Quezon City: Vibal Foundation, 2010), pp. 295–317.

[105] Its root word, *recoger*, is a broad term that primarily means to collect, gather, harvest. In other words, the word describes something that has been removed from its original location so that it may be used for a particular purpose. Its religious aspect is rooted in withdrawal from the mundane world, which leads one to meditation, seclusion, cloistering, and, presumably, to serve God's purpose. The word is interchangeable with the word *recolectar*, the root word of *Recoleto.*

[106] Rebecca Lee, "Iconic Womanhood, Liberal Discourse, and National Identity: Mercedes Valdivieso's *Maldita Yo Entre Las Mujeres* (1991) and Benjamín Vicuña MacKenna's *Los Lisperguer y La Quintrala* (1877)," *Latin American Literary Review* 35,69 (2007): 106.

[107] Camacho, "The Public Transcendence of Intimacy," p. 298.

with domesticity, chastity, and discretion, much of which translated to a certain level of seclusion or shunning of public life, such that "excessive visibility" on the part of a woman was considered a vice. A homebound existence was, in fact, considered the key to good breeding, because a secluded daughter's purity could "remain unscathed by the dangers of the world." Corporeal purity, in turn, mirrored one's spiritual purity. When in public, therefore, a *mujer recogida* observed "propriety in clothing" and a modest demeanor, taking special care in her body movements, "specifically to avoid anything provocative." Despite the perceived imperfections of their sex, women were, in fact, ascribed great potency in the sexually circumscribed Iberian world: they were seen as having a "humanizing, 'civilizing' influence ... in the family and consequently in society at large," especially if the woman's character was "correctly cultivated."[108] The inverse is, of course, equally powerful: that through inappropriate demeanor, a woman could and would incite inhuman, uncivilized, and wholly inappropriate behavior in men. The inversion of gender categories, even at a superficial level, was therefore likely to have been read not just as allegory but as signaling the inversion of social reality itself.

Cross-dressing was particularly provocative in the context of early modern Europe. Following the Biblical laws on civil and domestic life outlined in the Book of Deuteronomy,[109] to wear the clothing meant for the opposite sex was literally "an abomination to God" and "contrary to the laws of nature, which would give rise to many perils of human society." Specifically, for a woman to wear men's clothing was "a clear sign of masculine audacity and astonishing impudence in a woman's heart." It was also a sign that "she has already cast off her chastity together with her sense of modesty."[110] We can perhaps appreciate the level of outrage this transgression would have engendered in the Recoletos when we recall that, in their mother country of Spain, such "audacious females" had been subjected to the fiery, public *autos da fe* of the Spanish Inquisition for doing much less than what María Campan had done in the church at Tago.[111]

Recogimiento as a female ideal therefore addresses a perceived need for internal and external discipline to mitigate what were apparently considered to be "natural" female tendencies towards wayward, dangerous behavior—not just female audacity and impudence but the absence of morality itself. Presumably, these tendencies were fully realized in the actions of María Campan during the Caraga Revolt, to the absolute horror of the Recoletos who thought they knew her well. From this perspective, statements about her presumed piety as a "good Christian woman" were less about her demonstrated faith in God than they were about how she had internalized the social order—which at her level also meant the colonial order—and embodied it as a woman. The gravity that the Recoletos placed on her acts therefore becomes understandable once we see that, in their eyes, she had blasphemed against not only Christian doctrine but a key organizational axis of Western civilization.

Unlike María Campan, some *indias* did live up to this constrictive Iberian ideal of *recogimiento*. Along with the previously mentioned Magdalena Bacuyo, there were

---

[108] Ibid., pp. 310, 301, 298, 302, 303, 307, 308, respectively.

[109] Specifically Deuteronomy 22:5.

[110] Juan Luis Vives, *The Education of a Christian Woman: A Sixteenth-Century Manual*, ed. and trans. Charles Fantazzi (Chicago, IL: University of Chicago Press, 2000), pp. 108–9.

[111] See Mary Elizabeth Perry, *Gender and Disorder in Early Modern Sevilla* (Princeton, NJ: Princeton University Press, 1990).

other Lumad women who were held as exemplars of Christian womanhood. Known as the *beatas*, or "blessed women,"[112] they suggest that the Iberian missionaries were not entirely opposed to female prowess, as long as it was used in the service of their agenda.[113] One of these *beatas* was a Butuanon woman whose baptismal name was Isabel, to whom the Recoletos credited an untold number of conversions. In a report of her death in 1646, she was described as having "so much grace and gentleness of words that she seized the hearts of her hearers. To this she joined a modesty and bearing sweetly grave, by which she made great gain among those barbarians."[114] What is interesting about Isabel is that her complete embodiment of Christian ideals was so impressive to the Recoletos that they decided to utilize her feminine prowess to further their cause.

> Since so copious results were experienced through the agency of Isabel, both in the reformation of morals and in the many who were converted from their blind paganism, the fathers sent her to preach in the streets and open places where the people gathered to hear her—some through curiosity, and others carried away by her wonderful grace in speaking.[115]

Her work in public was not confined to preaching, for "[s]he also entered the houses of the obstinate ones who did not go to hear her in the streets." Before confining herself to a life of contemplation after she was widowed, she led a fairly active apostolic life, which included bringing catechism to "the stupid ones" and establishing a school in the village "to which the young girls resorted." Indeed, she was as full of *santo celo* as the Recoleto men.[116]

> One cannot easily imagine the diligence with which she sought souls; the means that she contrived to draw them from the darkness of heathendom. What paths she did not take! What hardships she did not suffer! She went from one part to another discussing with the spirit and strength, not of a weak woman, but of a strong man. The Lord whose cause she was advancing aided her; for the solicitation of souls for God is a service much to his satisfaction."[117]

The other *beatas* have similarly impressive apostolic resumes. Through exemplary *recogimiento*, in other words, Isabel and the other *indias* were able to transcend the presumed "natural" limits of their sex to earn the privilege of exercising their

---

[112] Though today the word is used for those who have been beatified or placed on the road to Catholic sainthood, in this context the title was given to extraordinarily pious indigenous women who took simple vows to serve the Catholic Church. Their status would have been something between that of a lay sister and a nun in a Religious order.

[113] See Luciano P. R. Santiago, *To Love and Suffer: The Development of the Religious Congregations for Women in the Spanish Philippines* (Manila: Ateneo de Manila University Press, 2005), pp. 40–42.

[114] Blair and Robertson, *The Philippine Islands*, vol. 36, p. 110. The awkward translation by James Robertson is quoted verbatim. The original intent of the description was likely that Isabel employed "great modesty and a gentle seriousness" in her apostolic work.

[115] Ibid.

[116] Ibid.

[117] Ibid.

prowess in public, as men were allowed to do. In contrast, women like María Campan were perceived as both dangerous and weak: feared for their feminine ability to incite others to action, while at the same time pitied for falling victim to their own innately perverse and animal qualities.

CONVERTING COLONIALISTAS

The special social mores expected of Christian converts had other implications for the relationship between converter and converted. An aspect of conversion not often addressed is the impact of the process on the missionaries themselves, especially after they have lived side-by-side with the natives for extended periods of time. While the phenomenon of "going native" among field-oriented researchers, in particular anthropologists, has long been recognized as a potential outcome of cultivating such socially intimate relationships, critical anthropologists tend to focus on the popular misappropriation of a romanticized nativeness by Westerners "playing Indian."[118] To appreciate the Lumad colonial experience, however, it may be worthwhile to ponder the extent to which the *colonialistas*, be they missionaries or soldiers, were, in a sense, converted to the Karaga social world, especially as their interactions evolved into ever more interdependent relationships. The social contract between priest and believer is complex enough in itself, but other equally intimate relationships would have arisen in this context, resulting from shared living conditions, religious practices, battle experiences, and outwardly expressed social standards and moral values. In other words, in the intensive social exchange between Lumad and Spaniard, both sides would have been affected.

Vicente Rafael's study of colonial-era conversion among the Tagalogs of Luzon tells us that the adoption of Castillian, and, by extension, Christianity was, more or less, a complex form of cultural accommodation performed by *indios* in the early colonial period.[119] In a comparable vein, Gauri Viswanathan situates Christian conversion in colonial India as part of a larger attempt to negotiate and accommodate the idea of modernity as a culturally relevant phenomenon, explaining Christian conversion in colonial societies as "signifying responses to internal changes that were already under way, and as a form of domesticating, and to some extent neutralizing" change.[120] However, these and other similar lines of interpretation dwell on the conversion phenomenon as a unidirectional development, especially when it took place within the context of colonialism. The cultural blindness of Spaniards, and Europeans in general, is a notable trope, one in which the native converts always seem to be doing all the heavy lifting in the cross-cultural experience.[121] Europeans, in fact, seem to have little significance in these particular arguments; what matters is the recognition that natives, whether in Filipinas, India, or elsewhere, had agency and used conversion to make modernity meaningful to and

---

[118] Philip Deloria, *Playing Indian* (New Haven, CT: Yale University Press, 1999). See also Shari M. Huhndorf, *Going Native: Indians in the American Cultural Imagination* (Ithaca, NY: Cornell University Press, 2001).

[119] Vicente Rafael, *Contracting Colonialism: Translation and Christian Conversion in Early Tagalog Society under Early Spanish Rule* (Ithaca, NY: Cornell University Press, 1988).

[120] Gauri Viswanathan, *Outside the Fold: Conversion, Modernity, and Belief* (Princeton, NJ: Princeton University Press, 1998), p. 41.

[121] See also Vicente Rafael, *The Promise of the Foreign: Nationalism and the Technics of Translation in the Spanish Philippines* (Durham, NC: Duke University Press, 2005).

for themselves. Southeast Asian acts of "localization" parallel the idea that religious conversion is a practical and concrete route for seamlessly accommodating a potentially problematic foreign object, such as the hegemonic Western notion of "modernity," into one's existing identity.

But what becomes of the converters? Peter Lape, writing about colonial contact in Southeast Asia, calls our attention to how the "myth of the primitive isolate"

> ... has contributed to the still living notion that contact between Europeans and "Natives" was an unprecedented event ... that completely transformed the foundations of "Native" social systems. The dramatic power of written accounts of "first contacts" has helped emphasize this notion, though in most cases it is not clear for whom the contact experience is a "first."[122]

Whatever was being digested culturally or psychologically by putative converts, the agents of conversion were also accommodating to this new relationship, even across the power imbalances that existed between such groups. The Lumad contact story is therefore woefully incomplete unless we begin to recognize their possible influence on the Iberians they fought alongside, lived with, worshipped with, and, at different moments, attacked and killed, all in very close quarters. There is not much primary source material to go on at the moment, but as we ponder the ways in which Christian conversion might be just another form of converting to modernity, we should not forget that moving into a larger, more "universal" Christian framework changes not just the converts and their relationships with each other. It also expands the missionary universe in making communication and interaction between Lumads and Europeans possible to begin with. By adopting new cultural markers, especially Christianity, the Lumad made themselves "legible" to Europeans, and we can assume that Europeans (at least the missionaries) mirrored their efforts by acquiring some cultural competency and a working knowledge of local languages. These efforts are also visible in the adoption of Lumad words like *mangayao, datu,* and *sacup,* as discussed in the next chapter.

We saw in the previous chapter how the indigenous peoples of Mindanao— Lumad and Moro peoples alike—were categorized by the missionaries and colonial officials. Those who converted were not only classified as allies of Spain but also considered to be people of noble character: trustworthy, peaceful, genteel, intelligent, compassionate, even handsome. For example, while the Kagayanon were still deemed "primitive" by European standards, they were considered exemplary, well-mannered, and inherently good-natured natives. This was, in part, due to their kin ties to the previously converted Butuanon people, who were similarly regarded as being nearly civilized. Meanwhile, those *indios* who would not convert were considered violent, irrational, impulsive, depraved, cruel, and unreliable, and possessed of many other negative traits because they worshipped "filthy" idols. This distinction was even more pronounced when compared to the Spanish assessment of the Moros: by their adherence to Islam, they were automatically classified as enemies of Christianity and therefore enemies of Spain. Moros, in fact, were routinely

---

[122] Peter V. Lape, "A Highway and a Crossroads: Island Southeast Asia and Culture Contact Archaeology," *Archaeology in Oceania* 38,2 (2003): 106.

characterized as *traidor*, or treacherous, and irredeemably so, as were their Lumad allies who made life dangerous for the Recoletos and other Spaniards.[123]

Yet in the passage from non-convert to convert, the same person who was labeled as a one-dimensional *traidor* somehow became a full human being considered capable of complex thought and demonstrating admirable qualities. Even the character of María Campan was converted in the post-Revolt accounting from a model Christian woman to a treacherous, sacrilegious creature, and then, it seems, back again. She and others may have redeemed themselves by returning to the Christian fold, but they were able to do so only because the missionaries believed that some "traitors" could be converted into good Christians. The real measure of success in conversion, as expressed by the Recoletos, was more than a simple matter of adherence to doctrine; there were larger aims, for in this context, a Christian identity represented more than just religion—it was what made civilization possible in the first place. In summing up their narrative of the early Kagayanon conversions, the Recoletos proudly concluded that these Lumad, once lost in "the desert of paganism," were now "converted into men who were useful to their God, their Country, and their King."[124] In other words, the Lumad were brought, through Christian conversion, into the light of the civilized, Western world, perhaps not as full citizens, but "useful" ones at least.

However, the core message communicated in the language of conversion and Christian identity presumes the successful transfer of shared norms and values, a presumption reinforced by joint participation in symbolic social interaction and other activities, especially Catholic rituals such as baptism, confession, and the Mass. In the Recoleto inquest, the Spanish witnesses' descriptions of Mangabo and his associates as "Christians and friends to the Spaniards," and of María Campan as one "whom the priests had once regarded as a very good Christian woman," tell us the extent to which Spaniards believed these Karaga to have shared their core norms and values. In codifying their deep sense of betrayal, these Spaniards also reveal how much they had been "converted" by the Karaga.

This dyad of trust and betrayal becomes even more significant against the backdrop of the *guerras piráticas*, or "pirate wars," which involved strategic assaults by Spain to contain the devastating raids being carried out against Christian settlements and other colonial outposts in northern Mindanao and the Visayas—sometimes even as far north as Luzon—by pirates from the Moro areas of Mindanao and Sulu.[125] That the Moros were a perpetual thorn in the side of Spaniards is apparent in the amount of attention devoted to them in the archival record. In at least two documents, military authorities officially requested permission to enslave

---

[123] Cushner, writing about the Americas, explains that missionaries "brought with them the same cultural prejudices as the Spanish soldiery. The only difference was that the [missionaries] believed that the Indian was capable of modifying his behavior." Missionaries therefore dealt with major cultural differences by trying to confront, in ethical and moral terms, the "apparently contradictory qualities [they] observed in the Florida Indians," by rationalizing that their positive character traits "could only have originated in a natural theology that disposed the Indian to goodness." Despite all of this, however, "the European could not see the Indian in his own terms." Cushner, *Why Have You Come Here?*, pp. 36–37.

[124] OAR, *Boletín de la Provincia de San Nicolas de Tolentino*, p. 71: " ... los convirtieron en hombres útiles a su Dios, a su Patria y a su Rey."

[125] See Vicente Barrantes, *Guerras Piráticas de Filipinas Contra Mindanaos y Joloanos* (Madrid: M. G. Hernandez, 1878).

any *indios mahometanos* they came across, for the crime of being Muslim. Spanish reports detailed the numerous violent attacks by Moros on Spanish-held territories, pointing out that the Moros targeted both the Religious and innocent natives. These accounts were then used as a justification for subsequent return attacks by Spanish troops, who were more often than not accompanied by native troops, including Karagas.[126]

The fact that the Spaniards at that time had a relatively recent history of violent antagonism against their own Moros in Europe explains the intensity of their response to these Moro raids. Like the Moors in Spain, these Moros of the southern Philippines were considered enemies of the "true faith" of Catholicism, which, during this period of colonial expansion, was essential to Spanish identity. After the conversion of the *datu* Inuc, Karaga warriors, just like their Butuanon and Kagayanon neighbors, began fighting alongside Spanish troops in anti-Moro raids aimed at protecting Christianized settlements and other Spanish interests. These alliances with the Karaga and other Lumad converts signified more to Spaniards than strategic military cooperation, they also signified, in part, an alignment of values and identities, a pact between Christians in league against the enemies of God.

We saw in the previous chapter that Moros did, indeed, target Spanish missionaries in these raids, and that some of them were tortured and killed, though it is difficult to say whether such attacks were carried out for any purpose other than calculated intimidation. Nevertheless, these missionary accounts emphasize not only their own suffering and martyrdom, but also that of their converts, at the hands of Muslims as incontrovertible proof of Christian devotion and zeal. In the same vein, Spanish accounts that address the Moro raids—such as *Relacion de la Valerosa Defensa de los Naturales Bisayas*[127]—tend to celebrate the active participation of the *naturales* in defensive actions as proof of their strong Christian identity, with the emphatic use of the inclusive pronoun *nuestro*, "we," at every turn.

Beyond the Lumad world, a wider reorientation towards Spanish colonial reality was also taking place. Due to limited personnel and marine resources, not to mention the fact that Mindanao was quite a distance from the capital in Manila, the colonial response to these Moro raids was neither timely nor decisive. Consequently, Moro pirates continued their attacks on the Christianized areas of northern Mindanao and the Visayas until well into the nineteenth century, when steam-powered boats began to give the Spaniards a major technological advantage in the water.[128] In contrast to Spain's unmistakably religious agenda, it is actually unclear whether Moro actions were in any way rooted in religious antagonism. As Thomas McKenna notes, "Prior to the late nineteenth century ... there is no direct evidence for Islamic clerics

---

[126] See, among others, (AGI, Filipinas, 27, N.63/30-06-1607), (AGI, Filipinas, 340, L.3,F.266r–267r/29-5-1620), (AGI, Filipinas, 330, L.4, F.5r–6r/1635), (AGI, Filipinas, 27, N.224/20-08-1637), (AGI, Filipinas, 27, N.64/04-07-1607), (AGI, Filipinas, N.112/25-07-1626), and (AGI, Filipinas, 331, L.8, F.61r–63v/1-5-1686).

[127] This, and a related publication entitled *Compendio de los Sucesos ... en Defensa de estas Christiandades e Islas de Bisayas*, both found in the Newberry Library vaults—(NL Ayer 2111.R38.1755) and (NL Ayer MS 1328)—refer to a massive attack by several Moro groups in June of 1754 that affected the Visayas archipelago from Leyte, in the east, down to Iligan and the northern coast of Mindanao.

[128] Madigan, "The Early History of Cagayan de Oro," pp. 123–27.

preaching anti-Spanish resistance to the general populace."[129] Moreover, the Moros' incorporation into Spanish colonial reality was commonly recognized, even internally, despite their widely celebrated resistance to all assertions of Spanish colonial power. For example, there is evidence that locally made Qur'ans dating back to the Spanish colonial period have the Magindanaw identifying themselves as part of *al-Filibin*, referencing the Spanish label of Filipinas as a toponym. [130]

Returning to the possible role of the Magindanaw Moros or any other outside forces in the Caraga Revolt, none of the witness testimonials refer to this purported involvement except to dismiss it as a ruse to scare up support for the revolt among locals, as the San Facundo account explicitly states. However, it is far more important to understand how the Lumad responded to the choice they thought they were given by the Moros: join the uprising or lose your heads. Because those who joined the uprising were expected to demonstrate their loyalty by killing Spaniards—including the Religious—the Lumad were faced with choosing between whether they would side with ethnic compatriots, in most cases their own kin, or protecting a few outnumbered foreigners. It is clear that, despite believing they were putting their own personal safety at risk, many Lumad chose the latter, which tells us two very interesting things: 1) that by 1631, after less than a decade of local missionary presence, Lumad identification with Christianity was, in Butuan and parts of Caraga and Siargao, strong enough to withstand a full-fledged anti-Spanish revolt; and 2) that the personal attachments of many Lumad in these contact areas, and by extension their loyalty and allegiance, lay squarely with the Religious and with Christianity, rather than with the Spanish Crown. The Religious were protected by, among others, the Butuanons both on the coast and in the interior, by Mangabo's brother-in-law in Siargao, and by Mangabo's son Zancalan. Ultimately, Mangabo himself spared the lives of two Recoletos for no apparent strategic reason, even though he had already murdered several other Spaniards without hesitation. The Recoleto accounts are uncharacteristically boastful of this outcome, and justifiably so.

Inadequate Spanish military support from the colonial centers of Manila and Cebu meant that isolated missions and Christianized communities in the Visayas and Mindanao had to rely primarily on their own initiative to defend their settlements and missions. The need to defend against the Moro threat was a powerful fact of the colonial experience in Mindanao, and a problem shared by both Lumad converts and Recoletos. It was also another important commonality that united the missionized Lumad. When we speak of Lumad resistance in the colonial period, this particular manifestation—resistance against Moro raids by Lumad Christians—is just as representative and true of their ethnohistory as the scattered anti-Spanish uprisings that we once thought were the norm.

---

[129] See Thomas McKenna, *Muslim Rulers and Rebels: Everyday Politics and Armed Separatism in the Southern Philippines* (Berkeley, CA: University of California Press, 1998), pp. 82–83.

[130] Gallop notes the use of the toponym *Filibin* to mark the location of the writer in two Qur'an manuscripts from the early nineteenth century found in the British Library. One, attributed to Musa bin Muhammad al-Ra'is al-Jakki, refers to the *masjid al-Jakki al-Hakari bi-Filibbin*. The other, copied by Abd al-Ghafur bin Ahmad, is self-provenanced as *fi qariyat Ahla al-ka'ina bi-baldat al-Filibin* (of the village of Ahla, in the land of the Philippines). Gallop explains that these notations may have been attempts to conform to Arabic practice in a formal, international context, but that references to *Filibbin* would not have been found in local, vernacular contexts, which were "always expressed in terms of the localised unit." See Annabel Teh Gallop, "From Caucasia to Southeast Asia: Daghestani Qur'ans and the Islamic Manuscript Tradition in Brunei and the southern Philippines," *Manuscripta Orientalia* 14,1 (2008): 32–56.

CHAPTER 5

YOUR SLAVES WHO SHALL SERVE YOU: THE HINTERLAND TRIBES OF MINDANAO SEEK PATRONAGE

To unearth the history of indigenous minorities like the Lumad, we are often left to dig through the more obscure parts of the colonial record in the hope that we manage to read something between the lines that no one has noticed before. It is extremely rare to find official correspondence between representatives of indigenous or Lumad communities and Spanish authorities. I therefore cannot exaggerate the importance of the documents from northern Mindanao, presented in this chapter, which allow us to examine more directly the power relations between Lumad peoples and the colonial state at different moments in the early colonial period.

The correspondence comes from three different communities, at different points in time, and, as such, these documents are vignettes rather than representative samples. Nonetheless, they are quite significant for illuminating some important elements of Lumad society in the eighteenth and nineteenth centuries, and for complicating our understanding of how colonialism was experienced elsewhere in the Philippines. First, though the documents in question are separated by both space and time, all refer to communications that took place between Spanish colonial agents and multiple indigenous leaders, or *datu*, revealing the highly diffuse, even acephalous, nature of indigenous political leadership at the time. Second, the explicit efforts by indigenous leaders to formalize ties with Spanish power and "harmonize" themselves with colonial bureaucracy challenges the common perception of Lumad peoples as isolated from historical events and foreign cultural influences. Last but not least, the concessions requested by and granted to the Lumad tell us that the balance of power during these periods was quite different from what one might expect. In fact, this pericolonial area appears to have been subject to intense political negotiation, with the indigenous Lumad retaining the upper hand even in areas that, at least on paper, had been subjected to the Spanish colonial taxation and tribute collection system since the late 1500s.

This chapter is built around three *expedientes*, or dossiers of correspondence, from two different Spanish archives, in which specific concessions are being negotiated to formalize relations between a Lumad group and the colonial state. The first *expediente*, found in the Archivo Provincial de los Agustinos Recoletos, located in Marcilla, Navarra, involves correspondence from the early 1700s and outlines specific demands in relation to vassalage, tribute, and missionization being put forth by *datus* representing the communities of the upper Tagoloán River in the province of Misamis in north Mindanao. The original letter was transcribed by Recoleto missionaries in a local dialect of the Visayan language, and reading it brings us as close as we will ever get to hearing a Lumad voice from the colonial period. Its significance to understanding the Lumad past therefore cannot be overstated. The same letter was later translated into Spanish as it became part of official correspondence, and a comparison of the original Visayan transcript with the Spanish translation, including the radically different cultural contexts in which certain terms were typically used, suggests that the messages sent by the *datus* and received by the colonial state may have been quite different.

The second and third *expedientes*, both located in the Archivo Histórico Nacional in Madrid, are internal memos which, though written entirely in Spanish, nonetheless provide a significant amount of useful data that flesh out Lumad ethnohistory in unexpected ways. The second *expediente* relates to comparable demands put forth by a different group of *datus* representing six different communities in Misamis in 1838, a little over a century after the first letter described above. In this document, the Lumad request conditional incorporation into Spanish dominion, principally through an explicit request for the intervention of colonial officials in local politics, as they ask for justices of the peace to be appointed among their *datus* "according to the example of the Christian settlements."[1] As in the first *expediente*, this second one outlines an attempt by Lumad leaders to secure major concessions in terms of fulfilling obligations related to tribute and corvée labor that were expected by Spain of all its native Philippine subjects. And, as in the first *expediente*, this letter includes an impassioned plea by concerned officials that Spain accept these costly demands because the Lumads and Lumad territories have become critically important to Spain's efforts to contain the piracy of the neighboring Moros.

The third and final *expediente* is a description, made in the course of a larger progress report on the state of the colony, of a treaty secured by the military governor of Caraga with the *mandaya*, or upriver peoples, under his purported jurisdiction in eastern Mindanao. Like the first two pieces of correspondence, this *expediente* specifies the military significance of these Lumad to the protection of Spanish interests in the south. However, it is also quite interesting for its incorporation of a key indigenous concept into colonial governance.

A MESSAGE FROM THE HEATHENS OF THE TAGOLOÁN HINTERLANDS

In this period, Tagoloán is of tremendous importance to the overall story of a very large number of Lumad communities in northeast Mindanao today. According to the official genealogy of at least one such community located deep in the interior, one of their most important ancestors, *Apu* Pabulusen, lived on the Tagoloán River approximately 250 to 300 years ago, depending on how one computes the space between each *tuad*, or generation.[2] As explained later in this volume, Pabulusen is considered a true, biological (not mythical) ancestor, one who is related to most, if not all, living Higaunon and Bukidnon, but also to many of their Manobo and other Lumad neighbors.[3] As related by William Biernatzki for the Bukidnon and Yumo for

---

[1] Archivo Histórico Nacional (hereafter AHN), Ultramar, 5155, Exp13,n2,f1r.

[2] Baliguihan Ancestral Land Claim (hereafter BALC), "Documented Proofs of the Historical Ethnic Origins and Long Term Settlement of the Higaunons of Baligiyan," supporting document for R10-CADC-012, Department of Environment and Natural Resources, Government of the Republic of the Philippines, 1994, section 1.2.

[3] See William Biernatzki SJ, "Bukidnon Datuship in the Upper Pulangi River Valley," *Bukidnon*

the Agusan Manobo, Pabulusen is also the primary actor in oral traditions about the origins of indigenous leadership that revolve around the myth of Kumbalan and Tawaga, who received from the king of Spain the symbols of political authority still used by Lumads today, as discussed in the next chapter. Baliguihan's genealogy similarly reveres Pabulusen "for starting the Higaonon *lagimu* or spiritual laws."[4]

These oral histories similarly relate the movement of Pabulusen's descendants out of Tagoloán and into the mountainous interior towards Sinakungan (in present-day Agusan del Sur province). Baliguihan's genealogical timeframe places Pabulusen in Tagoloán prior to 1744, and, considering that Lumads may change names several times in one lifetime, there is a possibility that the ancestor now known as Pabulusen was one of the Tagoloán *datu* named in the first *expediente*. This is a tantalizing possibility, but the only tenable statement we can make is that the matters discussed in this correspondence were likely relevant to the lives of Pabulusen and his immediate descendants, given the probability that they were living in Tagoloán during that period.

I mention Pabulusen not only to underscore the extraordinary cultural relevance of the first letter discussed below, but also to speak to the matter that may be of greatest concern to Mindanao specialists at this point—whether the correspondence discussed in this chapter actually pertains to the indigenous peoples of Mindanao, or whether it is an attempt to ascribe indigenous status to already Christianized Visayans who migrated from the northern islands during Spanish times. In my opinion, the answer is unambiguous: the relevant documents state clearly that the *datus* do not represent migrant Visayan converts, but local communities of *monteses* who, in the early eighteenth century, were living somewhere upriver in Tagoloán. This is an area that, today, three centuries later, is populated almost exclusively by descendants of settlers from other islands to the north, and is recognized as a clearly coastal, lowland, non-Lumad culture area.

The Tagoloán *expediente* is dated 1753, written for the most part in the hand of a single transcriber, and relates the founding of the upriver mission of Tagoloán in the province of Misamis.[5] It forms the whole of *legajo* (bundle) 61, folder number 3, of the Provincial Archive of the Order of Augustinian Recollects, Province of San Nicolás de Tolentino, located in Marcilla, Navarra, Spain. The date on the *datu* letter itself is October 6, 1722, which tells us this is a transcription of the original correspondence, now presumably lost.

The summary states that the basis for this collection of documents referring to Tagoloán is a letter written by the *infieles* (infidels, in both the religious and political sense) of the lake of Tagoloán.[6] We know from the previous chapter that Lumad *principales* in the early seventeenth century were literate and made use of letters to convey information to other communities, as was the case during the Caraga Revolt

---

Politics and Religion, ed. A. de Guzman and E. Pacheco, IPC Papers 11 (Quezon City: Ateneo de Manila University Press, 1973), pp. 15–50. See also Dionisio Yumo, "Power Politics of the Southern Agusan Manobo," *Mindanao Journal* 15 (1988): 3–47.

[4] BALC, "Documented Proofs," Section 2.2.

[5] The *expediente* itself is written on what appears to be handmade rice paper, extremely thin, delicate, and appealing to insects. As a result, different portions of the letter cited and its translation are not simply illegible but gone, i.e., the bit of paper on which it was written has been either broken off or consumed by insects.

[6] Archivo Provincial de los Agustinos Recoletos, Marcilla, Spain (hereafter ARM) leg 61, num 3, f1r–2v.

of 1631, when Karaga rebels attempted to gain the support of the *principales* of Butuan. We can therefore assume that the original letter was indeed written by the *datus* of Tagoloán, and that the transcription by a Spanish hand reflects the original phrasing and spelling they used. The letter declares their desire to recognize and accept the authority (*dar la obediencia*, lit. "give obedience to") of the king of Spain, but only under specific conditions, including:

1) that their missionary priest be assigned for life (*sea vitalicio*).

2) that they not be required to pay tribute in perpetuity, but in annual recognition of *vasallaje* (vassalage), married men will each pay a basket of rice, and single men will each pay half a basket.

3) that the priest, not the magistrate, be in charge of elections.

4) that they be given four pieces of artillery for their fortifications.

A note adds that the *fiscal* (municipal attorney) at first says no, then hesitates, and finally asks that the Provincial of the Recoletos be advised, and the entire agreement be approved.[7]

The letter, written in an archaic form of Visayan, discussed below, is followed immediately and unceremoniously by its translation into Spanish, which was done by *bachiller* Miguel García, according to its cover page. There are other letters transcribed in Spanish, including one in which the Lumad people of Tagoloán ask the Recoletos that they be ministered to by the priest Fray Juan de la Concepción, who, according to the second part of the same *expediente*

> ... had been in that Mission since the year 1620, and has managed to convince many infidels to be instructed in the principles of our Holy Religion, and although few among them are baptized, it is because the Missionary wishes first and foremost to prepare them such that their Christianization may be truly sound.[8]

This is a Recoleto document, obviously created with the involvement of Recoleto friars, and, as such, it was part of the bureaucratic record of their explicit missionary agenda. However, to find anything from this period written in an indigenous Philippine language is rare enough, and rarer still for the south. Therefore we should not ignore the Recoleto voice when it is being so informative, even though the focus of this chapter is the indigenous side of the equation.

In the compiled documents, there is a letter by Fray Concepción to the Father Provincial, Fray Benito San Pablo, in which he states his great desire to go to Tagoloán. In addition to other, more bureaucratic points, the documents advise that a stipend be allotted to provide for a second missionary to accompany Fray Concepción because the Order could not, in good conscience, place a lone Religious in such an isolated and difficult location (*en punto tan aislado y dificil*).[9]

---

[7] Ibid.

[8] ARM leg 61, num 3, f1v.

[9] Ibid.

The superiors are also informed that these particular *infieles* are quite peaceful and that not only are they responsive to the "sacred doctrine" preached by the Recoletos, they also have been expressing some active interest in conversion for a considerable time. Therefore, the sincerity of their motives in receiving a missionary should not be doubted, arguing that

> ... these heathens are obedient and inclined towards Our Holy Religion and that they have long made the same demands they are making now; one cannot show them to be acting in bad faith.[10]

These statements, particularly those by Fray Concepción, tell us that, at the time of the original writing, the Recoletos had already cultivated a relationship with the community of Tagoloán, such that the missionary priest had been working in Tagoloán for two years and had already managed to secure a few baptisms— despite the fact that Tagoloán remained a "wild" entity, a population of *monteses* outside the authority or sanction of either the Spanish empire or the Catholic Church. To underscore the intensity of this relationship between Fray Concepción and the Lumads of Tagoloán, the *expediente* adds that Concepción finds these particular natives positively inclined, in that they are

> without the other superstitious beliefs common to infidels of these islands; he [Concepción] furnishes as proof of their good inclinations their having spontaneously defended the garrison [*presidio*] of Cagayán on several occasions against the attacks of the Mindanaos [or Magindanaw Moros], plus several other representations they have made in order that they may be welcomed under the dominion of the King of Spain, something being done once again by three *principales* who are living with the Missionary with this very objective in mind.[11]

The letter adds that Concepción has asked for funds to build a church because "those natives are very fond of the magnificence of the service [the Mass]." The *expediente* goes on to note that Concepción had also made some "apostolic excursions" to other settlements. Initially, the Religious had planted a mission in the interior, along the Pulangi River, located south of Tagoloán, but they were forced to move to another location, called Pugasan, due to the unhealthy climate.

Therefore this correspondence was, for all intents and purposes, simply a formalization of the process of establishing an official mission and seeking financial support from the administrative wing of the Order. A major contrast between the Spanish and Visayan versions of the letter is that the Spanish version is loaded with legal terminology that does not appear in the Visayan, although the Visayan text may certainly be interpreted as according with the Spanish translation in terms of its most probable legal intentions. The Spanish text is therefore not a literal, but a legalistic, translation of the community's petition.[12]

---

[10] "... dice que estos infieles son dociles y afectos a Nuestra Sancta Religion y que siendo en ellos antigua pretencion la que ahora espresan, no debe rebelarse obren de mala fe." (ARM leg 61, n3, f1r).

[11] ARM leg 61, n3, f1v. Cagayán was the closest settlement to the west and the main Spanish presence in Misamis province.

[12] This is my translation of the letter from the Tagoloán *datus*, based primarily on the Visayan

Admiral who is our master:

There in [the settlement of] Caguindayon we who give notice are the *datus* who are all from these here towns upriver in Tagoloán, and who have gathered in the house of Cabayao but Manengo could not be with us because he was left in the town of Dalabahan[13] because he got sick. It is our joy and God's will that … we may not fall out of favor with Your Majesty, your dispatch arrived, and that of the Father Prior Fray Geronimo de San Miguel and of the Father Deputy Fray Juan de la Concepción brought to us by the [Father] Lieutenant [Fray] Nicolas Tolentino; and we the *datu* who have gathered among ourselves, these indeed are our names = the first ones to be baptized[14] are these = 1. Ca Bayao = 2. Ganayan = 3. Langundayon = 4. Catumbú = 5. Balagon = 6. Aliliton = 7. Suguib = 8. Anlas =

Those who consent = 1. Dalabahan = Buanun = Cagunad =

And before these two Witnesses who are Captain Miguel Tolon, and Captain L. P. Magon, we agree that all will agree to become the *sacup* of the King of Castilla, as we have noted in the message we sent to the Governor of Manila on account of the constrictions of our taxes, and that we will trust in the Spaniards and this is done with our free will. To admiral Andres García Fernandez and to the General in Cebu to please accept this as our word before the Governor of Manila so that these things for which we ask, if it could be approved by the Governor, that forever we are not to be taxed, and have no religious fee[15] to be paid in the church, and have no fee for weddings, and that we may be given our burials without fee … and that the *gantas*[16] will neither fall short of nor exceed the regulated amounts; and what

---

text, thus the peculiar tone and language of the letter follows a Visayan cadence. I have used the Spanish version as a supporting text, to compensate where applicable for the missing, unreadable, or ambiguous portions of the Visayan text. Dr. Aloysius Cañete was of substantial assistance in achieving a proper modern Cebuano translation of the Visayan text, but I take sole responsibility for any errors or deficiencies in the final interpretation presented in this chapter. My transcriptions of both the Visayan text (ARM, leg 61, num 3, HN25,f4r–5r) and the Spanish text (ARM, leg 61, num 3, HN25,f5r–6r) are included for reference as Appendix E, and cited according to line numbers where necessary. My clarifications are indicated between brackets, and original or equivalent terms are indicated by parentheses.

[13] In the *legajo*, this name is transcribed three different ways: Dalabahan, Dalabasan, and Dalabanan. This is most likely due to the close similarity of the letters *h*, *s*, and *n* when written in old cursive. Other names in the *legajo* likewise have single-letter variations in spelling. "Dalabahan," however, matches a name that appears elsewhere in Spanish archives as belonging to "a brave Bukidnon chieftain who helped the Spaniards fight against the Muslims." See Carmen Ching Unabia, "Gugud: A Bukidnon Oral Tradition," *Asian Folklore Studies* 44 (1985): 227, n. 6. Unabia cites Emma H. Blair and James A. Robertson, *The Philippine Islands, 1493–1898* (Cleveland, OH: Arthur H. Clark Company, 1903–09), vol. 46, p. 57.

[14] In the Spanish version, these names are introduced without any reference to baptism, i.e., simply as *los primeros y principales*. See Appendix E, line 57.

[15] The word *sanctorum* is used in the text. According to the online dictionary of the Real Academia Española (DRAE, www.rae.es/), this word was used in the Philippines in reference to an alms quota collected from each adult (age sixteen and over), whether native or *mestizo*, in order to sustain parochial services. It is a tithe, in other words.

[16] According to DRAE, a *ganta* is an indigenous Philippine volume measurement for dry goods and liquids equivalent to three liters, whereas a *cavén* is a unit measurement for dry goods equal to twenty-five *gantas* (see also le Roux et al. 2004: 336, n. 2). Both are still in use today. See also Pierre Le Roux, Bernard Sellato, and Jacque Ivanoff, eds., *Weights and Measures in*

we ask for is our Priest[17] and the four pieces of artillery [along with gunpowder] that we will grind[18] in our town. What we will give for the year is one *cavan* of rice from the married ones, a half from the bachelors; and as for Mr. Miguel Tulon, our wish with regard to him is that it remain possible that he doesn't leave us, and that we remain within the same *sacup,* and the same for Sebastian Balogilan, because they are the ones whom we follow [and who direct us in everything relevant to] our service and obedience to our Priest = _____

Mr. Admiral, should you consider us potentially helpful in battling against the Malanao [Maranaw], and we would not refuse but we are lacking fortifications for our town and secondly the people need to be guarding their fields at harvest time every year that we cannot just leave behind. This is our word. Our greetings to you [plural] and may God keep you to a year that is not … [In] Cabanglaan, October 6 of 1722. All of us who have authored this are your *ulibun* [slaves] who will serve you still, in the hope that you shall not abandon us: Dalabahan = Buanon = Cabayao = Gavayan = Langundayun = Cagunad = Catumbis = Alilitun = Suguib = Anlas = Balagon = Mr. Admiral Andres García Fernandez

In the Spanish version, the section requesting the freedom from tribute and religious fees is worded somewhat more explicitly and formally:[19]

In the presence of these witnesses … we conform and unite in order to … recognize the superior authority of His Majesty, may God keep him, the

---

Southeast Asia: Metrological Systems and Societies (Paris: École française d'Extrême-Orient and Institut de Recherche sur le Sud-Est asiatique, 2004), p. 336, n. 2.

The online conversion charts of the International Rice Research Institute clarify that, prior to 1973, one *caván* of rough rice was 44 kg, and one of milled rice was 56 kg; both were calibrated to 50 kg by 1973. The Philippine *ganta,* in turn, is distinct from the Malaysian *gantang,* which weighs 2.54 kg. See *World Rice Statistics 1993–94* (Los Baños, Philippines: International Rice Research Institute, 1995), pp. 258–59. However, in the Spanish text of our document, the amount of rice indicated for annual tribute is simply one *cesto,* or basket, of unspecified size.

[17] Here I translate *Padre* to Priest, because in the document the *datus* code-switch to Spanish in referring to "our priest." They do not refer to a formal title, as in the beginning of the letter, nor do they use the Visayan word for "father."

[18] The Visayan original asks for four *baríl* (the word used for "barrel" in north Mindanao Visayan today, from Spanish *barril*), then talks about grinding down or "milling" something unspecified. The word is from the root *galing,* used today for grain mills. My preliminary interpretation (and that of Cañete, see earlier note) was that this would refer to about four barrels of unhusked rice, corn, or another item to be milled. However, the Spanish version clearly states that they are asking for weapons (*pidimos qual piezas de Artilleria,* Appendix E, line 74), and the summary that opens the *expediente* itself specifies four pieces of artillery. In both versions, local agricultural production is mentioned separately, and the amount of tribute specified indicates that no subsidy of grain was needed by Tagoloán. Therefore, I can only conclude that the word *baríl* was used locally in 1722 to mean a kind of gun, as it is today in more northern Philippine languages like Tagalog. The grinding is most likely a reference to ingredients for gunpowder, which, at that time, needed to be ground together in a device very similar to a grain mill—a process called "corning." See Bert S. Hall, *Weapons and Warfare in Renaissance Europe: Gunpowder, Technology, and Tactics* (Baltimore, MD: The Johns Hopkins Press, 2001), pp. 68–104.

[19] See Appendix E, lines 60–71.

King of Spain, and we repeat anew that which we have sworn before the Governor of these Philippine Islands, in the City of Manila, as to the steadfastness and integrity of our trustworthy will, and with the will of the admiral Andres Fernandez García and of the General of the Province of Cebu, our Representation as such can be made manifest and evident, and accepted and secured if it seems to be so to the Governor ... that we are freed from tribute in perpetuity, and without the religious fee that is paid in the churches, and its fee for weddings, and burials as well be free of payment, and for this we might have the Special Decree carved in stone ... that *gantas* that may neither fall short of nor exceed the regulated amounts; and that for our Priest we request that he may be moved [here] for the whole [of his life].

The final paragraph is likewise interestingly worded in the Spanish version:

Mr. Admiral, we suppose that His Majesty would like for us to consult and prepare to wage war to the Malanao; we are not able to refuse as such, but we are impeded, first by our town not having any fortifications, and the other [reason being] the unavoidable care that the people must take in their rice farming and sowing, which, at present, is coming in [ripening] such that it is not possible to abandon it. And with this we close and salute Your Majesties many times over and may God keep you many [years], ad infinitum. Cabonlaan, October 6 of the year 1722. All of us who wrote this are your *esclavos* [slaves] who remain at the service of Your Majesties for always, unless you abandon us ... [20]

THE KING'S FAITHFUL "VASSALS" AND "SLAVES"

Regarding the nature of the relationship that the community of Tagoloán wished to establish with the king of Spain, as per their formal statement in the year 1722, the group of *datu* employ the indigenous term *sacup*, which is still in use today in several Philippine language groups to describe one thing as being part of a larger group of things. In general political usage, it refers to alliance networks that form around particularly strong or powerful individuals. Among Lumad peoples today, *sacup* refers to both the alliances that link *datus* from different settlements—often revolving around a particularly charismatic or well-respected *datu*—and the relationship between a *datu* and his followers.

Sacup is translated into Spanish as *vasallaje*, which in English would be "vassalage," which raises the question of the degree to which the Lumads' understanding of their traditional horizontal alliance formation (*sacup*) was distinct from the vertical feudal Spanish relationship of vassalage (*vasallaje*) to the king. We may therefore question how well each side may have appreciated, and perhaps exploited, the difference in these organizational structures. The interplay between these two concepts—and between foreign and indigenous political concepts in general—shows us a different aspect of the relationship between Lumads and the colonial state. Some things are lost in translation, but other things are also gained, on either side of this political relationship.

---

[20] See Appendix E, lines 81–88.

As mentioned earlier, the letter is for the most part comprehensible to someone today who knows Cebuano Visayan, which was and is the de facto trade language of the Visayas. But the indigenous usage of *sacup* three centuries ago is not as simple as looking in the dictionary, because Visayans in the seventeenth century used the word *haop* to refer to such inclusive groups. In modern Cebuano, the word is written as *sakup* and is defined as a subordinate, subject, or dependent. In the same dictionary, however, the word *ulipon*, a term routinely translated as "slave," is given as a synonym. *Sakup* appears as a cognate in present-day Tagalog as *sakop*, whose dictionary definition conveys a range of meanings: "subject; a person who is under the power, control, or influence of another; vassal; ... conquest; the thing conquered; ... territory over which jurisdiction extends."[21] In contrast, I apply an understanding of the *sacup*—and how it enables the type of confederation mentioned above—that is informed largely by modes of political organization among Lumad groups in the present day, as well as contemporary descriptions of political and social organization in the central and southern Philippines in the early colonial period.[22]

In political terms, the *sacup* delineates an alliance network that ties people together at various levels of society—whether amongst *datus*, or between *datus* and their followers, as opposed to a vertical or hierarchical type of tributary relationship. Describing the general features of social organization in the Visayas region in the early colonial period, William Henry Scott explains that the Visayan term *haop* (a cognate of *sacup*) is "any inclusive group, but especially one supportive of a person on whom they were dependent, like children on their parents or slaves on their master," adding further that kinship, whether real or fictive, would be an important determinant of membership in such a group. In the more densely populated Visayas islands, membership in a *hoap* could number up to a hundred households, and would therefore have much more pronounced hierarchies.[23]

At the center of the *sacup* is its head or leader, who was often referred to by the Spaniards as *rey* (sometimes *rrey*) or "king." Yet such a leader was neither king nor king-like, but simply another *datu* who, as *primus inter pares*, draws his fellow *datus* into his circle of influence and unifies them politically. This web of alliances, in turn, is a mode of political organization that echoes the *mandala* concept, described by O. W. Wolters as the indigenous political nucleus of Southeast Asian cultures.[24] As for the *sacup* leader, Scott gives us a range of titles acquired from Malay and Sanskrit, from *Saripada*, *Batara*, and *Rajah*, all of which imply a level of nobility, to indigenous

---

[21] See William Henry Scott, *Barangay: Sixteenth-Century Philippine Culture and Society* (Quezon City: Ateneo de Manila University Press, 1994), pp. 135–36. See also Rodolfo Cabonce SJ, *An English-Cebuano Visayan Dictionary* (Metro Manila: National Book Store, 1983), pp. 968 and 906, respectively. See Leo English CSR, *English-Tagalog Dictionary* (Metro Manila: National Book Store, 1993), p. 1132.

[22] The exception was and remains the hierarchical Muslim or *Moro* sultanates in western Mindanao and Sulu that dominated warfare in much of this area until the late nineteenth century. See Scott, *Barangay*, pp. 173–78.

[23] See ibid., p. 136. Scott here is relying on accounts from the early Spanish period, citing specifically the *Boxer Codex* of 1590 and Mateo Sánchez's *Bocabulario de la lengua Bisaya* of 1617.

[24] As described in O. W. Wolters, *History, Culture, and Region in Southeast Asian Perspectives* (Ithaca, NY: Cornell Southeast Asia Program Publications, 1999). See also Anthony Reid, *Southeast Asia in the Age of Commerce 1450–1680*, vol. 1 (New Haven, CT: Yale University Press, 1988), pp. 120–21.

titles, such as *pangulo* (or its Malay cognate, *penghulu*), which means simply "one who serves as the head," and *kaponoan*," from *puno*, "root or trunk."[25]

Within a *sacup*, a personalistic and symbiotic relationship is established between the individual and his allies. Scott, drawing from contemporaneous accounts in the sixteenth and seventeenth centuries, explains that

> These *datus* were part of ... a loose federation of chiefs bound by loose ties of personal allegiance to a senior among them. The head of such a chiefdom exercised authority over his supporting chiefs, but not over their subjects or territory.[26]

Depending upon the relationships among individual *sacup* members, there is the potential for members to coalesce into a temporary hierarchy for cooperative purposes, such as military defense, with the structure of the hierarchy itself based on any variety of cultural factors, such as local notions of social or spiritual precedence.[27] Today, individual Lumads typically identify themselves as being the *sacup* of the *datu* with whom they consult when difficult issues arise locally, and *datus* turn to their own networks to converse with other *datus* regarding supralocal issues. Today, instead of open warfare, these federations more often coalesce in response to the battle over ancestral land rights, presenting a united front against government bureaucracy or lowland businesses, or, in some cases, opposing factions formed by other *sacup* networks.[28]

As with any axis of social organization, inequalities are bound to develop based on the fact that all stakeholders are not created equal. Given that the title of *datu* is acquired as much by inheritance as by achievement, someone with proven military prowess will, by rights, be called to leadership before others in the same *sacup*. However, in principle, the *sacup* is a horizontal relationship, made hierarchical in practice only by the personal attributes of its members. With regard to the existence of such political hierarchies in acephalous or otherwise egalitarian societies, I would emphasize the coalition-building aspects of the *sacup* over any of its vertical aspects.

Related discussions pertaining to the larger Southeast Asian context describe the same type of horizontal coalescence by using the term "federation" or, alternately, "confederation." In a special volume on warfare in premodern Southeast Asia, Victor Lieberman points out the significance of this social phenomenon and its further consequences for larger identity formation. Referring to the work of Gerrit Knaap on Ambon, he remarks that

---

[25] Scott, *Barangay*, p. 128.

[26] Ibid., p. 129.

[27] Reid, *Southeast Asia in the Age of Commerce*, p. 123. On precedence, see Thomas Reuter, *The House of Our Ancestors: Precedence and Dualism in Highland Balinese Society* (Leiden: KITLV Press, 2002); and Andrew McWilliam, *Paths of Origin, Gates of Life: A Study of Place and Precedence in Southwest Timor* (Leiden: KITLV Press, 2002).

[28] One modern iteration of these federations are the so-called "unified CADT" (Certificate of Ancestral Land Title) coalitions throughout Mindanao, in which several autonomous communities have banded together successfully to secure legal title to their ancestral lands and deal more effectively with pressure from both the Philippine government and corporate ventures on their lands.

> Even before the arrival of Europeans … local groups formed federations, in effect proto-states, with a more or less stable identity that derived in large measure from their waging constant warfare … against rival federations.[29]

In the same special volume, Felice Noelle Rodriguez, without using the term "federation," also describes an identical phenomenon pertaining to the Visayas cultural region—of which the Lumad of adjoining northern Mindanao were a vital part. Political life during the early colonial period essentially "revolved around villages and supra-village federations. Dependent on the personality of powerful local warriors, the latter tended to be short-lived, unstable, if not also acephalous."[30]

In contrast to the horizontally structured, indigenous confederations that typified the *sacup*, the feudal *vasallaje* is, by definition, a vertical relationship, involving dependency, that ties a vassal (*vasallo*) to his lord (*señor*). As if to underscore the difference between *sacup* and *vasallaje*, the word *Señor* is also used in Spanish to refer to "the Lord" God. *Vasallaje* involves an obligation of obedience and servitude—principally in the form of military service—on the part of the vassal for the benefit of the lord, while the latter is supposed to provide to the vassal some form of protection and maintenance, for instance, by granting rights to farm land within the lord's territory. It is perhaps a truism that an ally is not the same thing as a vassal, and this is, of course, true for the Spanish empire. In other words, "an empire has no allies, only vassals."[31] In both Spanish and English, having a "lord" implies the subject's servility. The indigenous concepts pertaining to *sacup*, on the other hand, carry no such implication.

It is notable that, in internal state correspondence some decades after the 1753 letter, the word *vasallaje* disappears completely, and the indigenous term *sacup* is then adapted for Spanish use. It is transcribed thereafter as *sacop*, pluralized as *sacopes*. In 1778, the term *sacop* is used by the governor general's office in correspondence concerning area attacks by the Dutch elsewhere in island Southeast Asia.[32] Another example discussed towards the end of this chapter is an *expediente* that tells of the *reducción*, or settlement, in 1848 of several more hinterland *datus*, as well as some Moros, "along with a large number of their *sacups*" in Misamis province.[33] The term is still in use some decades later, appearing in the account of a journey through the interior of eastern Mindanao by the French anthropologist Joseph Montano.[34]

---

[29] Victor Lieberman, "Some Comparative Thoughts on Premodern Southeast Asian Warfare," *Journal of the Economic and Social History of the Orient* 46,2 (2003): 219. See also Gerrit Knaap, "Headhunting, Carnage, and Armed Peace in Amboina, 1500–1700," *Journal of the Economic and Social History of the Orient* 46,2 (2003): 165–92.

[30] Lieberman, "Some Comparative Thoughts … ," p. 216. See also Felice Noelle Rodriguez, "Juan De Salcedo Joins the Native Form of Warfare," *Journal of the Economic and Social History of the Orient* 46,2 (2003): 143–64.

[31] Ignacio Ramonet, "Vasallaje," *Le Monde Diplomatique* (Chilean edition), October 2002 http://www.lemondediplomatique.cl, accessed October 4, 2005. *"Un imperio no tiene aliados, sólo vasallos,"* written in reference to the United States of America but recalling the historical experience of Western Europe.

[32] Archivo General de Indias in Sevilla (hereafter AGI), Estado, 45, N.5/5/3r.

[33] "Con gran número de sus sacopes," in AHN, Ultramar, 5161, Exp 33, cover page.

[34] Joseph Montano, *Een Reis naar de Philippijnen* (Project Gutenberg, Ebook 13236, 2004), at http://www.gutenberg.org/etext/13236 (page 39), accessed November 30, 2007.

In this particular case, it is apparent that the European concept of vassalage did not take root in Lumad areas of Mindanao, and that the indigenous conceptualization of the proper relationship between such levels of political authority had prevailed—so much so that colonial officials apparently deemed it appropriate to replace the already familiar *vasallaje* with the indigenous word, Hispanized as *sacop/sacopes*,[35] as a political and administrative term, even in internal correspondence. At the very least, this complicates our picture of the power imbalance one generally expects to find in the relationship between "colonizer" and "colonized," and testifies to the inability of Spanish officials to impose their authority on this part of Mindanao in general, and on the Lumad in particular.

The distinction between the indigenous *sacup* and the Spanish *vasallaje* is not the only major cultural difference revealed by the translations of the Tagoloán text. In both versions of the text, the *datus* referred to themselves as "slaves" of the king. This word, in the particular Visayan dialect used in the text, is *ulibun*; it is *ulipon* in present-day Cebuano Visayan, *oripun* in Tagalog, and *esclavo* in the Spanish translation. Despite the uniform translation of these words into "slave" in English, we know from the Southeast Asian context in general, and from the Philippine context in particular, that what Europeans referred to as "slavery" in the early colonial period was quite distinct from "slavery" in Europe, the Americas, and Africa.[36]

On the nature of Southeast Asian "slavery," in general, Reid and others caution against assuming any similarity at all between European notions of "slavery" and Southeast Asian notions, explaining that "most of the Southeast Asian terms which early European travelers translated as slave could in other circumstances be rendered as debtor, dependant, or subject."[37] For the precolonial Philippines, Scott wrote that, given the inalienable rights and privileges of the average "slave," the indigenous category of *oripun* was such that "sociologically ... they constituted the class which in contemporary European society would have been called commoners."[38] Fenella Cannell goes even further, describing it as a type of proletarianism:

---

[35] Though at present I cannot determine the word's etymology, we can eliminate two possible linguistic roots for *sacup* or *sakop*. First, there is no such word or cognate in the encyclopedic dictionary of the *Real Academia Española*, nor does it register as familiar among the native Spanish speakers with whom I have inquired. Secondly, Scott's statement that the term *haop* was its Visayan cognate clearly tells us that *sacup* is not a Visayan word. Scott, *Barangay*, p. 136.

[36] For example, in Herbert Klein, *African Slavery in Latin America and the Caribbean* (New York, NY: Oxford University Press, 1988). See also Robin Winks, ed., *Slavery, A Comparative Perspective: Readings on Slavery from Ancient Times to the Present* (New York, NY: New York University Press, 1972).

[37] Reid, *Southeast Asia in the Age of Commerce*, p. 132. This is perhaps one of the few instances in which we are justified in "upstreaming" more recent descriptions to the distant past. Twentieth-century ethnographic research from Bukidnon by Biernatzki and from Agusan by Garvan, as well as my own personal knowledge of the actual usage of the word for "slave" by both Higaunon Lumads and Cebuano-speaking lowlanders in Misamis Oriental, corresponds exactly with descriptions of comparable populations from the eighteenth century in Mindanao and earlier. See Biernatzki, "Bukidnon Datuship." See also J. Garvan, *The Manobos of Mindanao* (Washington, DC: US Government Printing Office, 1941), pp. 22–26, 139–44, 184–86. See Oona T. Paredes, "People of the Hinterlands: Higaûnon Life in Northern Mindanao, Philippines" (Master's thesis, Arizona State University, 1997), pp. 132–39.

[38] Scott, *Barangay*, p. 133. See also Reid, *Southeast Asia in the Age of Commerce*, pp. 129–36.

> ... although debt-bondage was not (unlike European slavery) centrally defined by the idea of the "sale" of one person by another ... understood as the treatment of one person as equivalent to the inanimate property of another, we know that Filipinos were accustomed to think of a convertability between their labour obligations and tribute in other forms which could be substituted for it, a substitution which most people attempted to make, either in part or in total, and which was largely coextensive with a rise in social status. The most "exposed" persons in Filipino society were those with nothing at all ... to render within the *cycles of reciprocity*.[39]

Sather notes, however, that in Southeast Asia the debt that creates the bondage itself "was generally secondary to notions of obligation and fealty." Moreover, "slaves were not necessarily of lower status than the general population, and might at times attain considerable wealth and power," and that "there was generally less social distance between slaves and slave-owners" in Southeast Asia than in Europe and the Americas.[40] In other words, while being a "slave" in early modern Southeast Asia did involve "various degrees of non-freedom,"[41] it did not revolve around the type of social apartheid and abuse we have come to associate with the term, thanks not only to earlier European feudalism but also to the colonial-era trans-Atlantic slave trade and later types of human trafficking. There was thus a profound incongruity between the message Lumad leaders were sending and what Spain was officially receiving.

Given that Religious missions were integral to the Philippine colonial enterprise, one final translation must be examined, one with profound implications for these nascent allegiances, implications that cut through to core issue of identity. The Spanish word *fidelidad* (fidelity) touches on "faith" at a political and religious, as well as personal, level. It not only encapsulates the interdependence of the missionary and the colonial enterprises, it also hints at the personal ties that developed between the Recoleto missionaries and the Lumad. The word *infiel*, which is often translated as "heathen," literally means "infidel," and refers, in fact, to the totality of an individual's religious and political affiliation; that is, whether one's faith and loyalty (*fidelidad*) lie with the Spaniards. In the colonial period, Christianity and vassalage to the king were obviously tied together, even inseparable. In the case of the Tagoloán letter, even though all the *datus* in question were not yet baptized at the time of writing, their offer of vassalage to the king was founded on an earlier exposure to and accommodation of Catholic missionaries and their doctrine, without which a pledge of vassalage would have been inconceivable. To have been officially declared *fiel* or "faithful" was therefore a testimony not only to their favorable status in terms of religious indoctrination, but also to the Spanish perception of their general trustworthiness and reliability beyond the religious sense of the word. That is to say,

---

[39] Fenella Cannell, *Power and Intimacy in the Christian Philippines* (Cambridge: Cambridge University Press, 1999), p. 238, emphasis added.

[40] Clifford Sather, "Slavery," in *Southeast Asia: A Historical Encyclopedia from Angkor Wat to East Timor*, ed. Ooi Keat Gin (Santa Barbara, CA: ABC-CLIO, 2004), pp. 1222–23.

[41] Hans Hägerdal, "The First Invasion of East Timor: The Unknown Portuguese Conquest of the Seventeenth Century," NUS Southeast Asian Studies seminar series, February 13, 2012.

it was an assessment not only of their relationship to the Catholic Church, but also the quality of their character and their value as human beings.

This inseparability can be illustrated with reference to the application of the term *"infieles"* as an adjective to describe Muslim peoples. Given that Spain had almost a millennium of complex historical interaction with Muslim peoples on their home turf—defined by the bloody battle over Iberian cultural identity that was played out in the eight-hundred-year *Reconquista*—it should not be surprising that Spaniards had such paranoid and negative views about Muslims in general.[42] The Spanish use of the culturally loaded term *Moro* (Moor) to refer to Philippine Muslims therefore involved a direct conceptual link to their traumatic experience of the *Reconquista*. The related issue of religious fealty permeated almost every aspect of Spanish colonial interaction and policy in Filipinas, with regard not only to Muslims but also to non-Muslims. During the colonial period, in fact, there was no shortage of ink spilled in sweeping, acutely emotional denunciations of the Muslims of island Southeast Asia, who, beyond their alleged religious errors, were considered to be, by their very nature, irredeemably treacherous (*traidor*).[43]

From this perspective, the notion of cultivating alliances on multiple levels with the Lumad and other non-Muslim Philippine peoples therefore went beyond the usual methodologies of conquest. It may help to remember that Spanish conquistadors did not encounter the specter of Islam in the Americas, and in their conversion efforts there they did not have to contend with the constant presence of another politically powerful "world" religion. The idea that Spain would agree to major tax concessions and other privileges for the new converts of Tagoloán, located, as they were, in close proximity to Muslim Maranaw territory, becomes believable, even necessary, under these circumstances. The idea gains further legitimacy in light of previous Lumad cooperation in Spanish anti-Muslim campaigns mentioned in the previous chapter.

Finally, having pointed out that, in key points, the Visayan text and its Spanish translation appear to be conveying radically different messages to the king of Spain, I should make two observations before we proceed further. The first and rather obvious one is that the Spanish text, having been written by a Spanish scribe, would have been formatted to conform to administrative protocols, and therefore we cannot expect the Visayan document to have been translated literally because the result might well have been incomprehensible to the colonial bureaucracy. With the use of this administrative shorthand, we should not be surprised by the "mistranslation" of certain indigenous concepts that would have required further explanation. The

---

[42] See Tariq Modood for a deeper exploration of the historical antipathy of Europeans to Islam, and how this particular mode of "othering"—what Modood calls "cultural racism"—is more than mere religious intolerance because it appears to be an integral component of European self-definition. Tariq Modood, "Introduction," in *The Politics of Multiculturalism in the New Europe*, ed. Tariq Modood and Pnina Werbner (London: Zed Books, 1997), pp. 2–4.

[43] During my archival research in Spain in 2005, I was surprised to hear the very same language used by Spaniards in reference to Muslims currently residing in Spain, with one particularly opinionated man stating that their "treacherous" (*traidor*) nature was encoded in their very DNA and therefore immutable. I would agree entirely with Modood's statement that Muslims in colonial and modern times were/are "very much a part of 'the otherness' in the self-definition of the various peoples of [Europe]," an opposition that is manifested in the "racialisation" of Muslims (paralleling the racialization of Jews), such that the hostility towards Islam and Muslims is "more a form of racism than a form of religious intolerance." See Modood, "Introduction," pp. 2, 4.

second observation is less obvious: considering that the documents in this particular *expediente* are from the first half of the eighteenth century, and that previous Iberian visitors had already published a few cultural descriptions of the Philippines by this time, it is quite possible that at least some individuals within the colonial administration would have been aware of the differences between local political terms and the words *vasallaje* and *esclavo*, even if the king of Spain himself might not have known the difference. The Hispanized word *sacopes* is, in fact, found in many other Philippine documents preserved in the Archivo de Indias, the Archivo Histórico Nacional, and elsewhere for this and later periods. An example of one such document is discussed in the final section of this chapter. Moreover, the resident Recoleto missionaries, being both bilingual and close observers of Lumad culture, would have certainly understood the difference.

By the same token, I find no good reason to believe that the Tagoloán *datus* themselves did not fully understand what was involved in the *vasallaje* that was expected by the colonial government as part and parcel of recognizing the superior authority of the Spanish king. There is certainly nothing in the tone of the original Visayan text that suggests the signatories are oblivious to the nature of the relationship to which they were acceding, because at least some of their demands, which are identical in both versions, imply that they had been given information (most likely by the Recoleto missionaries) regarding the types of concessions a *vasallo* was expected to make, and the Crown's obligations of patronage that they could reasonably demand.

At the same time, there is also a very conditional tone to the Visayan text that indicates an awareness by the Tagoloán *datus* that they have the upper hand in the relationship with colonial officials. By mentioning their potential usefulness in battling the Maranaw, they appear to be playing to Spain's anti-Muslim sentiments as part of an effort to secure larger long-term concessions beyond a practical military alliance. The tone of the statement regarding the difficult demands of local agriculture also implies an awareness that, whatever demands Spain might try to secure from them related to any pledge of *vasallaje*, such demands would be, for the most part, unenforceable given their critical position vis-à-vis the Maranaw. This advantage is particularly significant considering the previous military advantage already demonstrated by the neighboring Kagayanon in the previous century.

It is not readily apparent from either the Visayan or Spanish text who the head of the Tagoloán *datus* may have been. Certainly no one is described explicitly as being of higher rank than the rest, nor is there any language in the Visayan text that suggests that there was a head to begin with. However, we can make several inferences from these documents regarding local politics and political organization in Tagoloán in the first quarter of the eighteenth century.

The texts mention that their signatories' decisive—and most recent—meeting took place in the house of Ca Bayao, which might signify his special status. However, the fact that the *datu* Manengo was so unfortunately "left behind" in Dalabahan's house suggests that a prior meeting had been convened in Dalabahan's home. It is, of course, possible that earlier meetings that were not necessary to mention had been held in the homes of other *datus*. But the manner in which the signatories to this declaration are mentioned in the original Visayan text suggests the presence of two political loci of power or influence in Tagoloán—Ca Bayao and Dalabahan:

> The first ones to be baptized are these: 1. Ca Bayao, 2. Gavayan,
> 3. Langundayon, 4. Catumbis, 5. Balagon, 6. Aliliton, 7. Suguib, 8. Anlas
>
> The ones who approve: 1. Dalabahan, 2. Buanun, 3. Cagunad.[44]

Dalabahan is also of potentially greater significance because the same name appears in Lumad oral traditions pertaining to the political history of northern Mindanao, discussed further in the next chapter.[45]

The order in which the names of the signatories are listed is the same in both lists, pointing to a possible correlation between list order and rank. But the most interesting aspect of these lists is the separation of the *datu* into two groups—*the first ones baptized* and *those who consent*—which clearly implies the existence of two distinct *sacups*, one of which had already developed a very close relationship with the Recoleto missionaries that, over two years of evangelization by Fray Concepción, resulted in the baptism of a handful of *principales*.

The implication is, of course, that the signatories had decided to cooperate for a common purpose, and that formalizing a political relationship with the Spaniards was a way of also doing the same among themselves without superceding any existing indigenous authority, thus maintaining the autonomy of each *datu* and each *sacup* of which he was the head. At the same time, despite the limits of the documents at hand, we cannot exclude the possibility that the unbaptized *datus* were already receiving catechism, or religious education, in preparation for future baptism. This possibility is fortified by the description of these particular Lumad presented by the Recoletos, i.e., that they are already inclined towards "Our Holy Religion."[46] If so, an earlier baptism—cited at the moment the request for incorporation is officially articulated—still points to the possible existence of two *sacups*, with one *sacup* already affiliated with the Recoleto missionaries through baptism.

CONCEPTUALIZING POLITICAL AUTHORITY

The concepts discussed above have great bearing on the relationship between Lumads and the colonial state. But I would also like to draw attention to the implications of the interplay between foreign and native political concepts, in particular what may have been lost in translation—and what might have been gained—by either side in this political relationship. And this study emphasizes the intricacy of a relationship that is complicated by issues of power, religion, and identity, such that it cannot be reduced to a willful imposition of dependency by the powerful upon the powerless. And what of the *datus'* motivation for working with Spanish concepts to begin with? Were they blissfully unaware of the discontinuity of these concepts, or did they conspire, with or without the missionaries, to subvert Spanish political bluster because they could?

Michael Laffan provides an interesting perspective on the entry of Arabic political concepts into Malay and Indonesian contexts that might well be applicable

---

[44] See Appendix E, lines 10–12.

[45] Unabia, "Gugud," pp. 213–19.

[46] During this period, the word "Religion" as used here referred to the doctrine of a particular Religious order, rather than to Christianity *per se*.

to the Philippine "translation" experience in general or, at the very least, to the case of our group of *datus* in Tagoloán. Laffan focuses on titulature, but includes other political concepts in his analysis, in which he states that, although Arabic terms

> ... were transplanted to new contexts as Islam spread, they did not necessarily replace existing words, nor did they necessarily force the speakers of languages other than Arabic to create new ones. Sometimes they were not embraced at all. For the case of Island Southeast Asia, [they] initially served to provide greater nuance to indigenous concepts, whether of rulership, of state, or sovereignty.[47]

Additional clarification makes it obvious that, working from the somewhat longer *durée* of the Islamic/Arabic presence in the same region, Laffan sees this aspect of Southeast Asian localization differently, arguing that, "rather than any process of translation ... the use of the political language of Islam represented the harmonization of a foreign tradition for local imperatives."[48] Or, more explicitly:

> ... the usage of Arabic titulature in the Malay context is more an aspect of the harmonization of the Islamic regal tradition than the translation of its forms and erasure of existing local structures. All such titles were most likely adopted by Southeast Asian rulers as part of the continuing process of adhesion to Islam. Over time the title of *sultan* served to denote connection with a far larger world—a world in which each claimed to be God's local representative, either with or without the support of the *'ulama*.[49]

Laffan notes the disparity between the adoption of such titulature and the actual governance of local rulers when he explains that this was neither a capitulation to foreign influences nor a replacement of local political concepts; instead, it was "a signpost for outsiders to Southeast Asia of an affirmation of Islamic juridical theory manifested at the diplomatic level."[50] In other words, even centuries of Islamization and the long-term adoption of Arabic titulature did not necessarily transform indigenous Malay ideas about political leadership and governance into Arabic ones. The harmonization of titulature is therefore more of an indicator of the relationship of Malays to the larger Islamic world: a cultural marker that signifies a claim and commitment to being part of the *'umma* and its broader ideas of political and social order, not to mention "the benefits of plugging in to a global network of trade."[51]

Spanish concepts like *vasallaje* and *esclavo* may appear secular when examined alongside Islamic political concepts that are explicitly religious, but Spanish colonial governance was no less intertwined with religious identity, in that those who remained unincorporated or otherwise outside the sphere of Spanish influence were branded as infidels. Positing a similar "harmonization" process for Lumad political

---

[47] Michael F. Laffan, "Dispersing God's Shadows: Reflections on the Translation of Arabic Political Concepts into Malay and Indonesian," *Malay Concordance Project*, n.d., p. 2, http://mcp.anu.edu.au/papers/laffan_apc.html, accessed November 14, 2012.

[48] Ibid., p. 12.

[49] Ibid., p. 6.

[50] Ibid., p. 7.

[51] Ibid., p. 6.

organization within the context of a theocratic colonial milieu opens us to a more nuanced understanding of the apparent coexistence of seemingly competing political concepts, and a better appreciation of the complexities of Lumad agency, as far as the Lumad colonial experience is concerned. Through religious conversion, and by formalizing ties with the king of Spain, the Lumad appear to have been doing more or less the same thing vis-à-vis the colonial state, and, beyond it, the European world. The pertinent networks of trade are beyond the scope of this study, but I have no doubt that Lumads would have also considered the potential economic benefits of being officially recognized as part of that powerful new *sacup*.

But what of the impact of this agreement on local politics? We already know through the colonial state's own usage that, over time, the indigenous concept of *sacup* would prevail in terms of actual governance in the Lumad areas of Mindanao. As to the concern that, by placing themselves under the dominion of the colonial state, Lumad *datus* would lose their legitimacy or power and become mere puppets of the state, Laffan explains that this was not the case with Malay rulers: "If anything, the role of the ruler as first among equals was in some cases strengthened with the advent of more direct colonial rule."[52]

This eager political expression of connectivity to a larger political universe may be relevant in terms of understanding the overall Lumad response to the missionary presence. For example, the incorporation of Spanish political elements within indigenous structures of political authority (discussed in the next chapter) may well signal attempts by the Lumad to "harmonize" with Spanish political and religious networks. Such connections, achieved primarily through missionization, religious conversion, vassalage, and other colonial interactions, also served to establish social and political connections among previously warring Lumad populations. The establishment and expansion of Catholic missions, therefore, brought more than the symbolic incorporation of Lumad peoples into the global European milieu—they also fostered the development of a broader pan-Lumad identity, one that would eventually cleave the Lumad world along religious lines.

In the next section, we move up one century but remain in Misamis province, this time casting an even wider net, as Lumad communities would request incorporation into the Spanish system of general administration and, notably, jurisprudence. In the nineteenth century, we find colonial authorities endorsing, with even greater enthusiasm, similar requests from Lumad *datus* for special concessions on taxation, defense, administrative autonomy, and Religious personnel, strongly implying a significant level collusion between *datus*, resident missionaries, and local politicians once again.

THE HINTERLAND TRIBES OF MISAMIS REQUEST PATRONAGE

The Archivo Histórico Nacional in Madrid holds many Philippine documents from the nineteenth century, including an *expediente* from northern Mindanao, dated 1838, in which *datus* from various hinterland tribes of Misamis (*las tribus monteses de Misamis*) are reported to have requested that *ministros de justicia* (justices of the peace, though the term translates literally to "ministers of justice") be designated among their *datus* or indigenous leaders, just as they are in the Christian settlements. The petitioners had reportedly expressed the desire to live under the protection of

---

[52] Ibid.

Spanish laws, on the condition that they would neither be required to pay tribute nor be enlisted for *polos y servicios personales* (corvée labor). This request by the Misamis tribes does not appear in their own words, but had reportedly been forwarded on their behalf by the local colonial administrators of Misamis. According to the *expediente*, the request was, indeed, granted.

The dossier's principal document, a letter to the Foreign Affairs office, or *Ultramar*, informs Spain of this request for patronage:

> Your excellency, the current *corregidor* [magistrate] of Misamis, in opinion number 200 directed to this government dated the 28th of the previous September [1837], declares that the hinterland tribes that inhabit Piao, Dicayo, Aluran, Layahuan, Labo, and Sicapa have implored him to request from the [government] that they annually designate justices of the peace among their *datus* or chiefs, according to the example of the Christian settlements,[53] and they wish as well to live under the protection of our laws and observe the policing regimen that these prescribe.[54]

This particular request is interesting because the *datus* are supposedly asking for some form of incorporation within the Spanish colonial system, "according to the example of the Christian settlements." But it also indicates that, while these communities—listed as Piao, Dicayo, Aluran, Layahuan, Labo, and Sicapa—are not necessarily interested in conversion to Christianity, they have enough familiarity with such Christian settlements to have decided that such a model was favorable, and potentially beneficial to their own welfare as non-Christian communities.

The request, as it is worded, also implies that some communities of *monteses* may have lacked the cultural or political resources for legal arbitration or adjudication during this period. The reason for this state of affairs is not explained, but if these different Misamis communities were autonomous from each other, as was typical, the request to the *corregidor* may easily have been part of a concerted effort by these

---

[53] The word used in the original, *reduccion*, and its verb, *reducir*, are most commonly translated within Philippine studies as "reduction" and "reduce," respectively. The sense of being "reduced" or "lessened" implies the wretchedness of a *de facto* forced conversion to Christianity. It is, in most senses, an exclusively negative and politically loaded term that is easily referenced in anticolonial rhetoric; it is a foregone conclusion that no free indigenous person in his or her right mind would choose to live in a more centralized settlement such as a *reducción*. I would argue that this interpretation has gained traction in scholarly discourse because, in popular imagination, the colonial *reducción* has been conflated with the forced resettlement into densely populated camps, also known as "hamletting." The practice of hamletting was used in both the American colonial and Republican postcolonial periods, especially during Martial Law, to allow the military to monitor and control a civilian population's movements with the objective of limiting their contact with antigovernment forces. However, forced resettlement was not the purpose of the *reducción* during the Spanish colonial period. The DRAE defines the historical use of *reducción* less controversially, describing it simply as a settlement of Christianized indians. Moreover, we are dealing in this chapter with the phenomenon of Lumads voluntarily requesting their own missionaries and their own *reducción*, something I would have found unimaginable before I witnessed this very same phenomenon in northern Mindanao among present-day Lumads vis-à-vis foreign Christian missionaries. In order to convey more accurately the usage of the word *reducción* within Spanish colonial policy, as opposed to the current Filipino anti-imperialist use of the term, I follow the DRAE definition.

[54] (AHN,Ultramar,5155,Exp13,n2,f1r).

communities to formalize relations among themselves at a higher level of political organization. One likely impetus for such an effort may have been the existence of endemic armed conflict, or what Filipinos like to call a "peace-and-order situation."

Whether this state of affairs was due to internecine conflict or conflict with other communities such as the Moros is not indicated directly in the letter. However, we know that Moro raiding was approaching its apex at this particular period in Philippine history, and though the strategic position of Misamis vis-à-vis the Moro territories is mentioned below as a possible long-term advantage to Spain, protection against such raids was not indicated as the primary reason for the *datus'* request. In fact, the focus of the request as worded indicates that they were primarily preoccupied with alleviating the tax burden on Lumads. It seems the prospect of gaining a strategic advantage against Moro raiding was mentioned by local colonial officials only to justify the loss of tax revenue to the larger colonial state, should the request be granted. This leads me to think that, if there was a "peace-and-order situation" at hand, it was more likely an intra-Lumad conflict, a situation consistent with general descriptions of indigenous political organization, as well as descriptions of widespread, endemic internecine conflict in the area at the time.[55]

Modern Lumad systems of adjudication (*paghusay*) are relatively well-represented in the ethnographic literature,[56] as are indigenous systems of adjudication throughout Southeast Asia.[57] There is little doubt that, even before the colonial era, Lumad peoples would have had their own legal traditions in place. The question is, why would Lumad *datus* then turn to outsiders for judicial intervention? And is it realistic to assume that they would have done so? In his study of colonial state expansion in northern Sulawesi, David Henley proposes "stranger-kingship," broadly construed, as a model of interaction with the colonial state.[58] "Stranger-kingship" refers to the phenomenon found throughout historical Southeast Asia and the Pacific, in which strangers are granted preferential political status, even overlordship, because of their perceived detachment from local factionalism, or the allure of their association with the outside world, or both. The position of the so-called stranger-king in local society was typically cemented through intermarriage

---

[55] See Montano, *Een Reis naar Philippijnen.*

[56] For example, in Biernatzki, "Bukidnon Datuship"; and Garvan, *The Manóbos of Mindanao.* See also Stuart Schlegel, *Tiruray Justice: Traditional Tiruray Law and Morality* (Berkeley, CA: University of California Press, 1970), for an extended description of Tiruray adjudication in western Mindanao. See also the description of leadership and adjudication among the Tausug by Thomas Kiefer. The Tausug are a Muslim, and therefore "Moro," group, but one that William Henry Scott says originated from a group that migrated out of Butuan (located to the east of Misamis; Butuan was the main trading port of north Mindanao) to Sulu in the late 1400s. The Tausug reportedly retained sufficiently close ties with Butuan, such that "as late as 1600, the sultan of Sulu, Batara Shah Tengah, appears to have been an actual native of Butuan." In other words, despite being established as a Moro group, today's Tausug and Lumad peoples may have had a shared ancestry, or at least a shared cultural origin. See Thomas Kiefer, *The Tausug: Violence and Law in a Philippine Moslem Society* (Prospect Heights, IL: Waveland Press, 1986). See also Scott, *Barangay*, p. 164.

[57] Reid, *Southeast Asia in the Age of Commerce*, pp. 139–40.

[58] David Henley, "Conflict, Justice, and the Stranger-King: Indigenous Roots of Colonial Rule in Indonesia and Elsewhere," *Modern Asian Studies* 38 (2004): 85–144. See also Hans Hägerdal, *Lords of the Land, Lords of the Sea: Conflict and Adaptation in Early Colonial Timor, 1600–1800* (Leiden: KITLV Press, 2012).

with indigenous elites.[59] Henley argues for "a more widespread appreciation for the usefulness of foreign authority as a way of controlling indigenous conflict and violence through various combinations of third-party mediation, impartial adjudication, and legal enforcement" fueled primarily—and realistically—by "the opportunism of local elites and would-be elites." The basic idea is that foreign colonial powers, having no local connections and therefore distinguished by "their aloofness from local rivalries," became the functional equivalent of the actual stranger-kings of the past, who played vital and symbolic roles in the perpetuation of local political order throughout the Austronesian world. The presumed impartiality of foreigners may have served a practical purpose in societies where competing indigenous leaders had no over-arching political or juridical authority to turn to for arbitration. In other words, their

> … mutual jealousy and distrust made it easier for them to accept outsiders (whose lack of local blood ties was supposed to help guarantee their impartiality) in the roles of arbitrators, judges, and enforcers of the peace than it was to create indigenous institutions with the same functions.[60]

With regard to the resolution of internecine conflict in such societies, there are several things to bear in mind. The reliance on foreign third parties does not necessarily mean that there were no indigenous jural traditions already in place, only that political leadership may have been too fraught or competitive to allow negotiations to take place. It is also possible that, under certain conditions of ongoing or impending conflict, political outsiders could and would have been used to usurp indigenous jural traditions and, with the emergence of a particularly powerful local ruler, consolidate the local political system to the extent that it was necessary or possible. The other side of the stranger-kingship coin, therefore, may be a cyclical model of political organization that oscillates between the fission and fusion of communities, an oscillation that may take place within one lifetime.[61] The interrelatedness of the groups involved—the fact that they are held together by complex ties of both culture and kinship—also seems essential to explaining the potential for both rapid alliance building, and the deep hostility that can develop

---

[59] Henley, "Conflict, Justice, and the Stranger-King"; and Hägerdal, *Lords of the Land, Lords of the Sea*.

[59] Henley, "Conflict, Justice, and the Stranger-King," p. 87

[60] David Henley, "Conflict, Justice, and the Stranger-King: Indigenous Roots of Colonial Rule in Indonesia and Elsewhere," *Modern Asian Studies* 38 (2004): 87.

[61] For example, as described for Timor and Maluku. See McWilliam, *Paths of Origin*. See also Leonard Andaya, *The World of Maluku: Eastern Indonesia in the Early Modern Period* (Honolulu, HI: University of Hawaii Press, 1993). The classic ethnography that describes this phenomenon of oscillation between egalitarian and hierarchical modes of political organization came not from island Southeast Asia but from the mainland. See Edmund Leach, *Political Systems of Highland Burma* (London: Athlone Press, 1954). Marshall Sahlins also points to a similar range of possibilities with regard to political organization, i.e., between "big-man" and "chiefly" types in Melanesia and Polynesia, respectively. Though Sahlins does not describe an oscillation, he does discuss how one type might evolve to resemble the other, and devolve back again, depending upon the level of economic stratification, demographic pressures, and various other factors. See Marshall Sahlins, "Poor Man, Rich Man, Big-man, Chief: Political Types in Melanesia and Polynesia," *Comparative Studies in Society and History* 5,3 (1963): 285–303.

upon the breakdown of such alliances, as was described for the "sibling wars" among the Meto of southwest Timor.[62] These cyclical patterns of alliance and alienation also have consequences for understanding the changing patterns of warfare among the Lumad and other island Southeast Asian peoples. The subsequent differentiation created by such oscillation may also be relevant to understanding any "ethnicized" performative diversity among interrelated groups, as well as a factor in explaining the confusing ethnic variation found in Lumad areas.[63]

To date, I have not yet encountered any narrative from a Lumad group comparable to that found by Tania Li for Central Sulawesi, in which Dutch colonizers are expressly credited with bringing peace and security to their area.[64] However, there is a narrative tradition among Higaunon Lumads in northern Mindanao according to which an important symbol of political legitimacy originated as a gift to two ancestors given by a foreign king, whom they visited in Manila by traveling from northern Mindanao on a magical boat. Upon returning to Mindanao, these two ancestors, named Kumbalan and Tawaga, assembled all of the area's *datus* for the first time, and it was at this assembly that Pabulusen, an ancestor common to Higaunons and some Manobo groups as well, was named the "supreme *datu*."[65] The same assembly produced the *balaud*, or body of customary laws and other legal traditions, including the *tampuda ha balagon*,[66] that are still followed by many Lumad groups today. As discussed in the next chapter, this narrative tradition may be based in part on actual events because one of the best known symbols of political legitimacy among the Lumad is a legendary "golden cane," which, in turn, closely resembles the cane of office given by Spain to native officials as a mark of authority throughout its colonies in the Americas as well as the Philippines.

Returning to the 1838 letter from the second *expediente*, the text makes it clear that while these Misamis communities saw the colonial state as providing a plausible nexus of judicial impartiality, they were also aware of the negative aspects of being drawn into its dominion and therefore sought to retain some degree of autonomy where they could. In the *expediente*, these communities, indeed, requested colonially appointed justices of the peace,

---

[62] McWilliam, *Paths of Origin*, pp. 152–53.

[63] Oona T. Paredes, "Studying Mindanao through Southeast Asian Ethnographic Themes," *Kinaadman* 22 (2000): 11–34.

[64] Tania Li, "Relational Histories and the Production of Difference on Sulawesi's Upland Frontier," *Journal of Asian Studies* 60,1 (2001): 41–66.

[65] Biernatzki, "Bukidnon Datuship," pp. 21–22. See also William Biernatzki SJ, "Kalabugao Community Study," unpublished manuscript, Institute of Philippine Culture, Ateneo de Manila University, Quezon City, Philippines, 1978, pp. 16–17, 40–42.

[66] The *tampuda ha balagon* is an arbitration ritual involving the slicing of a length of rattan (*balagon*). It is used to determine whether the conflict or other issue being adjudicated has indeed been resolved. If the rattan does not yield cleanly in one blow, then it is a sign that one of the parties involved is not fully satisfied with the adjudication, and the idea is that negotiations must continue until the ritual proves the matter closed. Noting the resemblance between the word *balagon* and the *datu* Balagon from the Tagoloán letter, I inquired among some Higaunon *datus* based southeast of Tagoloán and was informed that there could be no possible relation, because the ritual refers only to rattan and not to the name of a person.

... but on the condition that they neither pay tribute, nor are enlisted for *polos y servicios personales*, offering also to raise bulwarks for the defense of towns that form and to guard them with a number of men from each respective town ... Upon hearing this interesting point, the *asesor* [municipal counselor] and the *fiscal* unanimously agreed that the offer made by the aforementioned tribes should be granted, and that in order to do this, in accordance with the law as put forth in the Royal Decree of 1791, they asked that the accord should be put to a vote. Adhering to all that was stated by the *fiscal*, who found said proposal to be laudable, and having done so should support it, he said that the exemption solicited by said tribes with regard to *polos y servicios personales* should be understood with respect to community projects and projects of the province in general, but not those that pertain to the places that serve as their residences, or to the new towns that they establish; it is them and not others who should work on their own projects—but for a limited time and not in perpetuity, because it seems unjust that they enjoy the common assets of the province, [then] later neglect to contribute to the same.[67]

The author of the main document, Andres Geambas, then gives a brief description of the fertile and untapped province of Misamis, writing that in order to properly weigh the petition, Spain must bear in mind the possible advantages of acceding to the *datus'* request for exemption from tribute and the *polos y servicios personales*.

The character of the infidel *indios* that comprise the aforementioned tribes or hamlets is, according to the information of the aforementioned *corregidor*, naturally mild and peaceful; the lands they possess [are] excellent for agriculture, and the benefit they can give [us] ... [would be] fairly substantial because they are located at the point where the Moros most often gather or approach in their raids ...

In addition to this military benefit, the author points out the agricultural benefits to Spain if it could secure its hold on Misamis, concluding that:

With this information about the climate, soil, population, and production of such an important province, it is no secret from Your Excellency the special advantage that should accrue to Your Majesty's government not only [by] favorably receiving some *reducciones* that are being offered at so little cost, but also [by] supporting them and uplifting others, in order to colonize such an advantageous area ... [and] to have large and strong villages with which we [would be] extending our dominance in Mindanao, [allowing us] to assert ourselves over the Moros and minimize their piracy, and to [either] dislodge them little by little from the regions they occupy on that island, or bring them under our authority.

Another document outlining the fiscal administration of the province of Misamis, dated 1853, gives us an idea of how much of an exemption was granted to the *datus*

---

[67] (AHN,Ultramar,5155, Exp13,n2,f1r-1v).

in Misamis. According to this document, *naturales* or natives paid 5 *reales* per person, and *mestizos de Sangley* (or, Chinese mestizos) paid 12 *reales*, 17 *maravedis* per person.[68] However, the *tinguianes*,[69] or upland people, paid "a reduced rate according to the rates [*tasas*] that are required or set by current mandates."[70] While this does not tell us how much the uplanders were actually obliged to pay, nor, for that matter, how much local governments were ever able to collect, it is clear that the general taxation rules were not applied to the uplands. The document also tells us that, despite Spain's admission that it never exercised any direct control beyond sections of the coast, Spain nonetheless maintained the pretense of its territorial claim by documenting its "legal" authority to tax "subjects" in the interior.

Although this particular text appears a little over a century after the letter from Tagoloán, it is clear that the situation in northern Mindanao had not changed significantly, in that there remained *monteses* in the same province, Misamis, who had yet to be incorporated into the colonial state. It is indeed notable that these *monteses* were making—and being *allowed* to make—demands regarding exemption from taxes and labor obligations that were required of all lowland Filipinos by the colonial government. In the second *expediente*, from 1838, these exceptions were justified, in part, by Spain's strategic interests, and the potential military assistance offered by the *monteses* in holding the line against Moro incursions and territorial claims. Much was made of the territory's economic and agricultural potential as well. Given that this exchange was part of internal state correspondence, the wording of the document is significant in its apparent admission that, with regard to northern Mindanao at least, Spain was not in a favorable position to seize such advantages on its own. In the larger Mindanao and Philippine contexts, the weakness of colonial power in this area was so obvious that major accommodations in terms of taxation and other colonial obligations were necessary.[71]

The nationalist hero, José Rizal, characterized Spanish colonialism in general to similar effect:

> The term *conquest* cannot be applied to more than a few islands and only in a very broad sense. Cebu, Panay, Luzon, Mindoro, etc., cannot be called conquered. It was accomplished by means of pacts, peace treaties, and reciprocal alliances.[72]

---

[68] Venancio de Abella, *Ynstruccion para el Gobierno y manejo del Subdelegado de Hacienda de la provincia de Misamis D. Francisco de Hidalgo y Caballero* (Manila, 1853), p. 4.

[69] Derived from the northern Philippines word *tinggi*, for "high hill," with cognates in Malay. However, the term was used during the Spanish period to refer to upland peoples throughout the archipelago. While it has the same cultural connotations as the Spanish word *montes*, *tinggi* more specifically locates its subject at the top of a hill or mountain.

[70] De Abella, *Ynstruccion para el Gobierno*, p. 4.

[71] For a comparable case among the Iban vis-à-vis both the British and the Dutch in West Kalimantan, Indonesia, see Reed L. Wadley, "Punitive Expeditions and Divine Revenge: Oral and Colonial Histories of Rebellion and Pacification in Western Borneo, 1886–1902," *Ethnohistory* 51,3 (2004): 609–36.

[72] William Henry Scott, *Cracks in the Parchment Curtain and Other Essays in Philippine History* (Quezon City: New Day Publishers, 1982), p. 4. Scott was citing Rizal's comments in his annotated edition of Antonio de Morga's *Sucesos de las Islas Filipinas* (Paris: Garnier Hermanos, 1890 [1609]), p. xxxiii.

We can be skeptical of this claim with regard to certain parts of southern Luzon and the Visayas, specifically the cities and towns in which non-natives were most concentrated (including Cebu, to be sure). William Henry Scott was certainly right to introduce his translation of Miguel Lopez de Legazpi's official 1571 claim to occupy Manila, on the island of Luzon, with the following remarks:

> Despite due respect for Dr. Rizal, I doubted that these treaties dictated by victors to vanquished would, either then or later, be really reciprocal. Moreover, I suspected that they would betray their farcical nature by representing the conquered as not only willing but happy to accept defeat. The 1571 document did not disappoint this expectation [filled as it was with "the legal niceties of which Hapsburg imperialists were so fond"].[73]

However, with regard to Spanish dominion over the outer reaches of the archipelago, in pericolonial areas such as Mindanao, it did not move very far beyond "legal niceties." The *expedientes* discussed above show that Spain's grasp on the region remained weak well into the nineteenth century. Which brings us back to the question of what actually constituted colonial authority in the case of Mindanao. In the Lumad case, it is uncertain whether the murky political relationships discussed in this chapter constituted subjugation in the form of "colonial rule" or simply local alliance formation, confused by one-sided Spanish claims of overlordship.

SPAIN TREATS WITH THE MANDAYA NATION

A third and final text rounds out our perspective on the Lumad world in nineteenth-century Mindanao. It is a letter from 1839, found in an *expediente* of reports compiled by Luis Lardizabal, Governor General of the Philippines from 1838 to 1841, to *Ultramar* (Foreign Affairs) officials in Madrid.[74] The *expediente* basically consists of draft correspondence pertaining to the troubled state of the colony, with references to deadly pirate raids, hurricanes and other natural disasters, and general lawlessness by bandits (*malhechores*) who were plaguing various parts of the archipelago around that time. Though the rest of the colony seemed in disarray, only good news was reported for Mindanao. A formal treaty had very recently been concluded with the "Mandaya nation" in the district of Caraga, which in the early colonial period meant the east coast of Mindanao island, all the way down into what is now the province of Davao Oriental.

As mentioned in chapter one, *mandaya* was once a generic term for people of the hinterlands, applied broadly to people who lived in upriver areas. Today, Mandaya refers to a subgroup of Lumads in the former Caraga district, including the Mansaka, the Dibabawon, and the Karaga.[75] In the previous chapter, we also encountered the

---

[73] Scott, *Cracks in the Parchment Curtain*, p. 4.

[74] (AHN, Ultramar, 5155, Exp30,n1)

[75] As explained in the first two chapters, I resort to the pan-ethnic term "Lumad" precisely because the interrelatedness of the various named Lumad groups and subgroups remains not only problematic, but also confused. Different observers using different criteria will draw different distinctions, and even linguists do not necessarily agree on who is related to whom. Moreover, group names used earlier in the Spanish period do not necessarily match the names used today, and the exonyms applied by the Philippine government's successive offices for tribal affairs over the years barely match those used by Lumads in talking about themselves

Karaga peoples of the seventeenth century, who were characterized early on by
Spaniards as fierce and prone to extreme violence. This reputation appears to have
been carried over to the Mandaya of the nineteenth century, persisting to the end of
the Spanish period. Field observations by early twentieth century American
anthropologists Fay-Cooper Cole and John Garvan included remarks about
indigenous warfare and the highly defensive architecture of Mandaya houses.[76]
While the *expediente* does not specify which particular Mandaya settlements or
subgroups are covered under the aforementioned treaty, it is also quite safe to
assume that the treaty refers to Mandaya-Karaga peoples who had not yet been
missionized or been "pacified" into paying tribute.

The absence of proper Mandaya names and places in this letter is likely due to
the very general nature of the report to *Ultramar* officials by the governor general.
However, it is unlikely that a majority, much less all, of the Mandayas in the district
of Caraga subscribed to the conditions of this treaty. The reference here to the
Mandaya as a "nation"—rather than to a specific *datu* or *sakop* or settlement—instead
implies that several communities had agreed to this particular treaty with Spain. This
is particularly obvious when it is revealed that the Mandaya signatories had agreed
to consolidate themselves into one *reducción*, with a single *teniente corregidor* or
deputy magistrate to be chosen among the indigenous leadership to serve as
representative of all Mandaya people.

The letter, excerpted below, is addressed to the Secretary of State and the Office
of Overseas Shipping, Commerce, and Governance, with a dateline of Manila, March
7, 1839. This text is taken from the duplicate of the final letter at the Archivo
Histórico Nacional in Madrid: [77]

> I have the satisfaction of announcing to Your Excellency that the most
> zealous and learned military governor and politician of the province of
> Caraga, Mr. Enrique Olaguer y Felice, celebrated in the capital of said
> province on the 26th of August of last year [1838], in the name of Your
> Majesty and as entrusted by my predecessor, a [treaty of] capitulation to and
> acknowledgement of [orig., *una capitulación y reconocimiento*] the Spanish
> Crown made with the leaders or *caciques* of the Mandaya nation, peoples
> situated on the eastern coast of Mindanao and confined to the

---

today. See Frank LeBar, ed., *Ethnic Groups of Insular Southeast Asia*, vol. 2 (New Haven, CT:
Human Relations Area Files Press, 1975). Higaunon Lumads today, for example, invariably
refer to all other Lumads as "Higaunons," and have been known to apply this same autonym
to all "tribal" peoples. For the reverse among "Manobos," who in the early American colonial
period insisted that only uncivilized outsiders are *manobo*, see Garvan, *The Manóbos of
Mindanao*, p. 1.

[76] See Fay-Cooper Cole, *The Bagobos of Davao Gulf* (Manila: Bureau of Printing, 1911), and *The
Wild Tribes of Davao District, Mindanao* (Chicago, IL: Field Museum of Natural History,
Publication 170, 1913). See also Garvan, *The Manóbos of Mindanao*; and Schreurs, *Caraga
Antigua*, p. 139.

[77] This text is catalogued as the *duplicado* of the final letter, and contains exactly the same
information, using almost identical wording. However, it differs from the final letter in that it
is exclusively about the treaty with the Mandayas, and is written by Lardizabal in the first-
person. The final letter, on the other hand, reads like a summary of combined reports, written
in the third-person and containing other information pertaining to pirate attacks, *malhechores*,
and natural disasters. The final document is part of the same *expediente*, at (AHN, Ultramar,
5155, Exp30,n1).

aforementioned territory of Caraga, whose governor has named one from among the chieftains who will govern them with the title of *teniente corregidor*, and arranged the contribution that is to be paid as proof of vassalage, that from the beginning of the current year four silver *reales* [be given by] the *principales* of said nation, and two [by] their *sacopes* or inferiors in status and rank, excepting only the women and those younger than eighteen years. As said nation recognizes the legal sovereignty of Our Child Queen, Doña Ysabel the Second and her legitimate heirs,[78] the aforementioned Olaguer, in the name of Her Majesty and representing this government, has taken them under his protection, [such] that he will always support them against the enemies that disturb [their] peace, and give them the resources necessary in arms and munitions to repel whatever attempts those [enemies] might make; and for the purpose of better ensuring them their well-being, [he will make them] subject to the mellowing influence of our laws; he proposed to them—and they agreed—that they consolidate themselves and form a town, whose lands they have already begun to clear in order to enable this consolidation. This comprehensive treaty is made up of six articles that are being drafted, and as soon as we have completed the relevant paperwork, I will give a full testimonial to Her Majesty to whom, in any event, Your Excellency may now give notification of this matter.[79]

This final letter is distinct from the previous ones in that, although a treaty was apparently negotiated, there is no explicit language indicating that the Mandayas came willingly to the table; the letter states only that, in the end, they agreed to the terms of the treaty. Indeed, the use of the word *capitulación* to characterize the treaty suggests that the leaders of the Mandaya surrendered their autonomy to the superior forces of Spain. However, although it can be used to describe the turnover of military power to another party, the word *capitulación* generally refers to a publicly or legally recognized contract or pact between two or more parties, also encompassing, for example, prenuptial agreements.[80]

Even though there is no language pointing to special exemptions or any distinct advantage gained by the colonial state in this matter,[81] it is not difficult to see that Spain made financial concessions similar to those in the previously discussed *expedientes*, particularly with regard to the amount of tribute reportedly agreed upon

---

[78] Spain was in the middle of the First Carlist War at this time, due to a dispute over succession after the late king Fernando VII designated his daughter Isabel II as his heir. At the time the letter was written, Isabel was eight or nine years old, and the head of state was her mother, María Cristina de Borbón, who ruled as regent. The remark about loyalty to Isabel II and her legitimate heirs is significant due to the presence in the Philippine colony not only of known Carlists, but also large numbers of Basques, an ethnic group that in Spain formed a critical component of the Carlist cause.

[79] (AHN, Ultramar, 5155, Exp30,n2bis,f1r-2v[dup.]).

[80] This is the DRAE definition. In the broader history of European political discourse, the word "capitulation" was likewise used with reference to negotiated concessions in trade agreements, for example, with Ottoman Egyptians. What the Ottomans called "favorable preferences" granted to Europeans in trade were, in contrast, referred to by Europeans as "capitulations" to them by the Ottomans.

[81] At present, I am unable to find a copy of the original treaty with the Mandaya nation that was referenced in this letter, and therefore cannot say what was contained in the six articles mentioned in the text.

by the Mandayas. The tribute amount, set at four *reales* each for the *principales* and two *reales* each for those within their *sacopes*, is quite low when compared to twice the basic tribute amount set for the rest of Filipinas more 250 years earlier. Writing in 1583 to complain bitterly about the abuse of Philippine natives by the earliest generation of *encomenderos*, the Dominican Fray Domingo de Salazar, first archbishop of Manila, states:

> The tribute that all are commonly assessed is the value of eight *reales*, paid in gold or in produce that they gather from their lands; but this rate is observed like all other rules that are in favor of the *indios*—that is, it is never observed at all.[82]

While the reference to silver *reales* makes it tempting to infer the existence of a thriving cash economy in a peripheral area like Caraga by the early nineteenth century (especially when the first *expediente* from the previous century mentions only rice), Salazar's comment makes it clear that, from the very beginning, tribute could be paid in cash or in kind. By the middle of the nineteenth century, the rate of tribute was twelve *reales*, so we can quantify the Lumad discount at over 66 percent for the *principales*, and over 83 percent for their *sacup* members.

What is most notable in this document, once again, is the apparent judicial intervention of the colonial state in Lumad political organization, through the selection of a *teniente corregidor* for all Mandaya people, and the purported agreement by the Mandayas to live under the laws of the colonial state. While there is no language indicating that such an intervention was actively sought by the Mandaya *datus*, the previous *expedientes* show us that it is certainly possible that they did so. The reputation of the Mandayas for violence and the considerable distance of Mindanao from the colonial center also make it very likely that this treaty resulted from a similar request by these particular Mandayas. Whether this points to a "peace-and-order" problem of internecine warfare between different Mandaya settlements is not clear. From the viewpoint of the Mandaya, however, the political relevance of such a treaty is that it would provide them with an over-arching framework for the arbitration of disputes—one made of foreign laws and enforced by a foreign authority that superceded their internal squabbles.

As with the two previous *expedientes*, an important aspect of the treaty was military assistance, in the form of Spain's commitment to grant arms and munitions to the Mandayas, ostensibly for protection against attacks by their enemies. Whether these enemies were the Moros or other Lumads remains unspecified, but it is notable that, in the report to *Ultramar*, and by extension to the Queen Regent María Cristina, the governor general did not speak of Spain's enemies—only the enemies of the Mandaya nation. Moreover, the plague of Moro piracy was mentioned explicitly elsewhere in the *expediente* but not at all in the letter about the Mandayas—another notable omission. If individual *datus* were prompted to seek external intervention, leading to negotiations with the military governor of Caraga and a treaty of

---

[82] From *Affairs of the Philippine Islands* by Fray Domingo de Salazar OP, as translated in Blair and Robertson, *The Philippine Islands*, vol. 5, p. 211. Salazar was Archbishop of Manila from 1581–94 and was responsible for founding the Manila Cathedral. In his statement, Salazar adds that tribute collectors often exacted more than was required and abused the natives in other ways. There is a similar complaint filed by the Recoletos in reference to the Misamis area from the early eighteenth century.

capitulation with Spain, the enemies of the Mandaya nation were most probably other, more troublesome Mandayas.

The ultimate outcome of this treaty for the Mandaya is unknown. However, the letter itself outlines the most significant developments on the horizon: the creation of a Mandaya population center through the consolidation of several existing settlements; the creation of a confederation of several *datus* under the judicial authority of one *teniente corregidor*; and the parallel creation of a Mandaya political center through the consolidation of several existing *sacups*.

THE MINDANAO *SACUP* AS COLONIAL *FUERO*

In addition to the overall weakness of Spanish colonial power in Mindanao, there is another possible explanation for Spanish willingness—indeed, enthusiasm—in granting special concessions to such marginal communities in Mindanao.

In Spanish law of the Visigothic era, the foundation of all later Spanish legal traditions, there is a concept called the *fuero*, which is a legal charter through which the king could justify the granting of special rights and privileges to select entities, be they a class, estate, region, or group of communities. These special provisions might include concessions that were disadvantageous to the king's financial and political power, such as tax exemptions. The special status accorded the Catholic Church in Spain is one example of a long-standing *fuero*.

One province in modern-day Spain, Navarra, is legally designated as La Comunidad Forál de Navarra,[83] which can be translated to English as the "chartered communities of Navarra." In theory, each town in Navarra is politically independent, each with special tax arrangements and other administrative concessions not granted to towns in other Spanish provinces. According to public information provided by the Government of Navarra,[84] this special autonomy granted to the towns of Navarra, each with their history of independent "kings," has lasted for a thousand years. It was reasserted in the Middle Ages as the *Fuero General*, when customary law was formalized in the first half of the thirteenth century. Every subsequent legal adjustment, including Navarra's formal incorporation into Spain, was built on the foundations of the *Fuero General*. It is notable that Navarra is located in the foothills of the Pyrenees, making it the cultural and political borderland between the politically volatile Basque region and the rest of Spain. Since the latter half of the twentieth century, its largest city, Iruñea (Pamplona), has been the staging ground for repeated political action by Basque nationalists, including terrorist attacks by the separatist group ETA.[85] In the past, during the Franco era as well as during the Reconquista period that immediately preceded European colonial expansion, this area likewise was a sort of political borderland between opponents of and loyalists to Franco and the Catholic Monarchs in their respective eras.

---

[83] In the Basque language, *Nafarroako Foru Erkidegoa.*

[84] Gobierno de Navarra, "Los Fueros: Significado," official website of the Government of Navarra, http://www.navarra.es/home_es/Navarra/Asi+es+ Navarra/Autogobierno/Los+ Fueros.htm, accessed January 31, 2012.

[85] Euskadi Ta Askatasuna, or "Basque country and liberty," is a paramilitary organization that originally formed in 1959 to oppose the repressive Franco regime with violence and to fight for an independent Basque homeland. ETA has remained active even after the advent of democracy in Spain, and has since been declared a terrorist organization by the European Union and the United States.

It is perhaps a coincidence that the Recoleto order originated and evolved in Navarra and its surrounding areas, and that many of the missionaries who came to work in Mindanao during the early colonial period likewise came from there. Did the missionaries, while serving as both translators and religious workers, give Lumad leaders the idea to negotiate for special concessions from colonial administrators in the tradition of the Navarrese *fuero*? Bearing these factors in mind, it is possible to see the visibility and relative success of Lumad political negotiation less as an act of political resistance by marginal communities in Mindanao and more as the continuation of long-established Spanish legal precedent.

The concepts relating to religious conversion and indigenous warfare explored earlier have allowed us to flesh out a historically informed picture of local Lumad politics in action at three different points in the Spanish colonial period. The three sets of correspondence translated, summarized, and analyzed above provide surprising data and suggest many more equally interesting possibilities pertaining to earlier Lumad political organization and the place of Lumad groups within the colonial state. Far from isolating themselves from foreign influences, the Lumad appear to have actively engaged the colonial state to achieve their own political objectives. Given the tenuous hold of Spain on Mindanao itself, not to mention its deeply contentious relationship with the Moros on the western half of the island, it is not surprising that the colonial state responded enthusiastically to these requests for incorporation. The key to the Lumad advantage was their position as counterpoint to Moro domination of the southern reaches of Filipinas, making them critical to the state as potential allies even as they remained peripheral economically, demographically, and socially. In the next chapter, I discuss the enduring cultural and political legacy of this active engagement with the colonial state, and explore what its symbolic aspects might tell us about the colonial Lumad.

CHAPTER 6

THE GOLDEN CANE AND OTHER COLONIAL SYMBOLS OF INDIGENOUS AUTHORITY

There is a general impression in the Philippines that Spanish colonial authority did not penetrate significantly the interior of northern Mindanao, much less radically alter indigenous institutions. As I explained in my preface, upland peoples like the Lumad are still commonly conceptualized by scholars as "un-Hispanized" Filipinos. Yet, on the contrary, Spain left quite intimate marks on the common cultural heritage of the Lumad, marks not readily obvious without a broader appreciation of the early Spanish colonial period. A brief look at some modern cultural elements that are tied to Christian conversion in this part of the archipelago shows that the colonial-era presence of Spanish missionaries had a definite impact on Lumad social organization, not only in bringing about new ethnic constructs but also new political forms, the most significant and enduring of which are related to ideas about political authority.

In this final chapter, I discuss some common ancestral symbols of political and legal authority, as well as the specific offices of the so-called "supreme *datu*" and the enigmatic *masalicampo* (discussed later), and the manner in which they are embedded in Lumad ideas about political organization. I describe very briefly the symbols of political and legal authority that, as of the late twentieth century, remained important to the Higaunon and other closely related Lumad groups within the Manobo language family, which, as I explained earlier, is the largest, most diverse, and most widespread group of all language families found on Mindanao. I focus not on the specific features of the symbols themselves but on the significance of these symbols to our understanding of the role of the colonial period in the development of Lumad societies.

These symbols are relevant to a study of the Lumad colonial experience because they are, in fact, a poorly understood legacy of the colonial-era administration of the Lumad areas. A recognition of their origins places key Lumad traditions, and therefore Lumad peoples, squarely within the framework of the Philippine colonial experience. The colonial past also plays a significant role in how these offices are "remembered" in oral history, which has interesting implications for our general understanding of the Lumad past.

THE GOLDEN CANE

In northern Mindanao, several ancestral symbols of political and legal authority are shared by the Manobo subgroups. These include the *giling*, the *takalub*, and the *bagobal ha bulawan*. The most important item of the three is the *giling*, which is often described as a black stick of wood with markings that refer to the *balaud* or ancestral/customary law (i.e., the Lumad equivalent of Indonesian *adat*), especially as it pertains to the traditions of datuship.[1] According to oral tradition, the first *giling* was made by supernatural beings and granted to the ancestors to symbolize the rule of law.[2] Those who claim to be familiar with the *giling* say that it can never be photographed because it is a sacred object with non-human origins.[3]

The second item, the *takalub* (also, *taklobo*), is a bracelet made of pig tusks that symbolizes the authority of its holder to mediate disputes, though I have also heard it mentioned in passing with reference to shamanism. According to oral tradition, the *takalub* was given by the epic hero and immortal ancestor Agyu to one of his mortal sons, who then passed it on to his descendants, who keep it to this day.[4] Again, this item is claimed to be a supernatural object, and, therefore, like the *giling*, the true *takalub* has never been photographed.

The third item, however, came neither from the mythological ancestors nor the spirits, and appears to have less than supernatural origins. According to Lumad oral histories from northern Mindanao, the *bagobal ha bulawan*, or "golden cane," was given a long time ago to two men—brothers—living in northern Mindanao by a foreign king who lived in Manila. The golden cane is "a sign of leadership" that gives one "the authority to settle disputes."[5] It symbolizes such authority as embodied by Higaunon and Manobo customary law, a body of legal thought known

---

[1] In her compendium of Philippine verbal arts, Coben's chapter on the Bukidnon presents the *giling* as being the same thing as the *bagobal ha bulawan*, which I describe in the next section, though, in contrast, she implies that the Bukidnon are not aware of its colonial origins. See Herminia Meñez Coben, *Verbal Arts in Philippine Indigenous Communities: Poetics, Society, and History* (Quezon City: Ateneo de Manila University Press, 2009), p. 239. Though these venerated objects do sound quite similar in some ways, conversations with local people who profess to know about these things have always led me to believe that they are two separate items (rather than the same thing with different names), and therefore I feel more comfortable describing and discussing them as such, at this time.

[2] William Biernatzki SJ, "Bukidnon Datuship in the Upper Pulangi River Valley," in *Bukidnon Politics and Religion*, ed. A. de Guzman and E. Pacheco, IPC Papers 11 (Quezon City: Ateneo de Manila University Press, 1973), pp. 19–20. See also Dionisio Yumo, "Power Politics of the Southern Agusan Manobo," *Mindanao Journal* 15 (1988): 3–47.

[3] During my master's field research in 1994, local historian Jovenaldo Abalos described to me in detail the *giling* that he saw with his own eyes while studying the folklore of the Higaunon in Bukidnon province. According to him, he attempted to photograph the *giling* using his instant camera, to prove that it was "just a stick." However, he claimed that every frame on the roll turned completely black and the camera itself no longer worked normally after he attempted to capture the image— which he interpreted as proof not only of the supernatural power of the *giling*, but also to the fact that it does not want to be photographed.

[4] Biernatzki, "Bukidnon Datuship," pp. 20–21. See also Coben, *Verbal Arts*, pp. 239, 250. Agyu is one of the main characters of the *Ulaging* epic, an oral tradition shared by the Higaunon, Bukidnon, and other Manobo-speaking groups. It is also called the *Ulahing*, *Ulagingan*, or *Ulahingan*, and its story tells of the dramatic exodus of these people's ancestors, led by the family of Agyu, from famine and oppression to immortal life in a place called Nalandangan. In other sources, this epic is referred to as the *Banlakon*, the *Agyu*, the *Lenà*, the *Baybayan*, and by other names that refer to particular characters in the *Ulaging*. See, among others, Ludivina Opeña, "Olaging: The Battle of Nalandangan," *Kinaadman* 1,1 (1979): 151–227; Francisco Colom Polenda, "Ulegingen: A Prose Retelling of a Mindanao Epic," trans. R. E. Elkins, *Kinaadman* 16,2 (1994): 101–225; Elena Maquiso, *Ulahingan, An Epic of the Southern Philippines* (Dumaguete, RP: Silliman University Press, 1977); and E. Arsenio Manuel, *Agyu: The Ilianon Epic of Mindanao* (Manila: University of Santo Tomas Press, 1969).

[5] Yumo, "Power Politics of the Southern Agusan Manobo," p. 8.

most commonly as the somewhat untranslatable *bungkatol ha bulawan daw nangka tasa ha lana*, which was passed down from the ancestors. Augusto Gatmaytan refers to this body of customary law as the *bungkatol ha bulawan daw nang katas ha lana*, following the usage of Higaunons in the Minalwang area of Claveria, Misamis Oriental.[6] Maricel Paz Hilario uses an even longer term—*bungkatol ha bulawan daw nangka tasa ha lana ha pinaglaw*—adding that it is "difficult to translate but it refers to 'all that is good in Higaonon culture, which is to say the customary laws or rules and standards of the Higaonon way of life; it could be considered as the charter or constitution of the Higaonon.'" According to one of her informants, the Bukidnon *datu* Amay Tangkil, the "*bungkatol* is the most important attribute that a *datu* should have. It is an embodiment of several values that include: (1) *pabatun-batuna* (helping one another), *pahaon-haona* (loving, caring for, and freeing each other), (3) *palaglagimowa* (sharing with each other), (4) *pagpasayuda* (open communication), and (5) *matareng* and *huda daugon* (justice and absence of exploitation)."[7] It embodies much more than the simple reciprocity represented by this particular interpretation, despite the fact that in most quick English translations the *bungkatol* is misleadingly referred to as the "golden rule."

The most curious thing about the cane, however, is that the legend of its origins actually has an empirical, historical basis. *Bagobal* is the term used by the southern Agusan Manobo in reference to the cane,[8] but further west among the Higaunon and Bukidnon they call it the *bastún*, drawing on the actual Spanish word for a walking stick or cane, *bastón*.[9] This intriguing foreign connection within an indigenous tradition comes from the Spanish colonial practice of granting a "cane of office," usually decorated with silver, to native leaders in the Philippines.[10] In the late nineteenth century, when missionaries and colonial government officials were

---

[6] As written by the Minalwang Higa-onon Tribal Council, Inc. (MIHITRICO), in their "Ancestral Domain Management Plan," dated November 1997, produced in compliance with their Ancestral domain claim (R-10-CADC-114) awarded earlier that year. See also Augusto Gatmaytan, *Tenure and Community Resource Management: Case Studies from Northern Mindanaw* (Laguna, Philippines: World Agroforestry Centre/ICRAF Southeast Asia Regional Office, 2002).

[7] Maricel Paz Hilario, "Transforming Lives and Recreating the Environment Beyond the Sustainable Development Paradigm: Reflections from the Experiences of a Higaonon Community in Northern Bukidnon, Mindanao," *The Future of the Sierra Madre: Responding to Social and Ecological Changes*, ed. J. van der Ploeg and Andres Masipiqueña, proceedings of the Fifth International Conference on Environment and Development (Tuguegarao, Philippines: CVPED and Golden Press, 2005), pp. 278–79.

[8] Yumo, "Power Politics of the Southern Agusan Manobo," p. 9.

[9] William Biernatzki SJ, "Kalabugao Community Study," unpublished manuscript, Institute of Philippine Culture, Ateneo de Manila University, Philippines, 1978, pp. 16–17, 40–42.

[10] For example, see Ed C. de Jesus. *Tobacco Monopoly in the Philippines: Bureaucratic Enterprise and Social Change, 1766–1880* (Manila: Ateneo de Manila University Press, 1998), p. 15. See also Frank Lynch, "The Bukidnon of North-Central Mindanao in 1889," *Philippine Studies* 15,3 (1967): 472–73; and F. Landa Jocano, *Sulod Society: A Study in the Kinship System and Social Organization of a Mountain People of Central Panay*, Institute of Asian Studies Monograph 2 (Diliman: University of the Philippines Press, 1968), p. 26, n. 27. Curiously, however, there are not many Spanish archival sources that reference canes of office, which could mean that the cane was either politically insignificant from the Spanish perspective, or else taken totally for granted as a colonial practice, and therefore not worth noting in reports. See also the "gold-knobbed sticks" mentioned in Roy Ellen, "On the Contemporary Uses of Colonial History," *Journal of Southeast Asia Studies* 28,1 (1997): 85.

attempting to organize people on the Bukidnon plateau into permanent, "civilized" *pueblos* (towns), a *gobernadorcillo* (municipal officer) was appointed by the region's military governor to assist in collecting local taxes and ensuring local compliance with *corvée* labor obligations and other colonial laws. The Mindanao historian Mardonio Lao reports that this "*gobernadorcillo* had a cane and wore a special kind of hat as emblems of his authority and influence."[11] Therefore, the mythical cane, which is said to have been in the possession of *datus* for many generations, appears to be a wholly Spanish introduction to Lumad culture, perhaps introduced as recently as a century and a half ago.

In fact, the Lumad are not alone in incorporating a mythologized cane as an indigenous symbol of power or authority. It was common in Spanish colonial America, as well, including what is now the Southwestern United States, where it survives in some Native American Pueblo cultures.[12] In the Andes, it is not a cane but a staff made of black wood, adorned with silver, called the *vara*.[13] Similar objects were likewise used by the Portuguese in colonial Timor as tokens of office—in this case, it was a "scepter" called a *rota*.[14] The Portuguese apparently used it to appropriate existing political hierarchies in Timor, by complementing rather than disrupting them. A similar process is very likely to have taken place in the Lumad areas of Mindanao. Ricardo Roque describes a type of ritual exchange that took place between the indigenous *régulo*, or "cult and jural lords," and the Portuguese, which symbolized the reciprocal relationship that existed between them—as vassal and ruler, respectively:

---

[11] Mardonio M. Lao, *Bukidnon in Historical Perspective*, vol. 1 (Musuan, Bukidnon: Central Mindanao University Publications Office, 1985), pp. 39–40. For a distinctly different analysis, in which the cane of office (including the hat) is described as being one and the same with the *giling*, see Coben, *Verbal Arts*, p. 239.

[12] See Edward H. Spicer, *Cycles of Conquest: The Impact of Spain, Mexico, and the United States on the Indians of the Southwest, 1533–1960* (Tucson, AZ: University of Arizona Press, 1962), p. 390. I have Bill Biernatzki to thank for first connecting the dots for me. It is in his notes that I first encountered the story of the golden cane, which I then confirmed through other sources, and in our eventual correspondence he told me about a mystery novel by Tony Hillerman, in which a replica of just such a cane is the key to solving a murder. See Tony Hillerman, *Sacred Clowns* (New York, NY: HarperTorch, 1994). Encountering the Lincoln Cane, the symbol of the governor of the Hopi pueblo in which the murder takes place, the main character, Detective Leaphorn, recalls: "President Lincoln had ordered ebony and silver canes made and sent them to the leaders of the New Mexico Indian pueblos during the dark days of the Civil War. They were intended … as a signal that Lincoln recognized tribal authority, and to reward them for their neutrality and to keep them neutral. One of the Spanish kings, probably King Charles if Leaphorn's memory served, had done the same two hundred years earlier" (p. 210). Ten pages later, the current keeper of the authentic cane relates that "Lincoln sent nineteen of them out from Washington—one for each of the pueblos. The Spanish started it in 1620" (p. 220). The novel mentions later that while some pueblos had no canes left, others had a total of three such canes: one from the Spaniards, one from Lincoln, and one from Mexico after its independence from Spain.

[13] See Billie Jean Isbell, *To Defend Ourselves: Ecology and Ritual in an Andean Village* (Austin, TX: University of Texas Press, 1978), p. 85. As opposed to the word *bastón*, which is more specific to walking sticks (also ski poles), the word *vara* is used more generally for a stick or other length of wood (i.e., a synonym for the word *palo*).

[14] See Douglas Kammen, "Fragments of Utopia: Popular Yearnings in East Timor," *Journal of Southeast Asian Studies* 40,2 (2009): 394. I thank Douglas for all my cane-related citations for Portuguese Timor.

The Timorese *régulo* swore obedience to the government and assumed his or her tributary obligations. He then presented the governor with buffaloes, horses, and other valuables. Yet, in exchange, the governor reciprocated with the royal title, status ranks, and the tokens of office (the sceptre and the flag), while also presenting the *régulo* with alcoholic drinks, fabrics, and a formal reception at the palace.[15]

Did the Lumad and the Spaniards engage in the same type of exchange in an extensive way, or is the oral tradition of the golden cane the result of the ritual being adopted as a fashionable foreign trend by more interior populations, where it survives today? This is a question that deserves further study. In any case, the colonial pageantry described for Timor above sounds very much like the story of the two Kagayanon brothers who traveled to Manila to receive prestigious gifts, including a special cane, from a foreign king.

According to William Biernatzki, Bukidnon narratives regarding the origin of datuship in northern Mindanao place the source of the "golden cane" to the north of the archipelago, in Manila. Two brothers named Kumbalan (sometimes Gumbalan) and Tawaga lived in Cagayán sometime in the early Spanish period, one of whom dreamed of receiving certain gifts from Manila. No one comes to fulfill the dream, so Tawaga travels to Manila, taking a fantastic and dangerous voyage on his shield.[16] He lands on the beach in Manila and talks to several gatekeepers—first a sergeant and then others of increasing rank—until he reaches either a general (possibly the Governor-General) or a king (possibly referring to the king of Spain or his representative). This general or king gives Tawaga several items of value, including guns, gold, a special *kalù*, or hat, and the famous *bastún*, or cane, that subsequently became the symbol for political authority in northern Mindanao.

I have already mentioned the cane and hat's ethnohistorical significance as symbols of the *maestre de campo*'s, and, later, the *gobernadorcillo*'s, political authority throughout the colonial period. While I have found no description of this particular hat, when *datus* appear in public in an official capacity, they are generally identifiable by some type of head covering, called a *tangkulu* among the Higaunon, as can be seen in photos of indigenous leaders from various Lumad ethnic groups dating back to the early twentieth century, and probably earlier.[17] Whereas the most common *tangkulu* these days is a wrap-around hat, typically made of cloth with a red field and decorated with elaborate beadwork and fringes, I have also seen more humble versions, in the form of a red bandanna or towel wrapped around a *datu*'s head. Even if this modern head covering is not directly related to the *kalù*, covering the head appears to be an important marker of authority, possibly echoing the mythological *kalù* from Lumad political history. Coincidentally, hats also signified a connection to the Iberian world elsewhere in island Southeast Asia's history, among the Topasses, or the so-called "Black Portuguese," of nearby East Timor. Despite their deliberate identification with the Western world, symbolized by the wearing of

---

[15] Ricardo Roque, *Headhunting and Colonialism: Anthropology and the Circulation of Human Skulls in the Portuguese Empire, 1870–1930* (Hampshire: Palgrave Macmillan, 2010), p. 46.

[16] Biernatzki, "Bukidnon Datuship," pp. 21–22; Biernatzki, "Kalabugao Community Study," pp. 16–17, 40–42.

[17] See also John M. Garvan, *The Manóbos of Mindanáo* (Washington, DC: US Government Printing Office, 1941), p. 46, on the "headkerchief" worn throughout eastern Mindanao.

special hats, and self-identification as Portuguese, the Topasses were, in fact, of mixed and "constantly changing" descent, and were noted for their resistance to European colonial control. However, as with the Lumad, close ties with Catholic missionaries were important in creating Topass identity. Dominican missionaries apparently "enjoyed a role … that was not restricted to religious service," and "sometimes even headed military expeditions."[18]

Whereas the version of the *Ulagíng* epic reported by Biernatzki features the brothers Kumbalan and Tawaga procuring the golden cane, another version, taken from the *gugud* oral tradition of Bukidnon,[19] names a man called Ubatling, who is a younger brother of Kumbalan and "Migtawaga":

> According to the old folks, he [Ubatling] was made to swim the wide sea and landed in the plaza of Manila at the mouth of Digkaaldaw River, because there the sun never shines. There, he was given the cane which was considered the *sanggulan ho mga batasan ha taga Manila*.[20]

In the Ubatling version, the cane symbolizes the customary laws of the people of Manila, a place that even today is imagined by the denizens of upland Mindanao as being located at such a great distance—geographically, culturally, and politically—that it is not so much a physical place as it is an idea, something like "America" or another faraway, imaginary place. The story of the cane's foreign origins therefore appears to symbolize more than just an abstract notion of broader political authority; it also symbolizes the adoption of an existing set of truly foreign customary laws. Could this story be related to the perfunctory acknowledgment of Spanish political authority by indigenous *datu* leaders described in the previous chapter? Or did it symbolize more profound political developments? It is possible that the cane was also used to symbolize the consolidation of political authority across different communities that, in the past, would never have cooperated, a question explored a bit further below.

According to this *gugud*, Ubatling was said to be responsible for Kalambaguhan, the area now known as Cagayan de Oro City, while his older brothers, Kumbalan and Migtawaga, were responsible, respectively, for the central plains of Bukidnon and the upper Pulangi river area. Ubatling and his brothers were grandchildren of Bala-as[21] and his wife, Nangilayanen, "the ancestors of the Talaandig, Higaunon,

---

[18] Hans Hägerdal, "Colonial or Indigenous Rule? The Black Portuguese of Timor in the Seventeenth and Eighteenth Centuries," *IIAS Newsletter* 44 (2007): 26. Hägerdal notes that one of the two leading families among the Topasses, the Da Costas, had "Pampanger (Filipino)" ancestry—a historical linkage to Pampangos that surely deserves more study.

[19] The *gugud* is one of the several forms of oral tradition found among Lumad populations that are linguistically part of the Manobo family of languages. It contains elements of etiological myth, historical narrative, and eschatology, and is recounted in prose by a narrator called a *palagugud*. As with most of these oral traditions, the characters are not considered fictional but are regarded as true ancestors. The Gahomon flood story, discussed in the next section, and the core story of the *Ulagíng* epic, mentioned in the previous section, are both part of the larger *gugud* tradition.

[20] Carmen Ching Unabia, "*Gugud*: A Bukidnon Oral Tradition," *Asian Folklore Studies* 44 (1985): 219. Here the cane is called, literally, the legal code of the people of Manila.

[21] In this *gugud* tradition, the brother of Bala-as, named Bala-us, in turn became the ancestor of the Maranaw Moros. They were said to be the sons of a widow from another island. Both brothers arrived on Mindanao and married two orphaned sisters who found them wandering

Tagoloanon, and Pulangi-en."[22] In other words, the ancestors of perhaps the largest subgroup of Lumad peoples alive today. Ubatling and his brothers, in turn, were to become the founding ancestors of their respective areas.

Ubatling's sibling set also included a brother named Kuwabuwa, the *datu* charged with Sinakungan, mentioned later in this chapter; a younger sister named Gawhanen; and a brother named Dalabahan, said to be responsible for the area around the upper Cagayán River. In fact, the name Dalabahan also matches that of one of the early eighteenth-century *datus* of Tagoloán, noted in the first letter in chapter five, who had offered to become the *sacup* of the king of Spain. Given that the Tagoloán River area is immediately to the east of Cagayán, it is tempting to pin the story of this *gugud* to the 1720s. No matter how tantalizing, however, the association with actual historical events and persons must remain tentative at this time. Dalabahan is also named in yet another *gugud* as having been the only high-ranking leader to survive the last, presumably precolonial, great war between Lumads (an alliance of Talaandig and Manobo) and Moros (an alliance of the Maranaw and Magindanaw) on the high plains of central Bukidnon.[23]

THE *MASALICAMPO*

Early on in the colonial period, the aforementioned cane of office was usually given by the Spanish colonial government to selected native leaders whom they had bestowed with the honorary military title of *maestre de campo*. The "ebony, silver-topped cane" these men received was treated as a symbol of their special colonial office, a reward for having "distinguished themselves by some service for Spain or its government; for example, by fighting against the Moros for the Spanish flag."[24] In the sixteenth and seventeenth centuries, *maestre de campo* was the rank of a superior military officer who had command responsibility over several *tercios*, or Spanish infantry regiments. Prior to the sixteenth century, the *mariscal de campo* (literally, "field marshal") exercised comparable command responsibility, and today the rank would be equivalent to the Spanish *general de división* (major general), who falls below the *teniente general* (lieutenant general) in military rank.[25]

Datu Silongan of Butuan, one of the earliest Lumad converts ever named in historical records, was reportedly given the title of *maestre de campo* very early in the seventeenth century, but there is no word as to whether he was given a cane or other symbol of his favored position.[26] I did locate a document from 1606[27] that discusses

---

around what is now Lake Lanao. See Unabia, "*Gugud*," pp. 217–19. This, coincidentally, is the only local story I have come across that directly follows the "Stranger-King/Lords of the Land" theme relating to political power commonly found in Austronesian cultures, in which a man from another island achieves political legitimacy in a new land by marrying a local woman from the existing power elite, and goes on to become an important leader.

[22] Ibid., p. 219.

[23] Ibid., p. 213.

[24] Lynch, "The Bukidnon of North-Central Mindanao in 1889," pp. 472–73. See also Jocano, *Sulod Society*, p. 26, n. 27.

[25] These distinctions in rank are based on their historical definitions in the online dictionary of the Real Academia Española (DRAE; http://www.rae.es/).

[26] Peter Schreurs, *Caraga Antigua 1521–1910: The Hispanization and Christianization of Agusan, Surigao, and East Davao* (Cebu: University of San Carlos Publications, 1989), p. 112.

[27] (AGI [Archivo General de Indias], Filipinas, 19, R.8, N.116).

the transportation to Manila of three *datu* leaders from Mindanao, including one named Silongan, for official recognition by the governor-general as *maestres de campo*. Tantalizing as this potential match to our Butuanon *datu* may be, the three men in question are clearly identified in the document as leaders of the "Mindanao," which is what the Spaniards called the Magindanaw. Butuan was already a very familiar place to Spaniards at that time, so the fact that the place name of Butuan was not mentioned anywhere in the document indicates that the record is most likely about another "*datu* Silongan," namely Sirongan (sometimes Silonga), who was *rajah* of Buayan during roughly around the same period.[28]

Beyond this, I could find only one other archival record of this particular title being associated with someone identified as a *natural* or *indio* of the island of Mindanao. In 1727, a man in Iligan named Basilio Virtudes Tamparong, described as a "general of the natives of the Presidio and the jurisdiction of Iligan, on the border with the Moros" and recognized by the title of *maestre de campo indígena*, was approved to receive a stipend of six *pesos* monthly for his services.[29]

Centuries later, the Spanish Jesuit José Clotet would report in the late nineteenth century that a handful of elders in the Bukidnon and Misamis areas were referred to as *masalicampo*, which denoted a special status among their peers.[30] However, the nature of this special status was not explained further by Clotet or other outsiders. All we know is that, to this day, the *masalicampo* title still commands respect in many Manobo language family groups. Its cognates are also found among other Philippine ethnic minority groups—for example, the *maslicampo* of the Tagbanuwa of Palawan—but with no detailed description of what special authority or duty the title conveys.[31]

The word *masalicampo*, however, is very clearly a corruption of either *maestre de campo* or *mariscal de campo*, another curious vestige of Spanish colonialism buried deep inside Lumad culture. Even though we have yet to uncover more about the evolution of this phenomenon, the existence of this direct titular appropriation already establishes a strong colonial link among the Lumad as we know them today.

Conceptualizing the Supreme *Datu*

For the Higaunon Lumad, the golden cane is an integral part of their historical narrative that deals with the origins of the political authority of the *datu*. In fact, the cane symbolizes the roots of present-day political organization among the Higaunon, which, as discussed in the previous chapter, consists of independent *datus*, each with an acephalous *sacup* or individual sphere of influence that, at least in theory, has the organizational capacity and political will to coalesce temporarily—for the purpose of common defense—into a hierarchical structure organized, in part, along local ideas

---

[28] See Michael O. Mastura, *The Rulers of Magindanao in Modern History, 1515–1903: Continuity and Change in a Traditional Realm in the Southern Philippines* (Manila: Philippine Social Science Council Modern Philippine History Program, Research Project No. 5, 1979), pp. 100–2. See also Horacio de la Costa, *The Jesuits in the Philippines, 1581–1768* (Cambridge: Harvard University Press, 1961), pp. 303–7.

[29] (Archivo General de Indias [hereafter AGI], Filipinas, 333, L.13, F.41r-42r/17-10-1727).

[30] Lynch, "The Bukidnon of North-Central Mindanao," pp. 464–82.

[31] See Robert B. Fox, *Religion and Society among the Tagbanuwa of Palawan Island, Philippines* (Manila: National Museum Monograph 9, 1982), p. 124. See also Lynch, "The Bukidnon of North-Central Mindanao," pp. 472–73; and Jocano, *Sulod Society*, p. 26, n. 27.

of political and territorial precedence. Therefore, the golden cane also symbolizes the formation of possibly the first confederation of *datus* from across north-central Mindanao. In this organizational schema—again, in theory—different *datus*, along with their *sacups*, commit themselves to coalescing as needed into a hierarchical structure under one so-called "supreme *datu*."

Let us bear in mind here the fundamental nature of political leadership among the fiercely independent Lumad, based on what little we do know. The Lumad of earlier centuries were nothing if not politically pluralistic, and the word *principales*, usually translated into English as "chiefs," in fact applied not to a single, political office, but referred more generally to the leading members and families within the local population, including women and children. Lumad settlements were very clearly characterized as politically autonomous units, and more often than not the presence of multiple *principales* in each polity was noted with frustration by missionaries and other colonial agents. Today, government officials, NGO workers, anthropologists, and contemporary missionaries are likewise forced to deal with multiple loci of power within any given Lumad community, where there are typically several *datus* even in very small communities. Whereas in the past, Lumad leaders seem to have been easily identifiable, today outsiders are often unable to distinguish which men are the *datus*, especially when they do not wear their special accoutrements on a daily basis. As Gatmaytan explains, the *datus* "become active only when there is need for them; e.g., conflict-resolution or representation of the community to outsiders. Otherwise, they farm and cut rattan like anyone else."[32] Therefore, the operational "supremacy" of any single *datu*, whether inside his own community or as part of a larger network, is tolerated by necessity as a transitory commission.

Fay-Cooper Cole reports that a "chief *dato*" ruled Central Bukidnon before colonial influence reached the area. He actually writes that this was the case "before the coming of the Spaniards," but I found nothing in the Spanish archives to support this notion.[33] This "chief *dato*" may very well be a reference to the ancestor Pabulusen, who, as explained further below (and elsewhere in this volume), was considered a true ancestor and, according to Higaunon oral histories, was once given control of nearly all of Higaunon territory. Pabulusen is also said to have been the first *datu* to be selected as holder of the golden cane and the special hat—the very same symbols of legal authority acquired by Kumbalan and Tawaga from the king of Manila.[34]

A few so-called "supreme *datus*" have also been recognized by local government officials in Bukidnon, Misamis Oriental, and Agusan in the present day, but I have not encountered a single *datu*—including, notably, the man once officially recognized by lowlanders as the "Supreme Datu of Gingoog"[35]—who has admitted that such a person exists. They made it clear to me that the idea of a "supreme *datu*" or even a "chief *datu*" who could extend his jurisdiction beyond their respective *sacup* and

---

[32] Augusto Gatmaytan, "Issues in Community Resource Management in Northern Mindanao," ICRAF Southeast Asia Policy Research Working Paper 19, Laguna, Philippines, 2001, p. 37, n. 39.

[33] Fay-Cooper Cole, *The Bukidnons of Mindanao* (Chicago, IL: Chicago Natural History Museum Fieldiana 46, 1956), p. 79.

[34] Biernatzki, "Kalabugao Community Study," p. 42.

[35] *Datu* Manlindahay Mandahinog.

claim to rule a whole region was, in a word, inconceivable. The "Supreme Datu of Gingoog" was, in fact, regarded by other Higaunon people as simply another *datu* in a larger constellation of his peers, albeit the one who had the misfortune of dealing most directly with lowland government officials.[36]

The temporary formation of hierarchical political structures among fundamentally acephalous peoples—for the sake of political collaboration—bears some resemblance to the possible manner in which chiefdoms in Polynesia evolved out of more fragmented, egalitarian big-man networks, as described by Marshall Sahlins. I refer in particular to the apparent cycling between more decentralized or fragmentary political structures and more centralized ones under a "paramount chief."[37] Any number of factors would have brought about such transitions; even the presence or absence of such basic connections as kinship, extant political alliances, or economic ties between individual leaders will have "provided structural avenues for at least temporary expansion of political scale, for consolidation of great into even greater chiefdoms."[38] Indeed, Sahlins's description of "big-men" as a political type in Melanesia closely resembles the role played by more prominent *datu* leaders in Lumad society, in that they can be an "indispensable means of creating supralocal organization: in tribes normally fragmented into small independent groups, big-men at least temporarily widen the sphere of ceremony, recreation and art, economic collaboration, of war too."[39]

The next section explains how such a confederation of *datus* from normally fragmented, autonomous communities may have been conceptualized, and explores the role of Spanish colonialism in facilitating this notion of pan-*sacup* cooperation, even if it may never have actually been realized on a grander, pan-Lumad scale.

GENEALOGIES OF THE FIRST SINGAMPO

Let us now return to the ancestors Tawaga and Kumbalan, who, in some oral traditions at least, brought the golden cane to Cagayán in northern Mindanao. It is said that, upon their return, Tawaga organized the first-ever *singampo*, or conference of *datus*, in Dumalaging, central Bukidnon, to create a regional alliance among all the different *datus*.[40] This new type of political conference then decided as a body to assign the region's first overarching political authority to *Apu* Pabulusen. In oral history, therefore, Pabulusen assumes what appears to be a newly created supralocal role among the other *datus*: that of paramount leader. It is also Pabulusen, whose designation *Apu* marks him as true ancestor, who carries us past colonial-era mythology and into modern Lumad bloodlines. As explained in the previous chapter, he is identified in some Higaunon genealogies as being from the Tagoloán

---

[36] Oona T. Paredes, "People of the Hinterlands: Higaûnon Life in Northern Mindanao, Philippines" (Masters thesis, Arizona State University, 1997), pp. 136–39. See also J. R. Nereus Acosta, "Loss, Emergence, and Retribalization: The Politics of Lumad Ethnicity in Northern Mindanao (Philippines)" (PhD dissertation, University of Hawaii at Manoa, 1994), p. 181, n. 32.

[37] See Marshall Sahlins, "Poor Man, Rich Man, Big-man, Chief: Political Types in Melanesia and Polynesia," *Comparative Studies in Society and History* 5,3 (1963): 287, 298.

[38] Ibid., p. 295.

[39] Ibid., p. 292.

[40] Not to be confused with the more recent major *singampo* events, such as one that took place during the late 1960s in the Tapel river area of Bukidnon. See Coben, *Verbal Arts*, pp. 240–41.

river valley in Misamis Oriental,[41] while one Agusan Manobo version says that Pabulusen was the son of a woman named Gahomon who traveled towards the east, eventually settling in the Agusan valley with him.[42] Biernatzki also reports that Pabulusen settled in Sinakungan (located in southern Agusan, to the east of Tagoloán), where, in accordance with the story of Kumbalan and Tawaga related above, he became the first *datu*.[43] Pabulusen is also noted in one detailed genealogy "for starting the Higaonon *lagimu* or spiritual laws."[44] While the genealogies of different settlement groups will show variations with regard to the order of distant ancestors, they all show descent from this common ancestor, *Apu* Pabulusen.[45] If there had, indeed, been a historical supreme *datu* among the Lumad in colonial Mindanao, it is most likely to have been him.

The ancestral commonalities of the different Lumad groups in northern Mindanao is an important underlying facet of this story. It is reportedly marked in the *giling*, mentioned earlier as a magical symbol of customary law, that the Higaunons and Manobos—essentially all Lumads who are part of the Manobo language family—are "fingers on a hand" in terms of their overall relatedness. According to their folklore, the Higaunon and other Manobo peoples are related not only culturally but genealogically as well.[46] Various stories in Higaunon mythology also relate that they, along with all Manobos, came from the same female ancestor, *Apu* Gahomon[47]—a remarkable claim in itself, given that, according to Biernatzki,

---

[41] Baliguihan Ancestral Land Claim (hereafter BALC), "Documented Proofs of the Historical Ethnic Origins and Long Term Settlement of the Higaunons of Baligiyan," Supporting document for R10-CADC-012, Department of Environment and Natural Resources, Government of the Republic of the Philippines, 1994, Section 1.2.

[42] Yumo, "Power Politics of the Southern Agusan Manobo," pp. 7 and 43 n.1.

[43] Biernatzki, "Bukidnon Datuship," p. 19.

[44] BALC, "Documented Proofs," Section 2.2.

[45] Ibid., Section 1.1.

[46] Biernatzki, "Kalabugao Community Study," p. 96. However, some of Biernatzki's informants claimed that "[a]ll Bukidnons are descended from *Apu* Limbubungan," who in turn was descended from *Apu* Pabuluson (p. 110). Limbubungan is important because, in some oral traditions, he is the father of Tawaga and Kumbalan, who received the cane and hat from the foreign general or king according to Higaunon narratives. Genealogies carry individual variations but are taken very seriously, so it would be impossible to establish one version as the standard. In fact, my two major sources of genealogical information on the Higaunon also claim descent from Adam and Eve, even though only one of these genealogies was provided by Christian converts, so clearly we have only begun to scratch the surface with regard to this subject. See Biernatzki, "Kalabugao Community Study," p. 115. See also BALC, "Documented Proofs."

[47] There is another dimension to the Gahomon story, included in Yumo's version from the Agusan Manobo, that clearly points to the incorporation of elements from the story of the Biblical flood: *Apu* (ancestor) Gahomon, a pregnant widow, is told by a voice to inform the people that a flood is coming and that it would engulf the high mountains. This is to cleanse the world from sin. Whoever will survive would be considered people of God. They are the clean people who would listen to the laws of God. *Apu* Gahomon then tells this to the people but they do not believe her. They assume that, if it were to flood, the waters would never reach the mountains where they lived. Sure enough, the earth becomes dangerously flooded, because a giant crab (*kayumang*) has blocked the drain, known as the *pusud hu dagat* or "navel of the ocean." *Apu* Gahomon secures herself in a wooden box (*baúl*) that was sealed to prevent water from coming in. When the water rises high, the people ask the help of *Apu* Gahomon, but the widow tells them it is already too late ... Meanwhile, a big snake (*sawa*) appears out of nowhere and tosses the *baúl* towards the top of Sinalagaw mountain ... The *sawa* then fights

Higaunons consider Manobos to be "wild" and "without law."[48] But this ancestral link is relevant in that the same story has also been recorded from the Agusan Manobo.[49]

In Biernatzki's Bukidnon version of the golden cane's origins, the *bagobal ha bulawan* was eventually given to another man named Mandagbol, who was likewise situated in Sinakungan (southern Agusan), as Gahomon and Pabulusen were. The *datu* Mandagbol was known for having been "once the holder of the *giling*"—prior to the arrival of the cane, that is—and he moved from Dumalaging (in Bukidnon, and the commonly agreed location of the first *singampo*) into Sinakungan (in Agusan) after marrying into a local kin group. Yumo adds that a hereditary path to datuship was established in Sinakungan by the intermarriage of *Apu* Gahomon's female descendants with seven men, five of whom were from Higaunon areas.[50] Coincidentally, one of these Higaunon men was from a place called Baligi-an, and in a present-day Higaunon settlement called Baligiyan or Baliguihan, located in the same general vicinity, the common genealogy likewise notes that some of their ancestors lived in Sinakungan about 180 years ago.[51]

Given the importance of Pabulusen as a uniting figure in Higaunon and Manobo oral traditions, especially those related to the golden cane, early political unification, and the first *singampo*, it is quite possible that "Mandagbol" represents an alternate name for Pabulusen.[52] The practice of changing names throughout one's lifetime was

---

the *kayumang* until it unblocks the drain, allowing the waters to recede. Gahomon then sends a crow and a parakeet to find any survivors. They see that Noah, in his ark (*paragat*), "was the only survivor of the people from the sea [*dumagat*]." In another version of this story, however, the pregnant Gahomon is the only survivor due to pure luck. All her children born before the flood drown. There is no *baúl*, no survivor-seeking bird, and no warning about cleansing the world of sins and sinners. See Yumo, "Power Politics of the Southern Agusan Manobo," pp. 7–8. Note that *baúl* is Spanish for a storage trunk.

It is tempting to point to the appearance of Noah's Ark here as conclusive proof of Christian influence in ancient Lumad traditions, but Unabia says that it is more likely the result of Islamic influences, due to the use of Muslim terms throughout the version of this story she recorded from the Talaandig, as well as the fact that "the narrator [Anastacio Saway] lives close to the borders between the Bukidnon and Maranao territories, and his story covers the origin of the people of central Mindanao which includes the Muslim Magindanao and Maranao." See Unabia, "*Gugud*," p. 207.

In any case, the flood story clearly relates something about the origins of today's Manobo-speaking peoples, including all the descendants of Pabulusen, such as the Higaunon and Bukidnon. This ties the Gahomon flood story solidly to Southeast Asian, rather than Christian, tradition, as similar flood ethnogenesis myths are widespread in Southeast Asia. These flood myths typically feature a great deluge that leaves only two survivors who have no choice but to repopulate the land through a sexual union that is categorically abnormal, usually shockingly incestuous in nature. See Dang Nghiem Van, "The Flood Myth and the Origin of Ethnic Groups in Southeast Asia," *The Journal of American Folklore* 106,421 (1993): 304-337.

[48] Biernatzki, "Kalabugao Community Study," p. 96.

[49] Yumo, "Power Politics of the Southern Agusan Manobo," pp. 6–7.

[50] Ibid., p. 8.

[51] BALC, "Documented Proofs," Section 2.2.

[52] Please note that the significance of matching names from genealogies to names in Lumad oral tradition is tricky because postmortem renaming is reportedly a common cultural practice among many Lumad groups. It is currently not possible to determine whether the similarities between some names preserved in modern genealogies, colonial archives, and indigenous oral traditions are due to coincidence or actual historical confluence. The most I hope to gain by pointing out these mesmerizing convergences is to pique the interest of those who might be in

once common among the Higaunon. It could also be that the name of Pabulusen, a very important ancestor, has simply been conflated with this tangle of events after the fact. Despite his great prominence in oral traditions, or perhaps because of it, there is no consensus on Pabulusen's precise place in the larger mythical genealogies within Higaunon and Manobo oral tradition. Some genealogies identify Pabulusen as Gahomon's husband, while in others he is named as one of her children. In fact, in some flood myths, he is both.[53] At this point, without a more detailed study, we are limited to pure speculation.

Given that Gahomon is present in the Mandagbol version, it is not so farfetched to suggest that Mandagbol might simply be Pabulusen's name as remembered by the southern Agusan Manobo. According to the Higaunon version, the descendants of Pabulusen eventually left Sinakungan about 180 years ago, as mentioned above. They then settled in Baligiyan, which straddles the Misamis–Agusan border, and eventually became known by a different tribal name. Presumably this refers to the people who later became the Higaunon. Given that the Higaunon and Manobo settlements in this area are similar and share so much culturally, it is not so farfetched to believe that this oral tradition is a narrative of the actual, historical migrations of these population groups.

In any case, I present these different, sometimes conflicting, oral histories because they clearly point to a major political development taking place in the time of Pabulusen that, at the minimum, affected north Mindanao Lumad communities from as far west as Dumalaging (now part of Bukidnon province) all the way north to Tagoloán, and southeast from there to Sinakungan (now part of Agusan del Sur province). This major political development, one involving both migrations to the interior and the political reorganization of this part of the Lumad world, may have taken place anywhere from the beginning of the eighteenth century to the first half of the nineteenth century, depending on how one uses the genealogies to compute the *tuad,* or spaces between generations.

We can formulate a possible scenario based on the shared elements of the oral histories outlined above. First, there was a major gathering, or *singampo,* that took place sometime in the first half of the nineteenth century, perhaps even earlier. As described in chapter three, this was a period of great transition in northern Mindanao, marked by a substantial increase in the number of Recoleto missionaries, during what I refer to as the second mission period. Due in part to this missionary intensification, the second mission period was the time when Mindanao as we know it began to emerge.

Second, there is no dispute as to where events took place. The *singampo* took place in Dumalaging, Bukidnon, and it involved the common ancestors of today's Higaunon and Manobo communities from what are now the provinces of Bukidnon, Misamis Oriental, and Agusan del Sur. The participants in the *singampo* included notable parties from the Tagoloán and Sinakungan valleys. It is also clear that the individual eventually chosen by the *singampo* as the first "supreme" *datu* with supralocal authority was—like the ancestor Pabulusen—not originally from Sinakungan but decided to settle there.

---

a better position to tackle the subject.

[53] See footnote 47, above. The pregnant Gahomon gives birth to a boy, with whom she mates (because no one else is available), and from this incestuous union he becomes the ancestor Pabulusen.

Other aspects of these events are much less clear. For example, while male leadership was the order of the day in the *singampo*, we know that the female ancestor Gahomon had an important role to play, possibly as either the wife or the mother of Pabulusen. She also could have been a highly respected *bae* or female authority figure.[54] However, Gahomon plays a mythological role in Higaunon and Manobo creation stories as well, as she is the putative "Eve" from whom all her people are descended. Given such complex possibilities, Gahomon's likely role vis-à-vis the *singampo*, and other developments in Lumad political organization, is open to endless interpretation and remains undefined.

An important question, however, is why the *singampo* was organized to begin with. Let us take into account three factors: the origins of Pabulusen and others in Tagoloán, as indicated by various oral traditions; the mission history of Tagoloán; and the intensification of mission work at this particular time, which would have had a significant impact in Bukidnon, where the *singampo* took place. The events remembered in these oral traditions may be related to both a revitalization movement that emerged in response to intensifying Christianization, and later, a more literal movement of people away from the centers of Christianization.

If people from Tagoloán did relocate to a remote place like Sinakungan—which is remote even in the present day—they may have done so as cultural refugees, seeking a return to ancestral practices or perhaps following new religious practices, as suggested by the genealogy mentioned in chapter five. The first *singampo* of oral tradition could signify the creation of a new religious path for the area's Lumadnon, a path tied to neither ancestral nor colonial authority structures. The creation of such a path would explain not only the necessity of such a large gathering of *datu* from throughout the region, but also why new ideas about political authority would be discussed and negotiated, and why the participants in this gathering would even consider incorporating wholly external symbols like the *bastún*. In other words, with the *singampo*, the Lumadnon may have been creating a new, potentially radical, tradition in response to a new political and social milieu.

In one way or another, the threads of oral tradition surrounding the first *singampo*, which led to the selection of the first "supreme" *datu* as keeper of the golden cane, suggest that there is some historical truth in the stories of Lumad movement away from their coastal brethren, a move undertaken to escape the new and intensified colonial reality that was emerging in the second mission period.

IMPLICATIONS FOR LUMAD ETHNOHISTORY

It is ironic that these "indigenous" symbols, narratives, and mythologies—commonly perceived as ancient local traditions established since "time immemorial"—are, in fact, rooted either in a Spanish colonial practice that was once used globally, or in the Lumad experience of Spanish colonization. Important aspects of Lumad political organization appear to be products of Western expansion rather than of "original" or pre-Hispanic Philippine culture, including symbols of authority

---

[54] The *bae* is almost always glossed by researchers and officials as the "female *datu*," as if the two offices were interchangeable but for gender. However, this is not necessarily correct. As an indigenous authority figure in many different Lumad societies, the *bae* is even more poorly defined and underappreciated than the *datu*. The way political organization is gendered in these societies remains to be thoroughly investigated.

like the cane and the hat, special titles like the *masalicampo*, and even the development of key concepts surrounding datuship itself.

However, I assembled this chapter not merely to underline the importance of appreciating more fully the impact of Spanish colonization on the indigenous cultures of Mindanao, but to highlight Lumad innovation as well. If nothing else, the case of the "golden cane" in Lumad traditions compels us to study further an aspect of the Philippines' Hispanic heritage that has been completely overlooked: the "Hispanization" of supposedly "un-Hispanized" upland groups. The examples in this chapter encourage us to modify what we now know about the Lumad colonial experience in several significant ways.

First, the acquisition of Spanish colonial symbols and titles by the Lumad tells us that Lumadnon were active stakeholders in the colonial enterprise. These symbols and titles could not be acquired except through service to the Spanish Crown, which in this period of Mindanao's colonial history typically involved fighting against Spain's principal enemy in the region, the Moros. We now know that the Lumadnon, rather than violently rejecting any outside influence on their cultural traditions, welcomed the presence of Spanish missionaries. They actively participated in mission life as well as in major military campaigns against the Moros, fighting under the banner of Spain. In a few instances, they also conducted minor operations against Lumad "outlaws," as in the aftermath of the Karaga revolt. We know from this and the previous chapters that the Lumad allied themselves with the Spaniards, particularly with the missionaries, in pursuit of their own interests. They actively sought colonial intervention with regard to enhancing security, considerable economic freedoms, and the structuring of internal community protocols related to political authority and legal adjudication. This is a far cry from the popular image of the fierce Lumadnon as the last true bastion of anticolonial resistance.

Second, the appropriation of Spanish colonial symbols and titles to legitimize and represent political authority among Lumad peoples shows us that we should never forget how very Southeast Asian they are. The Southeast Asian habit of "localization"—in which outside elements are readily appropriated and easily incorporated into local culture—is significant in explaining the remarkable openness of the Lumad and other island Southeast Asians to the influence of external entities. The enduring significance of these symbols and titles among the Lumad also tells us that Spanish colonialism had a more profound impact on this pericolonial area than previously acknowledged.

Finally, oral traditions about a pan-ethnic political confederation among the Lumad, in the form of the first *singampo* and assignment of the golden cane, tell us that, during the colonial period, a diverse body of Lumad peoples—from different family groups, different settlements spread out over three different provinces, and distinct dialect groups—once found enough common ground for cooperation and collaboration. Our still limited knowledge leaves undetermined the number of different territories and peoples who were represented in this confederation. A more thorough study of oral traditions about these interrelated Lumad political genealogies would shed more light on this intriguing moment in Mindanao's colonial history and deepen our appreciation of the Lumad experience.

AFTERWORD

RESPECTING PLACE

> History, exactly like the utterly naïve anthropological concept of culture, is not something that people just have: it is something that they often must struggle against, whether they want to or not.[1]

The preceding chapters paint a picture of Lumad life in northeast Mindanao during the early colonial period. We find the Lumad spread throughout the region in small communities, with an occasionally larger settlement concentrated around a particularly influential *datu*. Most of their settlements appear to have been in areas that today are regarded as thoroughly "lowland," in that they are occupied by Visayan Catholics who had settled there over the past two centuries as part of both the natural growth of Christianized populations and the resettlement efforts of Recoleto missionaries in the course of optimizing their conversion efforts in north Mindanao. Given the early conversion of the aforementioned coastal Lumad communities, we can assume that at least some of today's coastal "lowlanders" are descended from Lumad converts who chose to live in a missionary-organized settlement or *reducción* in the first mission period. These early Lumad converts would have undergone the same process of Hispanization as all other converts elsewhere in the archipelago. We also know, based on oral traditions, that some Lumads pulled up stakes and left to find less Hispanized accommodations, time and again. This was true throughout the first mission period, particularly in relation to issues of taxation, Moro raiding, local unrest, and really anything else that might have struck the autonomous, independent-minded Lumadnon as impinging on their freedom. The impulse to escape troubles by running to the interior has become a familiar response among the Lumad in Mindanao—a recurring motif of their existence—as culturally resonant then as it is now. This would have become more pronounced when other Christians—from the Visayas and elsewhere—began to arrive more systematically as the overall colonial project rolled on and intensified over the centuries.

This scenario, and the fact of early Lumad conversion, does not lessen or invalidate the cultural integrity of Lumad peoples, nor does it make them less "indigenous" than we have always believed them to be. On the contrary, it gives remarkable credence to the deep, recurring Lumad oral traditions that tell of flights away from the coast to escape a variety of destructive or otherwise negative forces that were disrupting normal life. The epic of Agyu, for example, centers on the Lumad protagonists' magical escape from cultivated, coastal areas at sea level to an interior, higher-elevation place—an uncultivated land, free from controlling outsiders—during a time of extreme crisis that permanently destroys Agyu's community. As mentioned in the previous chapter, the *Ulagíng* has as many versions

---

[1] Gerald Sider, "Can Anthropology Ever Be Innocent?," *Anthropology Now* 1,1 (2009): 47.

as the different Higaunon and Manobo groups that carry it as part of their tradition. But despite the plot varieties in circulation, the tale repeats, in all known cases, this trope of a traumatic population displacement from the coast to the interior, from lower lands to higher lands, from "civilization" to a wilderness devoid of dwellings, crops, and livestock, a new, unfamiliar place in which they are expected to start everything over from scratch.

The Higaunon and Manobo ancestor named Pabulusen, who dates back to approximately three hundred years ago, around the late seventeenth century, and who has occasionally appeared in the *Ulagíng,* is likewise described as having led his people away to a new place where his descendants now live, in order to preserve or revive cultural ways or "laws" that were considered under threat in their original settlements. Presumably, these refugees also left behind those of their brethren who chose not to follow, possibly leading to a fissioning of their community that would have been traumatic in itself. One Manobo oral tradition that evokes precisely this sort of trauma tells of two brothers from many generations ago who parted ways over a book. One brother believed in the promise of this book and decided to pursue literacy and academic learning, becoming what colonial observers would have called "civilized." The other, meanwhile, was not impressed by what the book had to offer, rejected his brother's newfangled ways, and resolved to remain true to his ancestral traditions by moving deeper into the interior of Mindanao.[2] This is not a cautionary tale to promote educational values but a discourse on the development of cultural differences between coastal and interior peoples in this part of Mindanao, one that may not be historical in the normal sense but nonetheless ties broader Lumad past and pastness to wider Philippine, Southeast Asian, and global history. In light of what we know about the early conversion of Lumad peoples in this area, we might also read into this story a statement on the profundity of difference that has since developed, over many generations, between converts and non-converts in the region.

Despite its relatively ancient points of reference, this story of migration and fission is also a very modern trope, one found in all present-day Lumad narratives of encounters with outsiders, in which the arrival of settlers presents Lumadnon with a difficult choice, one with bitter consequences all around. Escaping to higher ground means remaining autonomous and true to ancestral cultural traditions but also abandoning the ancestral land and leaving crops to be harvested by others. Staying put and defending one's rights to the land means risking abuse and exploitation by lowlanders, as well as losing one's culture as the next generation assimilates. In the minds of modern Lumad peoples, this is their eternal dilemma, one that is now exacerbated by the fact that, in the increasingly crowded interior of Mindanao, there is no other place to go. In their minds, they are slowly being engulfed by a creeping tide of poor migrant settlers who desperately stake their claims even in the deepest, roughest interior mountains, leaving them with no other place to run except—as my dear friend Tahak likes to say—"up our rear ends."

Thus, the ethnohistory of Lumad peoples can be ultimately distilled into a question of place: the various physical locations they have occupied on the island of Mindanao represent not only a history of residences and settlement, but also a

---

[2] Augusto Gatmaytan, "Constructions in Conflict: Manobo Tenure as Critique of Law," in *Control and Conflict in the Uplands: Ethnic Communities, Resources, and the State in Indonesia, the Philippines, and Vietnam,* ed. Filomeno Aguilar Jr. and Angelina Unson, Institute of Philippine Culture, Culture, and Development Series No. 1 (Quezon City: Ateneo de Manila University Press, 2005), p. 63.

manifestation of the increasingly marginal place they occupied in Philippine society and history as the colonial period unfolded. As the few written records of these areas were archived and forgotten over the centuries, so were the stories of the Lumad ancestors whose lives remain deeply embedded in the landscape, and in fragments of Lumad cultural memory. Given the interpretive challenges involved in writing out an academically respectable ethnohistory of the Lumad colonial experience that would be readable globally, yet also meaningful locally, this study has been very much an academic thought experiment, one in which I have attempted to put the Lumad back in their rightful place.

I originally began this study as an attempt to locate and establish Lumad peoples, in general, as authentic participants in the Philippine colonial experience. I wanted to historicize them so that they may be more easily recognized as equal stakeholders in the Filipino nation: as integral rather than external to it, for the Lumad and other minority peoples have generally been regarded as living in a world apart by "mainstream" Filipinos. For Mindanao, this marginality has become normalized in part because histories of the island usually begin in the late 1800s, after the return of the Jesuits, when coastal Mindanao was no longer the domain of Lumad peoples. Histories since then have focused almost exclusively on either the areas ministered by Jesuits, or on the more politically compelling Moro areas. Beyond this narrow and myopic historiography, the standard ethnographic data regarding on the Lumad that have been collected and presented to the world by anthropologists since the early American period have tended to convey a cultural timelessness. Often it is as if, in the midst of all the authentic Filipino history that was in the making, the Lumad appeared suddenly out of a time warp, somehow fully formed *in situ*, without having undergone the traumatic passage and meaningful transformations their lowland brethren had to struggle with over four centuries of foreign occupation.

But those NGO workers, missionaries, and others who work regularly in Lumad areas already know that even the seeming isolation of the mountains has not immunized the Lumad from the economic, social, and political forces of the coastal areas. From the perspective of Lumad cultural and political realities, therefore, such "histories" tell an extremely shallow and one-dimensional story. Yet this historiography still colors how most of us conceptualize the Lumad, how we assess the validity and urgency of their claims to ancestral land and cultural autonomy, and how haphazardly we pass judgment on the rightfulness of their place in both Mindanao and the Filipino nation. Those already concerned with Lumad culture know that this study is more than just a prelude or backstory to the more commonly found narratives of the area's history: respecting place is, ultimately, a matter of respecting human rights.

In terms of place, this study pushes us to appreciate the true weight of colonial authority in a pericolonial region like Mindanao during the first mission period. In this case, although Spain was able to establish the pretense of colonial administration, it was unable to impose what we generally think of as colonial rule. With the exception of small coastal fortifications built a few decades after missionaries first arrived, military reinforcements were middling to nonexistent in the earliest part Mindanao's colonial period. Even as late as the nineteenth century, the Spanish colonial government was desperately seeking ways to secure the political allegiance of the indigenous peoples of northern and eastern Mindanao by granting them tax concessions that were not offered to those living in the more fully incorporated parts of the colony. The contrast with Spanish dominance in the Visayas and Luzon could not be more stark. That said, it would be a mistake to suggest that Mindanao did not also experience a significant level of colonization.[3] Even the pericolonial experience was meaningful enough to realign the entire island politically and to leave a permanent mark on its indigenous peoples. This shows us how fuzzy a term like "colonial" can be, and that there is a very wide range of political relationships possible, spanning from total subjugation and repression to total resistance, with all manner of negotiation and accommodation in-between.

To see Lumad peoples clearly also requires a reorientation of our latter-day narratives to articulate Lumad Mindanao within larger regional and world history. In this particular case, we can recognize that the Lumad are culturally distinct today precisely because of their significant contact with Spanish colonialism, as opposed to the lack of it. Though there are few traces of this legacy in Lumad material culture, we do find it in women's multi-colored "traditional" clothing styles across different groups in northern and central Mindanao, such as those described for Bukidnon by Fay Cooper-Cole. Their full, voluminous skirts and close-fitting jackets with wide sleeves, decorated with appliqué and embroidery, may be considered distinctively "ethnic" today, but were "actually derived from European dress styles."[4] Beyond material culture, the impact of colonization is also recognizable in important oral traditions. Contact references from both the Spanish and American colonial eras are sprinkled throughout different tellings of the *Ulagíng* epic, as previously mentioned. It is notable, however, that in many versions of this tale, the hero Agyu and his followers are lifted up into a saucer-like vessel called a *salimbal*, ascending by means of an enormous magical rope pulled upwards by a male deity, and remain there for a period of time before continuing their other adventures.[5] The episodes with the *salimbal* represent the experience of boarding not an extraterrestrial flying saucer, but a large Spanish ship, as viewed or otherwise imagined by Lumads in previous centuries.[6] Not only are these indicators of direct contact between Lumad ancestors and the colonial state, they are also but a few of the many elements of "indigenous" Lumad culture apparently drawn from their very own colonial experience, as opposed to survivals from pre-Hispanic culture that were preserved due to the avoidance of contact.

---

[3] See, for example, John Leddy Phelan, *The Hispanization of the Philippines: Spanish Aims and Filipino Responses, 1565–1700* (Madison, WI: University of Wisconsin, 1959). See also the more recent work of Linda Newson, *Conquest and Pestilence in the Early Spanish Philippines* (Honolulu: University of Hawaii Press, 2009). Both otherwise excellent studies of the Philippine colonial experience exclude any real analysis of Mindanao, dismissing the impact of Spanish colonization there as historically insignificant in the face of stronger Islamic influences.

[4] Herminia Meñez Coben, *Verbal Arts in Philippine Indigenous Communities: Poetics, Society, and History* (Quezon City: Ateneo de Manila University Press, 2009), pp. 233–34. Coben cites Roy Hamilton, ed., *From the Rainbow's Varied Hue: Textiles of the Southern Philippines* (Los Angeles, CA: University of California Fowler Museum of Cultural History, 1998), pp. 15–102. See also Fay-Cooper Cole, *The Bukidnons of Mindanao* (Chicago, IL: Chicago Natural History Museum Fieldiana 46, 1956), p. 24.

[5] Oona T. Paredes, "True Believers: Higaunon and Manobo Evangelical Protestant Conversion in Historical and Anthropological Perspective," *Philippine Studies* 54,4 (2006): 534–37.

[6] I owe this particular insight to Ron Jennings of the New Tribes Mission, who is a long-term resident of one Higaunon community in Misamis Oriental province and fluent in the Higaunon language.

We have long needed an image of Spanish-era Lumadnon—ancestors of today's Higaunons, Manobos, Karagas, and others—as living, breathing, dynamic individuals whom we can locate, geopolitically and historically, on their own terms, and not solely in reference to their Moro neighbors in south and west Mindanao. In allowing our sense of Lumad history to evolve, we are able to deepen the history of Mindanao as a whole and relocate it in the pastness of the Philippines as a nation.

I originally explored the phenomenon of Lumad-missionary contact in order to circumvent the underlying epistemological problem of what to write Lumad ethnohistory from, given that all written records for the first mission period come from missionary and colonial transcripts. I fully expected to find a confirmation of many of the commonly accepted ideas about modern and ancestral Lumad peoples that all Filipinos inherit, including the image of their aggressive resistance to conversion, colonial authority, culture change, and the call of the modern world in general. I anticipated writing a history of rebellion and repression, rather than of conversion and collaboration. What I found instead compelled me to appreciate the implicit modernity of the colonial-era Lumad, as demonstrated by their willingness to entertain a coexistence with new people, new ideas, and new things. They apparently exploited the potential of the colonial milieu where they could, seizing opportunities to establish a more structured relationship with colonial authority, however distant. They opened certain political avenues for themselves that enabled them to retain their political autonomy, lower the taxes they owed to Spain, and gain access to a greater cache of arms and ammunition. Conversion also brought with it a degree of cultural legitimacy vis-à-vis Europeans, which, in turn, had a lasting impact on relationships with old friends and new enemies. At the very least, we now see how active the Lumad were in terms of their own conversion to Christianity, just as they were active in transforming their own cultural milieu. Accepting their agency here not only compels us to appreciate the impact of the colonial period on a people who are defined in the present as those who were "never" colonized; it also complicates how we conceptualize their present-day differentiation from other Filipinos.

With regard to conversion itself, this study also points to the possibility of a curious mirror effect among European missionaries, at least in a few cases. The indigenous peoples of Mindanao—Lumad and Moro peoples alike—were categorized by the missionaries and colonial officials in two general ways. Those who converted were not only putative allies but also deemed to be of noble character, i.e., trustworthy, peaceful, genteel, intelligent, compassionate, even handsome. For example, the Butuanon and Kagayanon, while presumably remaining coarse by European standards, come across as exemplary colonial subjects in the colonial records. Thanks to their conversions and their pledges of vassalage to the Spanish Crown, they are seen as well-mannered and inherently good-natured natives in the retrospective conversion narratives. In contrast, those who resisted Spanish influence, including conversion, were considered violent, irrational, impulsive, depraved, cruel, and unreliable, stigmatized by a host of negative traits. The Muslim Magindanaw and other Moro groups were, in fact, routinely characterized as *traidor*, or treacherous, and irredeemably so, as were some of the more steadfast of their Karaga allies who had instigated the 1631 revolt. The same category was used for any *indio* or *natural* who made life too dangerous for the Recoletos, Spaniards, and native Christian converts when they were within spearing distance. Yet we also saw that, in the passage from non-convert to convert, the same person who had once been labeled a one-dimensional *traidor* somehow transcended this treacherous nature and became a full human being, capable of complex thought and demonstrating admirable qualities. Even the character of childhood convert María Campan, whose notorious actions in the Karaga Revolt became the focus of missionary shock and outrage, was converted in the post-Revolt accounting, transformed from a model Christian, to a profoundly treacherous, sacrilegious woman, and then someone worthy of returning to the fold once again.

Our impulse might be to see these colonial-era missionaries and their compatriots as culturally narrow creatures who compelled powerless others to adopt their language and cultural markers before they would condescend to listen or see them as real or human. This is certainly a widely acknowledged element of colonial contact. But having observed modern foreign missionary activity among modern Lumad, in which inequalities of power remain, along with differential access to modern knowledge and technology, I can say with some authority that missionization is never a single story. Racism and prejudice may be one story we already know, but it is not the only story, certainly not the whole story. This study has posited mainly that religious conversion—to Christianity, in these particular cases—was able to provide an overarching social and political framework that enabled new kinds of interaction, negotiation, cooperation, and alliance formation among previously antagonistic Lumad communities throughout an area that was originally more preoccupied with revenge raiding. But it is quite obvious that the same process also enabled novel relationships between missionary and missionized, and, therefore, more generally between Lumads and Europeans. Regarding the first mission period—and other situations of native-missionary contact throughout the Philippines—we know that whatever new realities were being digested culturally or psychologically by the Lumad, by both converts and non-converts, their relationships to and with the agents of conversion, and by extension various agents of the colonial state, also had to be accommodated. On both sides. The potential duality of the conversion process is certainly something that deserves further attention within the context of Philippine history.

This study also delved into the nature of political organization and political leadership among the Lumad, an issue that I hope to address more substantially with future field research. So far, we find that, in terms of the classic political types in anthropology, the Lumad political figure known as the *datu* is something of a chimera: part chief, part "big-man," and, occasionally, part shaman, all depending on the specific demographic structure of his community, and the particular context in which the *datu* is observed in action.[7] The *datu* are the critical Lumad actors in the conversion narratives I have presented here, and they remain highly relevant in Lumad life today, not only internally in their respective communities but also in terms of Lumad political interaction with outsiders. They are also familiar to most Filipinos as an indigenous political category, but are almost always conflated with political types from the considerably larger, more socially and economically stratified Philippine lowland ethnic groups, such as the chiefs of the Tagalogs and Visayans of previous centuries, and the sultans of the Magindanaw. *Datu* is, in fact, a popular

---

[7] While *datus* are *the* primary political actors in any give Lumad community, in most circumstances the *datu* is supposed to be indistinguishable from any other Lumad in that he is expected to farm and otherwise live just like everyone else. See Augusto Gatmaytan, "Issues in Community Resource Management in Northern Mindanao," *ICRAF Southeast Asia Policy Research*, Working Paper 19 (Laguna, 2001), p. 37, n. 39.

adjective among lowlanders used to mark someone who has amassed considerable material wealth, especially in Mindanao. This popular use of the word shows that the Lumad brand of leadership—as well as the nature of a *datu*'s "followership," or *sacup*—remains poorly understood. We have yet to appreciate fully the most basic aspects of datuship, such as how a *datu* manages to exercise political influence in unstratified communities and in the presence of other equally respected *datus*, or even how a *datu*'s authority is acknowledged and recognized in the first place.

The same is true for the nature of the *sacup*, the *datu*'s individual sphere of influence characterized by horizontal relationships and interdependence. Among lowlanders today, the cognate term *sakop* denotes a social and economic dependent within a highly stratified patron-client type of relationship—such as an employee or a servant—which is fairly common among the Tagalogs and other large ethnic groups in the lowlands. This definition, in turn, ties in with lowland notions of a "*datu*" who stands apart due to economic wealth. The acephalous quality of the Lumad *sacup*, which is marked by egalitarianism, independence, and the presence of multiple loci of leadership—other *datus* within the same community—is totally forgotten. There is much to explore and understand in this particular area of Lumad culture.

This study evolved from my earlier short-term field research with the Higaunon Lumad that exposed me to some of the oral histories and epics and compelled me to ask more questions about the history of northern and eastern Mindanao.[8] This field encounter also opened for me a new window through which to view the missionary-Lumad encounter and brought the question of earlier Lumad religious conversion to the fore. In observing the modern manifestations of these phenomena *in situ*, I was able to appreciate the strong agency of converts and non-converts alike, even under the pressure of evangelical Christian proselytizing, and the dual nature of religious conversion that is rooted in the cross-cultural interaction between proselytizer and proselytized. Typical academic descriptions and critiques of Western missionary work do not—and perhaps cannot—portray the full reality of this encounter on the ground, for such intimate relationships eventually grow beyond the introduction and acceptance (or rejection) of externally derived scriptures and doctrines.

Last but not least, for this anthropologist at least, the act of translation— from seventeenth and eighteenth century "Castillian" and "Bisaya" to twenty-first century academic English—became a critical mode of discovery, teaching me much more about my subject matter and providing some of the most surprising, and most interesting, findings of this study. For me, the process of methodologically translating these texts also involved a symmetrical process of "untranslating" and detaching such historical texts from their prior ideological uses. The dual nature of this process made it much easier for me to step outside of the larger frameworks in which data from the colonial period have been previously interpreted, allowing other histories and other voices, such as those of the Lumad, to be heard. If only for this reason, my "first contact" with primary sources was well worth my permanent graduation to bifocals.

---

[8] See Oona T. Paredes, "People of the Hinterlands: Higaûnon Life in Northern Mindanao, Philippines" (Master's thesis, Arizona State University, 1997).

ONE FINAL STORY

I did not walk into the Lumad world until I was an adult, despite the fact that I had spent most of my childhood in northern Mindanao, and that my coastal hometown of Medina had been visited for centuries by an assortment of Lumadnon seeking trade. Once I began my research, however, a cultural veil was lifted and, like someone wearing magic lenses, I began to see traces of the Lumad everywhere and in everything I encountered back home. I even found them wrapped inside my family's history, as my late grandmother enthusiastically recalled how she would anticipate their arrival at the end of every harvest at her Chinese grandfather's dry goods store. They came to trade their cash crops and forest products for food, alcohol, and the sorts of goods that Pacific Rim anthropologists would call "cargo." Oddly and colorfully dressed, speaking in heavily accented Bisaya, they were to my grandmother as exotic as they were familiar. I imagine she regarded them with the same childish awe as I did the Muslim women I saw on day trips to Cagayan de Oro city, sparkling like proud butterflies in their gold-threaded veils and dresses.[9]

When I finally came to know individual Lumads, I was struck by the fact that, beyond the sound bytes of a seemingly well-rehearsed contact rhetoric that, in effect, merely bounced back to outsiders their own simplistic misconceptions about Lumad existence, and despite the Lumads' relative geographical isolation, they actually had quite a sophisticated understanding of their place and purpose in this world. They also had an incisive sense of humor that both referenced and contested this understanding. In pulling regional, national, and world events into the orbit of their political and cultural milieu, they made clear to me that they did not consider themselves to be on the periphery of anyone or anything. As far as they were concerned, they were just as integral to the real world as anyone else, even if lowlanders were prevented by their pathetic ignorance and prejudice from recognizing this fact.

Sometimes the irrepressible wit of their metanarrative rivaled the best Monty Python sketches. Once I tried to take a picture of two elderly women in a Higaunon village who were looking particularly photogenic one day, wearing some colorful beaded jewelry around their necks, arms, and ankles. So they did what most older Higaunons do when faced with a camera: they scowled at the lens and stood still as statues. I remarked that it made them look mad, which elicited some mockery from others present. "Don't look so angry," they teased the women, "She'll get scared and call the military!"[10] Everyone giggled nervously, male and female alike, chiming in with progressively cruder comments until my subjects finally loosened up. Now smiling in the bright sunlight, the ladies' composure was again sabotaged by heckling. "Try to look pathetic, will you!" one of their relatives pleaded, "We're trying to convince her that Higaunons are abused and oppressed!" This unleashed a cascade of riotous laughter, engulfing everyone within hearing range. One of the men apologized melodramatically for his relatives' "uncivilized" manners, facetiously repeating some lowland stereotypes and epithets that he had no doubt

---

[9] The more subdued, less colorful Arab styles of *hijab* were not yet in vogue in Mindanao when I was a child.

[10] A reference to the painful history of military intervention due to the "peace-and-order situation" in the Misamis uplands. See Oona T. Paredes, "Higaunon Resistance and Ethnic Politics in Northern Mindanao," *The Australian Journal of Anthropology* 8,3 (1997): 270–90.

contended with all his life. Finally, the giggling subsided, and I was able to take a proper, though far from candid, photograph.

My experience of the Lumad in general, and the Higaunon in particular, is full of moments like this. And to me such moments illustrate that, even as they struggle to communicate a vital political and social statement about lowlander prejudice, they will actively contradict any neat intellectual constructs we might try to apply to their situation (at least those they are aware of). They certainly do not let the outside world define who they are, much less who they ought to be. Nor do they struggle with the things that bog down outsiders (lowlanders, scholars, state officials) who, in the process of trying to understand the Lumad, obsess over what is culturally "authentic" and what is not. The same can be said with regard to language, dress, food, housing, and other markers of ethnic identity. When we relocate the Lumad as peoples *within* history, the dynamic picture that emerges differs quite radically from the nationalist iconography that requires them to stagnate as peoples *without* history.

Smiling for a photo opportunity does not erase the reality of lowlander and state-based prejudice, nor does it invalidate the righteousness of Lumad claims to define and maintain their own lands, cultures, and identities. In this sense, the perspective of Lumad ethnohistory presented in this study, though based on cautious archival and anthropological research, is really more for the enlightenment of outsiders than for the benefit of the Lumad. After all, they already know who they are, and they don't fret over any of the contradictions that seem to be engendered by their very existence. The onus is on the rest of us to catch up with them and fully appreciate that fact.

Appendix A

Abbreviations

PARES Portal de Archivos Españoles (http://pares.mcu.es/)

AGI Archivo General de Indias in Sevilla, Spain

AHN Archivo Histórico Nacional, in Madrid, Spain

ARM Archivo Provincial de los Agustinos Recoletos, Marcilla, Navarra, Spain

BN Biblioteca Nacional, in Madrid, Spain

NL Newberry Library, in Chicago, Illinois, USA, specifically the Ayer Collection

OAR Orden de los Agustinos Recoletos, or Order of Augustinian Recollects

SJ Society of Jesus, or the Jesuits

VFL Vatican Film Library, at St. Louis University, Missouri, USA

APPENDIX B

A NOTE ON TRANSLATION AND ORTHOGRAPHY

Spanish is not normally used in the Philippines. However, growing up in a former colony of Spain, I was exposed to a few stock Spanish words and phrases. In fact, my particular ancestry also exposed me to a much wider range of Spanish grammar and vocabulary than most Filipino children I knew. But Spanish is certainly not my first language, more like my fifth, and I learned to read it properly only as an adult.

I received some formal language training as an undergraduate, and benefited greatly from additional training and language immersion during my archival research in Spain. However, for the most part my linguistic abilities have been acquired through patches of independent self-study that intensified only when archival research was in the cards. Whatever deficiencies or quirks appear in my translations and interpretations of text should, therefore, be blamed on my somewhat esoteric language formation, and not on my language teachers or my relatives or Filipino culture in general. Nor should those native or more advanced speakers who assisted me on occasion be held responsible for any errors that may surface.

I tried as much as possible to capture what I consider to be the essential meanings conveyed by the text, while staying true to its phrasing to preserve the uniqueness and foreignness of its voice. This means that, where translation to English was required, I tried to be as literal in my translation as possible to convey and clarify the meaning of the particular text without adding new words or expressions through which other ideas might enter.

With a few exceptions pertaining to archaic text, the Spanish language words and phrases used in this study have been revised to follow the present-day conventions of the Real Academia Española (RAE). To clarify the deeper meanings of particular words, I relied for the most part on the arbitration of the RAE *Diccionario de la Lengua Española*, cited in the text as DRAE (see http://www.rae.es, available for public use).

For the pronunciation of indigenous Philippine terms, unless otherwise indicated, emphasis falls by default on the second to the last syllable, a notable exception being the term *lumad*. Adjacent vowels retain their individual pronunciation, resulting in a hiatus or sometimes a glottal stop. For example, the word Higaunon is pronounced /hi-ga-U-non/. Last but not least, minimal diacritical marks are used here for the sole purpose of guiding the reader's pronunciation. For example, the place name Tagoloán is pronounced /ta-go-lo-AN/. However, diacritical marks are not commonly used when Philippine languages are rendered in written form.

APPENDIX C

ON THE CITATION OF ARCHIVAL SOURCES

When I cite archival material that is available in published or book form, it appears in the footnotes as part of my general list of references cited, along with other published or otherwise publicly disseminated media. For the remainder, being primary sources in manuscript, microfilm, or map form, most of which do not have titles, I employed a practical citation style that allows the reader to locate the item in its respective repository, verify its contents, and perhaps find additional uses for that particular source. The title and its author, if available, are sometimes also indicated as part of the text or in a note. I have tried to provide as much information as possible to facilitate this verification process and encourage additional research. At the very least, I provide all the information necessary for readers to locate the items cited in this study and request a viewing of the material in question. For additional information on each of these collections, links to related online resources are provided below.

Archivos Estatales, **Spain**
Documents from the state archives (*archivos estatales*) of Spain, such as the Archivo General de Indias (AGI) and the Archivo Histórico Nacional (AHN), are cited following their newly reorganized and totally computerized catalog system. The citation provides the exact information to write on the document order form or type into the computer in order to submit a request for the archive's staff to retrieve or locate the document. The only additional information I provide is naming the archive itself.

For example, (AHN,Ultramar,5155,exp13,n1,f1r) refers to *legajo,* or document bundle number 5155, in the *Ultramar* (Overseas/Foreign Affairs) section of the Archivo Histórico Nacional, specifically the right (*recto*) side of the first sheet of document number 1, found inside dossier (*expediente*) 13.

Portal de Archivos Españoles **(PARES)**
This was formerly called *Archivos Españoles en Red* (AER, Spanish Archives Online). PARES uses its own citation style that differs only slightly from that used in the state archives, and is noted here by the initials PARES preceding the actual archive name and catalog information. See http://pares.mcu.es/

Because both these Spanish systems—the *archivos estatales* and PARES—are relatively new, the citation style will differ somewhat from that used by earlier researchers. However, a search function is available in some of these archives through which one can easily find a document's new location using the old *signatura,* or catalog number. Please refer to the following websites:

AGI   http://www.mcu.es/archivos/visitas/indias/indias.html
AHN   http://cvc.cervantes.es/obref/arnac/nacional/
BN   http://www.bne.es/

Archivo de los Recoletos, Marcilla, Navarra, Spain
This archive has no formal system of citation, so I devised my own using the following abbreviations:

leg   *legajo,* or bundle number
num *número,* or folder number
doc   *documento,* or document number indicating its order of appearance in the folder
f   *folio,* or sheet number
r/v   manuscript side, whether front (r, for *recto*) or back (v, for *verso*)

For example, (ARM leg 61, num 3, doc HN25, f1r) indicates the front side of the first sheet of a document marked "HN25" inside folder number 3 located within *legajo* 61.

Newberry Library, Chicago, Illinois, USA
Documents from the Newberry Library are cited using their catalog information, or, where available, their Library of Congress call numbers. See www.newberry.org

Vatican Film Library, St. Louis, Missouri, USA
The Vatican Film Library holds a complete copy, on microfilm, of the Pablo Pastells Collection, from the Jesuit Provincial Archive in Sant Cugat, Barcelona, Spain. It contains transcriptions from the turn of the twentieth century of selected records pertaining to the Jesuit order that are found in the various state archives of Spain. I also consulted relevant sections of the microfilmed Archivo Romanum Societatis Iesu (ARSI), but do not cite them for this particular study. For materials in the Pastells microfilm collection, I indicate the number of the film roll and the page number of the microfilm copy itself, rather than the now-defunct Spanish catalog numbers originally copied by Pastells. See http://www.slu.edu/libraries/vfl

APPENDIX D

MINDANAO MISSIONS OF THE RECOLETOS, FIRST AND SECOND MISSION PERIODS

This table presents a compilation of mission statistics for the first and second mission periods in Mindanao, drawn from Recoleto sources. The numbers represent the number of people per mission, referred to as *almas*, or souls, that they claimed to serve. More specifically, the numbers are supposed to represent only the *bautismos verificados*, or certified baptisms, credited to the Recoletos. The actual number of people living in or otherwise attached to each mission would therefore have been greater, if unbaptized souls would have been included.

There are minor discrepancies between the three sources listed below, primarily with regard to the dates when particular missions were said to have been established. In some cases, all that I could verify was that the missionaries had indeed been working in a particular place, based on the mention of place names in passing in other texts. For the first mission period, there is no master list of Recoleto missions with conversion figures catalogued over time.

Province	*Pueblos* and *visitas* (year established)[1,2,3]	*Almas,* 1622–1623[1]	*Almas,* 1749[1]	*Almas,* 1778[1]	*Almas,* 1830[1]	*Almas,* 1851[1]	*Almas,* 1861[1]
Misamis	Cagayán (1622)	1,800	—	—	7,505	11,095	11,682
	Misamis	—	—	—	3,877	3,830	5,147
	Jasaán	—	—	—	3,993	3,262	4,796
	Balingaság	—	—	—	—	4,812	6,628
	Yponan	—	—	—	—	—	3,790
	Subtotal for Misamis	**1,800**	**—**	**—**	**15,375**	**22,999**	**32,043**
Agusan	Butuan (1596/1622)	1,500	—	—	6,493	7,558	5,202
	Linao/Bunawan (1624)	1,600	—	—	—	—	766
	Talacogon	—	—	—	—	—	980
	Subtotal for Agusan	**3,100**	**—**	**—**	**6,493**	**7,558**	**6,948**

(cont.) Province	Pueblos and visitas (year established)[1,2,3]	Almas, 1622–1623[1]	Almas, 1749[1]	Almas, 1778[1]	Almas, 1830[1]	Almas, 1851[1]	Almas, 1861[1]
Camiguin	Catarmán (1622)	600	—	—	10,316	7,401	10,707
	Sagáy	—	—	—	—	4,282	2,923
	Mahinog	—	—	—	—	—	2,397
	Mambajao	—	—	—	—	—	3,708
	Subtotal for Camiguin Island	**600**	**—**	**—**	**10,316**	**11,683**	**19,735**
Surigao	Surigáo	1,200	—	—	7,284	7,411	4,909
	Mainit (1622)	—	—	—	—	—	3,567
	Gigaquit (1622)	1,600	—	—	—	4,015	4,548
	Cantilan (1622)	—	—	—	4,863	4,310	4,519
	Dinagat Is.	1,200	—	—	—	—	2,502
	Siargáo Is.	4,000	—	—	—	—	—
	Cacub (Siargao Is.)	—	—	—	2,194	5,185	2,386
	Cabuntóg (Siargao Is.)	—	—	—	—	—	3,541
	Subtotal for Surigao/Siargao	**8,000**	**—**	**—**	**14,341**	**20,921**	**25,972**
Caraga	Tandag, *misión de San Juan* (1622)	1,200	—	—	2,177	3,919	5,161
	Tandag, *visitas* only	—	—	—	3,066	—	—
	Tago	1,800	—	—	—	—	—
	Bislig, *misión de Caraga*	2,000	—	—	1,078	4,870	6,208
	Bislig, *visitas* only	—	—	—	2,139	—	—
	Cateel	1,200	—	—	—	—	—
	Baganga	1,600	—	—	—	—	—
	Subtotal for Caraga	**7,800**	**—**	**—**	**8,460**	**8,789**	**11,369**
GRAND TOTAL		**21,300**	**20,560**	**30,904**	**54,985**	**71,950**	**96,067**

[1] Los Recoletos en Mindanao, *La Época* (Madrid), June 29, 1891, num. 13.948, p. 1.

[2] *Estado Correspondiente al Año de 1863, que manifiesta los Religiosos existentes en la Provincia de San Nicolás de los Agustinos descalzos en las Islas Filipinas y en las diversas casas de ella…*, 20 May 1863, San Sebastian, summary by Fr Claudio del Arco, on the order of Fr Provincial Juan Felix de la Encarnacion. (Newberry Library [NL], Ayer, 2143.A81 A8 1863, Folio Sheet 3)

[3] *Estado Correspondiente al Año de 1877, que manifiesta los Religiosos existentes en la Provincia de San Nicolás de Agustinos descalzos en las Islas Filipinas y en las diversas casas de ella…*, 15 May 1878, Manila, summary by Fr Gregorio Sesma de la V. del Rosario, on the order of Fr Provincial Aquilino Bon de Sebastian. (NL, Ayer, 2143.A81 A8 1863, Folio Sheet 2)

APPENDIX E

TRANSCRIPT FROM THE ARCHIVO PROVINCIAL DE LOS AGUSTINOS RECOLETOS REGARDING THE FOUNDING OF THE MISSION OF TAGOLOÁN

The text (ARM leg 61, n3, f4r-6v) is a 1753 copy of correspondence from the *datus* of Tagoloán, in northern Mindanao, with the original dated October 6, 1722. The first part is in a local dialect of the Visayan language, followed by its Castillian version. Black lines (━) represent text that is missing due to physical deterioration of the manuscript, or otherwise presently undecipherable.

1   [f4r] Almirante nga Agalun nam━

2   [f4v] Diha sa caguindayon came, managpahibalo ay ang manga c━ datoan nga

3   tanan dinhi ni yning manga Calungsolan sa Ylaya sa Tagaloan, Ugnagtigum came

4   sa balay ni Cabayao apan si Manengo uala maha uban canamo cay naha bilin

5   salongsod ni Dalabahan Cay na saquit ug ano palaman namo ━utman sa Dios

6   nga dimo cami hisauaan Ym━ ymung despacho ug sa P. Prior Fr. Geronimo de

7   S^n Miguel ug sa P. Vicar━ Fr. Juan de la Concep^n. Nga mao ang Alferez Nicolas

8   Tolenti━ ug came ang nanag Cavildo mga manga Ca Datoan mao quini ang

9   manga ngalan namo =

10   Ang ma ha ona nga pa Bunag mao quini = 1. Ca Bayao= 2. Gavayan= 3.

11   Langundayon= 4. Catumbis= 5. Balagon = 6. Aliliton = 7. Suguib = 8. Anlas =

12   Ang mi oyon = 1= Dalabahan = Buanun = Cagunad =

13   Ug sa atubangan ni ynin duha ca manga Testigos Nga ang Capitan D^n Miguel

14   Tolon, Ug ang Cap^n D^n L. P. Magon, Nga ━ oyon cami nga tanan ugmisugot

15   sapag papasacup sa Hari sa Castila nga guidongangan namo ang among polong

16   nga naha ona sa Señor Governador sa Man^{la} cay ang pagcahugot sa among buis ug

17   amo salig came sa manga Castella ugangay man sa buut. Sa Señor Almirante D^r

18   Andres Garcia Snz ug sa Señor Gral sa sugbu nga y padangatman quining amung

19 polong sa atubangan sa Señor Gov^{or} sa Man^a apan quining amung
pinangangayo

20 con tumanun unta sa Señor Governador nga uay pagbuhi namo sauay-
catubtuban

21 ug uay ▬ctonum ug uai hatag sa pag casal, uguay paglimos sa ▬▬▬ga

22 hatagan cami sa among calingunan ng▬ ang chinantanan ug ang

23 gant ▬▬▬▬▬▬▬▬

24 ▬▬▬▬▬▬▬

25 [f5r]maoy mangaylu canama ang among P^e ug ang upat ca baril nga ygaligun

26 namo sa among lonsod = _____

27 ~ Ang y hatag namo camang sa tuig ngatanan tag sacaba guid a▬ otunga

28 saolitao ug si D^n Mig^l Tulon ang buut namo dina ▬un Canama ug ang yiang

29 manga sacop, ug si Sebast^n Balog▬an, Cay maoi pagasondon sapag servi

30 sa among Padre = _____

31 Señor Almirante buut ca cahang ama catugbung came sapagcauil sapag
gubat,ta sa

32 Malanao dili came arang dumili apan naulang cami sa among pag ngilap sa
amung

33 lon sod ug ycaduha ang pagbantay sa manga tauo sa ylang manga oma cag-
tuig sa

34 pag bus uae sa human nga di árang cabí yaan namo ma ona ang polong namo

35 comosta camo sadaghan uyamot ug bantayan camo sa Dios sa tuig nga dili
may▬

36 Cabanglaan y octu^e 6 de 1722 ▬S Came nga tanan ang tag sulat niyni ang
inyong

37 manga ulibun nga manga servi canino guihapon ug diman ninyo biyaan
Dalabahan

38 = Buanon = Cabayao = Gavayan = Langundayun = Cagunad = Catumbis =

39 Alilitun = Suguib =Alnas = Balagon = Señor Almte Dr Andres Garcia Frnz

40 Digo lo el Bachiller Miguel de Urrutia Capellan de la Capilla real Nuestra
senora

41 de la Encarnaz^n que lo fue de esta Armada de Cargo de Sor Almirante D^n
Andres

42 Garcia fnrz que es ver▬ queel escrito adjunto de la foxa antecedente es el
mismo

43 que ▬tieron los prinzipales Infieles de los Montes y Riveras ▬io de
Tagaloan, en

44 respuesta de otro que les remitio el ▬^r Almirante por mano del Alferes
Nicolas

45 Tolentino ▬tural de este Pueblo de Cagayan y por ferverdad lo fir▬ en 8 del S

46 del 1722. B^er Mig^l de ▬rrutia=

47 ▬ ^te nro ámo = Grandecima alegria ha sido p^a nosotro▬

48 ▬lo voluntad, luego q llegue E Mre de Campo D^n Nia▬

49 ▬ noticia su llegada al precidio ▬ Cagaian, âl ▬▬▬

50 [f5v]taste nos participamos Unos a otros todos los Princip^les a▬ estos Pueblos
de

51 la laguna de Tagoloan, y nos juntamos y congrega^s en la cassa y morada de

52 Cabayao, pero Manengo falt a la junta nra, por que se quedo en el Pueblo de

53 Dalabahan p^r enferma y es felicidad nra y V━lun^d D━na q para que con Vmd
no

54 caygamos en falta lleg━ su despacho, y el del P^e, P^{or} fr Geronmino de S^n Migu━

55 del P^e Jilario fr Juan de la Concepss^n q trajo el Alfz, Nicolas Tholentino y los
que

56 nos juntamos y congregamos los prinçip.^{les} En con falta son los sigu^{tes}
nombrados

57 = Los primeros y princip^{les} son = prim^o Cabayao = segunda Gabayan = tercera,

58 Langondayon = quarto, Catumbis = quinta, Balagaon, = sexto Aliliton =
septima,

59 Suguib = Octabo, Anlas = Los que se conforma^n y siguieron, Prime^o Dalabahan
=

60 segundo, Buaron = tercera, Caguna = En presencia de estos testigos el Capp^n
D^n

61 Miguel Tulon, y el Capp^n D^n Pedro Magon nos comforma^s y Unimos para a

62 ━ y rendirnos a la obedien^a a su Mag^d que Dios gu^e El Rey de Espna, y

63 Repitimos nuebo lo que tenem━ prometido al Sor Governa^r de estas Yslas
Philip^s

64 en la Ciu^d de Manila p^a la firmeza y entereza de nra voluntad fiados y con

65 voluntad del Sor Alm^{te} D^n Andres Fern^{ez} Garcia, y del Sr Gral dela Prov^a de
Zebu,

66 puede hacer manifiesto y patente esa nra Representac^n, admitidas y
conseguida si

67 le parece al Señor Govr seamos E━ tos, y libres del trbuto perpetuam^{te} y sin el

68 santoru━q pagan en las Ygleçias, y sus obençiones de Casam^{tos}, y ━tierros
tamb^n

69 libres de pagar, y que p^a esto, tengamos ━çial Decreto esculpido enbronçe, y
que

70 en orden alp━ de la Chinan━ y gantas, que ni falten, ni sobren según

71 ━en; y que Nro P^e que se pedimos sea portoda su ━ga en esto mu━nza; y

72 que p^a las elecçiones de ━

73 [f6r]llo y sus Ministros lo haga el P. Minro, y no venga el Alcalde a Viçitarnos ,
ni

74 otro por su Comiz^{on} y pídimos qual piezas de Artilleria para fortaleçer y
guardar

75 nro ━ llo = A lo que podemos obligarnos a al año en Reconoçim━
Vasallaje

76 el tributar un cesto de arros el cassa^o y el ━tero medio cesto; Y D^n Miguel
Tulon

77 lo que pedimos y suplicamos siendo posible no nos quite, ni nos separe con
toda

78 sug^{te} ael agregada, y assi mesmo sebastian Balaguilan a quienes siguiremos y

79 quien es en todo nos dirigeran para el servicio y obedien^a a Nro P^e Ministro =

80 _____ _____ _____

81 Sor Alm^{te}, suponemos q Vmd gustará de que basemos p^a consultar en orden a
que

82 demos guerra a Malanao; no podemos dejar de admitir si assi fuera, pero nos

83 embarasamos, lo primero no tener fortaleza nro Pueblo, y lo otro el cuidado

84   inescusable de la g^te en sus labranzas y sementaras de arros que al prese^te se
     halla
85   espisando que no es posible poder desamparar y con esto cessamos y
     saludamos a
86   Vmds muchas Veces y les qu^e Dios mu^s P, y infinitos. Cabonlaan y octu^e 6 del
87   1722 an^s ━ = ━━mos todos los que escrivimos esta sus esclavos que han de
88   servier a Vmds smpre sino nos dejan, y d━━ ran = Dalabahan = Buanon
89   =Cabayao = Gabay━ Langundayon = Cagunad =Catumbis = Alili━ Suguib
90   =Anlas =Balagon =
91   Certifico yo El B^er Miguel Garcia Cler━━bitezo, Domiciliario de esta
92   Arzpdo, de Manila ━go, y encargo del Sr D^n Thoribio Joseph M━Cosio,
93   Marquez de Torre Cam°, Cavallero ━━ de Calatraba Gov^or y Cap^n Gral, de
     esta
94   s━pinas y p━id^te de la R^l Audz^a y charz━━ qu━
95   [f6v] recide, tengo trasumptada la Carta Referido escrita en Idioma bisaia por
     los
96   princip^les del Pueblo de Cabonlaan en la Castellana y va fiel y verdaderam^te
97   trasumptada segun y como alcanz━ a enten━ sus terminas y propoçiones sin
98   añadir, ni gu━ y porque conste donde conbenga di esta en qual ━ Diz^e de
     1722 a^s
99   = B^er Miguel Garcia= _____

INDEX

SOUTHEAST ASIA PROGRAM PUBLICATIONS
Cornell University

Studies on Southeast Asia

Number 61 *A Mountain of Difference: The Lumad in Early Colonial Mindanao*, Oona Paredes. 2013. ISBN 978-0-87727-761-3 (pb.)

Number 60 *The Kim Vân Kieu of Nguyen Du (1765–1820)*, trans. Vladislav Zhukov. 2013. ISBN 978-0-87727-760-6 (pb.)

Number 59 *The Politics of Timor-Leste: Democratic Consolidation after Intervention*, ed. Michael Leach and Damien Kingsbury. 2013. ISBN 978-0-87727-759-0 (pb.)

Number 58 *The Spirit of Things: Materiality and Religious Diversity in Southeast Asia*, ed. Julius Bautista. 2012. ISBN 970-0-87727-758-3 (pb.)

Number 57 *Demographic Change in Southeast Asia: Recent Histories and Future Directions*, ed. Lindy Williams and Michael Philip Guest. 2012. ISBN 978-0-87727-757-6 (pb.)

Number 56 *Modern and Contemporary Southeast Asian Art: An Anthology*, ed. Nora A. Taylor and Boreth Ly. 2012. ISBN 978-0-87727-756-9 (pb.)

Number 55 *Glimpses of Freedom: Independent Cinema in Southeast Asia*, ed. May Adadol Ingawanij and Benjamin McKay. 2012. ISBN 978-0-87727-755-2 (pb.)

Number 54 *Student Activism in Malaysia: Crucible, Mirror, Sideshow*, Meredith L. Weiss. 2011. ISBN 978-0-87727-754-5 (pb.)

Number 53 *Political Authority and Provincial Identity in Thailand: The Making of Banharn-buri*, Yoshinori Nishizaki. 2011. ISBN 978-0-87727-753-8 (pb.)

Number 52 *Vietnam and the West: New Approaches*, ed. Wynn Wilcox. 2010. ISBN 978-0-87727-752-1 (pb.)

Number 51 *Cultures at War: The Cold War and Cultural Expression in Southeast Asia*, ed. Tony Day and Maya H. T. Liem. 2010. ISBN 978-0-87727-751-4 (pb.)

Number 50 *State of Authority: The State in Society in Indonesia*, ed. Gerry van Klinken and Joshua Barker. 2009. ISBN 978-0-87727-750-7 (pb.)

Number 49 *Phan Châu Trinh and His Political Writings*, Phan Châu Trinh, ed. and trans. Vinh Sinh. 2009. ISBN 978-0-87727-749-1 (pb.)

Number 48 *Dependent Communities: Aid and Politics in Cambodia and East Timor*, Caroline Hughes. 2009. ISBN 978-0-87727-748-4 (pb.)

Number 47 *A Man Like Him: Portrait of the Burmese Journalist, Journal Kyaw U Chit Maung*, Journal Kyaw Ma Ma Lay, trans. Ma Thanegi, 2008. ISBN 978-0-87727-747-7 (pb.)

Number 46 *At the Edge of the Forest: Essays on Cambodia, History, and Narrative in Honor of David Chandler*, ed. Anne Ruth Hansen and Judy Ledgerwood. 2008. ISBN 978-0-87727-746-0 (pb).

Number 45 *Conflict, Violence, and Displacement in Indonesia*, ed. Eva-Lotta E. Hedman. 2008. ISBN 978-0-87727-745-3 (pb).

Number 44 *Friends and Exiles: A Memoir of the Nutmeg Isles and the Indonesian Nationalist Movement*, Des Alwi, ed. Barbara S. Harvey. 2008. ISBN 978-0-877277-44-6 (pb).

Number 43   *Early Southeast Asia: Selected Essays*, O. W. Wolters, ed. Craig J. Reynolds. 2008. 255 pp. ISBN 978-0-877277-43-9 (pb).

Number 42   *Thailand: The Politics of Despotic Paternalism* (revised edition), Thak Chaloemtiarana. 2007. 284 pp. ISBN 0-8772-7742-7 (pb).

Number 41   *Views of Seventeenth-Century Vietnam: Christoforo Borri on Cochinchina and Samuel Baron on Tonkin*, ed. Olga Dror and K. W. Taylor. 2006. 290 pp. ISBN 0-8772-7741-9 (pb).

Number 40   *Laskar Jihad: Islam, Militancy, and the Quest for Identity in Post-New Order Indonesia*, Noorhaidi Hasan. 2006. 266 pp. ISBN 0-877277-40-0 (pb).

Number 39   *The Indonesian Supreme Court: A Study of Institutional Collapse*, Sebastiaan Pompe. 2005. 494 pp. ISBN 0-877277-38-9 (pb).

Number 38   *Spirited Politics: Religion and Public Life in Contemporary Southeast Asia*, ed. Andrew C. Willford and Kenneth M. George. 2005. 210 pp. ISBN 0-87727-737-0.

Number 37   *Sumatran Sultanate and Colonial State: Jambi and the Rise of Dutch Imperialism, 1830-1907*, Elsbeth Locher-Scholten, trans. Beverley Jackson. 2004. 332 pp. ISBN 0-87727-736-2.

Number 36   *Southeast Asia over Three Generations: Essays Presented to Benedict R. O'G. Anderson*, ed. James T. Siegel and Audrey R. Kahin. 2003. 398 pp. ISBN 0-87727-735-4.

Number 35   *Nationalism and Revolution in Indonesia*, George McTurnan Kahin, intro. Benedict R. O'G. Anderson (reprinted from 1952 edition, Cornell University Press, with permission). 2003. 530 pp. ISBN 0-87727-734-6.

Number 34   *Golddiggers, Farmers, and Traders in the "Chinese Districts" of West Kalimantan, Indonesia*, Mary Somers Heidhues. 2003. 316 pp. ISBN 0-87727-733-8.

Number 33   *Opusculum de Sectis apud Sinenses et Tunkinenses (A Small Treatise on the Sects among the Chinese and Tonkinese): A Study of Religion in China and North Vietnam in the Eighteenth Century*, Father Adriano de St. Thecla, trans. Olga Dror, with Mariya Berezovska. 2002. 363 pp. ISBN 0-87727-732-X.

Number 32   *Fear and Sanctuary: Burmese Refugees in Thailand*, Hazel J. Lang. 2002. 204 pp. ISBN 0-87727-731-1.

Number 31   *Modern Dreams: An Inquiry into Power, Cultural Production, and the Cityscape in Contemporary Urban Penang, Malaysia*, Beng-Lan Goh. 2002. 225 pp. ISBN 0-87727-730-3.

Number 30   *Violence and the State in Suharto's Indonesia*, ed. Benedict R. O'G. Anderson. 2001. Second printing, 2002. 247 pp. ISBN 0-87727-729-X.

Number 29   *Studies in Southeast Asian Art: Essays in Honor of Stanley J. O'Connor*, ed. Nora A. Taylor. 2000. 243 pp. Illustrations. ISBN 0-87727-728-1.

Number 28   *The Hadrami Awakening: Community and Identity in the Netherlands East Indies, 1900-1942*, Natalie Mobini-Kesheh. 1999. 174 pp. ISBN 0-87727-727-3.

Number 27   *Tales from Djakarta: Caricatures of Circumstances and their Human Beings*, Pramoedya Ananta Toer. 1999. 145 pp. ISBN 0-87727-726-5.

Number 26   *History, Culture, and Region in Southeast Asian Perspectives*, rev. ed., O. W. Wolters. 1999. Second printing, 2004. 275 pp. ISBN 0-87727-725-7.

Number 5	*Southeast Asian Ephemeris: Solar and Planetary Positions, A.D. 638–2000,* J. C. Eade. 1989. 175 pp. ISBN 0-87727-704-4.
Number 3	*Thai Radical Discourse: The Real Face of Thai Feudalism Today,* Craig J. Reynolds. 1987. 2nd printing 1994. 186 pp. ISBN 0-87727-702-8.
Number 1	*The Symbolism of the Stupa,* Adrian Snodgrass. 1985. Revised with index, 1988. 3rd printing 1998. 469 pp. ISBN 0-87727-700-1.

SEAP Series

Number 23	*Possessed by the Spirits: Mediumship in Contemporary Vietnamese Communities.* 2006. 186 pp. ISBN 0-877271-41-0 (pb).
Number 22	*The Industry of Marrying Europeans,* Vũ Trọng Phụng, trans. Thúy Tranviet. 2006. 66 pp. ISBN 0-877271-40-2 (pb).
Number 21	*Securing a Place: Small-Scale Artisans in Modern Indonesia,* Elizabeth Morrell. 2005. 220 pp. ISBN 0-877271-39-9.
Number 20	*Southern Vietnam under the Reign of Minh Mạng (1820-1841): Central Policies and Local Response,* Choi Byung Wook. 2004. 226pp. ISBN 0-0-877271-40-2.
Number 19	*Gender, Household, State: Đổi Mới in Việt Nam,* ed. Jayne Werner and Danièle Bélanger. 2002. 151 pp. ISBN 0-87727-137-2.
Number 18	*Culture and Power in Traditional Siamese Government,* Neil A. Englehart. 2001. 130 pp. ISBN 0-87727-135-6.
Number 17	*Gangsters, Democracy, and the State,* ed. Carl A. Trocki. 1998. Second printing, 2002. 94 pp. ISBN 0-87727-134-8.
Number 16	*Cutting across the Lands: An Annotated Bibliography on Natural Resource Management and Community Development in Indonesia, the Philippines, and Malaysia,* ed. Eveline Ferretti. 1997. 329 pp. ISBN 0-87727-133-X.
Number 15	*The Revolution Falters: The Left in Philippine Politics after 1986,* ed. Patricio N. Abinales. 1996. Second printing, 2002. 182 pp. ISBN 0-87727-132-1.
Number 14	*Being Kammu: My Village, My Life,* Damrong Tayanin. 1994. 138 pp., 22 tables, illus., maps. ISBN 0-87727-130-5.
Number 13	*The American War in Vietnam,* ed. Jayne Werner, David Hunt. 1993. 132 pp. ISBN 0-87727-131-3.
Number 12	*The Voice of Young Burma,* Aye Kyaw. 1993. 92 pp. ISBN 0-87727-129-1.
Number 11	*The Political Legacy of Aung San,* ed. Josef Silverstein. Revised edition 1993. 169 pp. ISBN 0-87727-128-3.
Number 10	*Studies on Vietnamese Language and Literature: A Preliminary Bibliography,* Nguyen Dinh Tham. 1992. 227 pp. ISBN 0-87727-127-5.
Number 8	*From PKI to the Comintern, 1924–1941: The Apprenticeship of the Malayan Communist Party,* Cheah Boon Kheng. 1992. 147 pp. ISBN 0-87727-125-9.
Number 7	*Intellectual Property and US Relations with Indonesia, Malaysia, Singapore, and Thailand,* Elisabeth Uphoff. 1991. 67 pp. ISBN 0-87727-124-0.
Number 6	*The Rise and Fall of the Communist Party of Burma (CPB),* Bertil Lintner. 1990. 124 pp. 26 illus., 14 maps. ISBN 0-87727-123-2.

Number 5   *Japanese Relations with Vietnam: 1951–1987*, Masaya Shiraishi. 1990. 174 pp. ISBN 0-87727-122-4.

Number 3   *Postwar Vietnam: Dilemmas in Socialist Development*, ed. Christine White, David Marr. 1988. 2nd printing 1993. 260 pp. ISBN 0-87727-120-8.

Number 2   *The Dobama Movement in Burma (1930–1938)*, Khin Yi. 1988. 160 pp. ISBN 0-87727-118-6.

Cornell Modern Indonesia Project Publications

All CMIP titles available at http://cmip.library.cornell.edu

Number 75   *A Tour of Duty: Changing Patterns of Military Politics in Indonesia in the 1990s.* Douglas Kammen and Siddharth Chandra. 1999. 99 pp. ISBN 0-87763-049-6.

Number 74   *The Roots of Acehnese Rebellion 1989–1992*, Tim Kell. 1995. 103 pp. ISBN 0-87763-040-2.

Number 72   *Popular Indonesian Literature of the Qur'an*, Howard M. Federspiel. 1994. 170 pp. ISBN 0-87763-038-0.

Number 71   *A Javanese Memoir of Sumatra, 1945–1946: Love and Hatred in the Liberation War*, Takao Fusayama. 1993. 150 pp. ISBN 0-87763-037-2.

Number 69   *The Road to Madiun: The Indonesian Communist Uprising of 1948*, Elizabeth Ann Swift. 1989. 120 pp. ISBN 0-87763-035-6.

Number 68   *Intellectuals and Nationalism in Indonesia: A Study of the Following Recruited by Sutan Sjahrir in Occupation Jakarta*, J. D. Legge. 1988. 159 pp. ISBN 0-87763-034-8.

Number 67   *Indonesia Free: A Biography of Mohammad Hatta*, Mavis Rose. 1987. 252 pp. ISBN 0-87763-033-X.

Number 66   *Prisoners at Kota Cane*, Leon Salim, trans. Audrey Kahin. 1986. 112 pp. ISBN 0-87763-032-1.

Number 64   *Suharto and His Generals: Indonesia's Military Politics, 1975–1983*, David Jenkins. 1984. 4th printing 1997. 300 pp. ISBN 0-87763-030-5.

Number 62   *Interpreting Indonesian Politics: Thirteen Contributions to the Debate, 1964– 1981*, ed. Benedict Anderson, Audrey Kahin, intro. Daniel S. Lev. 1982. 3rd printing 1991. 172 pp. ISBN 0-87763-028-3.

Number 60   *The Minangkabau Response to Dutch Colonial Rule in the Nineteenth Century*, Elizabeth E. Graves. 1981. 157 pp. ISBN 0-87763-000-3.

Number 57   *Permesta: Half a Rebellion*, Barbara S. Harvey. 1977. 174 pp. ISBN 0-87763-003-8.

Number 52   *A Preliminary Analysis of the October 1 1965, Coup in Indonesia (Prepared in January 1966)*, Benedict R. Anderson, Ruth T. McVey, assist. Frederick P. Bunnell. 1971. 3rd printing 1990. 174 pp. ISBN 0-87763-008-9.

Number 48   *Nationalism, Islam and Marxism*, Soekarno, intro. Ruth T. McVey. 1970.

Number 37   *Mythology and the Tolerance of the Javanese*, Benedict R. O'G. Anderson. 2nd edition, 1996. Reprinted 2004. 104 pp., 65 illus. ISBN 0-87763-041-0.

Copublished Titles

The Ambiguous Allure of the West: Traces of the Colonial in Thailand, ed. Rachel V. Harrison and Peter A. Jackson. Copublished with Hong Kong University Press. 2010. ISBN 978-0-87727-608-1 (pb.)

The Many Ways of Being Muslim: Fiction by Muslim Filipinos, ed. Coeli Barry. Copublished with Anvil Publishing, Inc., the Philippines. 2008. ISBN 978-0-87727-605-0 (pb.)

Language Texts

INDONESIAN

Beginning Indonesian through Self-Instruction, John U. Wolff, Dédé Oetomo, Daniel Fietkiewicz. 3rd revised edition 1992. Vol. 1. 115 pp. ISBN 0-87727-529-7. Vol. 2. 434 pp. ISBN 0-87727-530-0. Vol. 3. 473 pp. ISBN 0-87727-531-9.

Indonesian Readings, John U. Wolff. 1978. 4th printing 1992. 480 pp. ISBN 0-87727-517-3

Indonesian Conversations, John U. Wolff. 1978. 3rd printing 1991. 297 pp. ISBN 0-87727-516-5

Formal Indonesian, John U. Wolff. 2nd revised edition 1986. 446 pp. ISBN 0-87727-515-7

TAGALOG

Pilipino through Self-Instruction, John U. Wolff, Maria Theresa C. Centeno, Der-Hwa V. Rau. 1991. Vol. 1. 342 pp. ISBN 0-87727—525-4. Vol. 2., revised 2005, 378 pp. ISBN 0-87727-526-2. Vol 3., revised 2005, 431 pp. ISBN 0-87727-527-0. Vol. 4. 306 pp. ISBN 0-87727-528-9.

THAI

A. U. A. Language Center Thai Course, J. Marvin Brown. Originally published by the American University Alumni Association Language Center, 1974. Reissued by Cornell Southeast Asia Program, 1991, 1992. Book 1. 267 pp. ISBN 0-87727-506-8. Book 2. 288 pp. ISBN 0-87727-507-6. Book 3. 247 pp. ISBN 0-87727-508-4.

A. U. A. Language Center Thai Course, Reading and Writing Text (mostly reading), 1979. Reissued 1997. 164 pp. ISBN 0-87727-511-4.

A. U. A. Language Center Thai Course, Reading and Writing Workbook (mostly writing), 1979. Reissued 1997. 99 pp. ISBN 0-87727-512-2.

KHMER

Cambodian System of Writing and Beginning Reader, Franklin E. Huffman. Originally published by Yale University Press, 1970. Reissued by Cornell Southeast Asia Program, 4th printing 2002. 365 pp. ISBN 0-300-01314-0.

Modern Spoken Cambodian, Franklin E. Huffman, assist. Charan Promchan, Chhom-Rak Thong Lambert. Originally published by Yale University Press, 1970. Reissued by Cornell Southeast Asia Program, 3rd printing 1991. 451 pp. ISBN 0-300-01316-7.

Intermediate Cambodian Reader, ed. Franklin E. Huffman, assist. Im Proum. Originally published by Yale University Press, 1972. Reissued by Cornell Southeast Asia Program, 1988. 499 pp. ISBN 0-300-01552-6.

Cambodian Literary Reader and Glossary, Franklin E. Huffman, Im Proum. Originally published by Yale University Press, 1977. Reissued by Cornell Southeast Asia Program, 1988. 494 pp. ISBN 0-300-02069-4.

HMONG

White Hmong-English Dictionary, Ernest E. Heimbach. 1969. 8th printing, 2002. 523 pp. ISBN 0-87727-075-9.

VIETNAMESE

Intermediate Spoken Vietnamese, Franklin E. Huffman, Tran Trong Hai. 1980. 3rd printing 1994. ISBN 0-87727-500-9.

Proto-Austronesian Phonology with Glossary, John U. Wolff, 2 volumes, 2011. ISBN vol. I, 978-0-87727-532-9. ISBN vol. II, 978-0-87727-533-6.

To order, please contact:
Mail:
Cornell University Press Services
750 Cascadilla Street
PO Box 6525
Ithaca, NY 14851 USA

E-mail: orderbook@cupserv.org

Phone/Fax, Monday–Friday, 8 am – 5 pm (Eastern US):
Phone: 607 277 2211 or 800 666 2211 (US, Canada)
Fax: 607 277 6292 or 800 688 2877 (US, Canada)

Order through our online bookstore at:
www.einaudi.cornell.edu/southeastasia/publications/